To Alexandra Simou

With special thanks to super-editors
Melissa Oliver, Tzviya Siegman and Julie Kerr.

C O N T E N T S

CHAPTER 3
WHAT KIND OF RESTAURANT?

CHAPTER 4
RAISING THE MONEY

CHAPTER 5
EQUIPMENT AND DECOR

67

CHAPTER 6
THE BAR

77

CHAPTER 9
HYGIENE, HEALTH, AND SAFETY
145

CHAPTER 10
PUBLIC RELATIONS
157

INTRODUCTION

In the decade since the last edition of this book was published there have been changes and developments, but no major revolutions. Happily, the industry has expanded mightily and will continue to do so. There were more than 870,000 restaurants in the United States in 2003 with sales of $426 billion. In 2004, the number of locations had climbed to 878,000 and sales to $440 billion. This is expected to represent 4 percent of the U.S. gross domestic product. The restaurant industry is the nation's largest private-sector employer, employing more than 12 million people, or nearly 9 percent of the work force. More than four out of ten adults have worked in the industry at some time in their lives — for many youngsters, it's almost a rite of passage. The franchise option has become more attractive because it enjoys great success. Diet fads have had to be accommodated, and the popularity of the Atkins Diet has boosted business for steakhouses—not that they were ever ailing. There has been a dramatic increase in the number of very expensive restaurants, with investments in the tens of millions not uncommon.

The smoking ban in public places, which of course includes restaurants, has spread almost nationwide. To the surprise and relief of many, in the nine months after the ban was introduced in New York, sales tax receipts on food and drink rose by 12 percent and employment in the hospitality industry increased. At the same time, there was an 11 percent decrease in the smoking rate, in part attributable to the ban. Many smokers wish they didn't have the habit anyway, and the enforced discipline of having to refrain when dining in restaurants may have provided them with more incentive to stop. Some would-be diners who liked a restaurant, but would never go there because the place was always so darned smoky, have come in from the cold. Since smoking customers can find no sanctuary in another restaurant, they will probably continue drinking and dining at their favorite restaurants, possibly from time to time joining those huddled groups who've stepped out to the street for a smoke. Hospitality industry workers will be grateful for no longer having to risk the effects of passive smoking (i.e., being exposed for eight hours a day to the carcinogenic exhalations of others).

Many customers are so hooked on *the restaurant experience* that they seem incapable of price resistance.* There are restaurants whose *tasting menu* costs more than $300, and the $50 Kobe burger is now almost a cliché. A Beefeater martini at a New York hotel can cost $13. For the price of two cocktails you could buy a liter bottle of Beefeater's gin and have a home experience. But home is clearly not the same as being at a New York City Hotel, for you are unlikely to glimpse Tom Cruise or Ivana Trump there. Coffee shops on city corner sites paying $30,000 a month in rent make a profit because people will cheerfully pay $7 or more for an elaborate cup of coffee.

There is enormous curiosity for new experiences and the exploration of different cuisines. New York now has restaurants of almost every ethnicity, including Ethiopian, where the customers sit on the floor, and Tibetan (at least five), complete with banging gongs, chanting monks, pictures of the Dalai Lama, incense, and yak milk. Ethnic restaurants seem to do well, especially with the younger crowd, because they offer a small adventure at reasonable prices. Recent immigrants tend to be pleasant and friendly, usually offering a warm greeting and ambiance that makes a welcome change from the occasional snarled "Two?" (often with two of the maitre d's fingers raised just to make sure the incoming customers get the message), which is still, alas, to be encountered here and there.

The range of foods available, and avidly consumed, has expanded so much that gourmet stores are now Aladdin's caves of fascinating, delicious items. Many new foods are thrust upon the consumer public by determined corporations. If breakfast cereals hadn't been invented, what would we do with all that corn? Florida's citrus industry might well have been abandoned had concentrated juice not been invented, thus assuring a supply of drinks even in years of poor crops. The introduction of the idea of breakfast juice and fruity cocktails also helped. Fishermen have to trawl deeper as stocks of fish which swim in the upper layers of the ocean diminish, so that tilefish, monkfish, and orange roughy have become standard items. Kangaroo, wild boar, and ostrich meat are attracting adventurous diners.

Television and media coverage of food and restaurants has vastly increased interest in the subject—indeed it's become a genre in its own right. There are several cable channels devoted entirely to the subject. The world of food is a godsend to editors and producers who need to fill so many newspaper and

*The United States currently has 3.8 million high net worth individuals (HNWIs), up from 2.1 million in 2001. An HNWI household is defined as one that has $1 million in investable assets, not including property.

magazine pages and 24 hours of TV and radio time. TV programs are cheap to produce—until, of course, the star chef's fees start to soar. Burgeoning battalions of celebrity chefs and restaurateurs command acres of press and hours of television time. The faintest quirk of speech or manner will turn a TV chef into an international celebrity with iconic power almost overnight, and, as Emeril might say, "bring things up a notch." One multimillionairess TV chef recently regaled her audience with the correct way to boil an egg, and no one seemed to find this particularly ridiculous. The omelet pan she recommended sold millions. Fly-on-the-wall documentaries in which irate chefs insult, and even assault, their employees, enjoy high ratings among viewers.

A jaundiced eye might observe that Livy, the Roman historian, was convinced that the root cause of the decline of the Empire was the growing obsession with food that developed after the opening up of the spice routes to the Orient. Lowly cooks became senior members of the household, and the population became soft. The number-one medical problem in the Western world today is obesity, and many partly blame the food industry. But it could be argued that restaurant dining should be encouraged. A major reason for widespread obesity is the thoughtless and haphazard consumption of junk food throughout the day. Getting schoolchildren (and servicemen) to eat salad is a challenge. No matter how attractive school and armed forces chefs make the fruit and salad bar, it is largely ignored in favor of eggs, hamburgers, and french fries. You can lead a horse to water . . . .

If people ate only three times a day, in restaurants, they would be discreetly restricted to the discipline of commercial portion control, and would probably benefit from it. While portions are sometimes large, restaurants don't usually offer second helpings. Also, salad consumption in restaurants is part of the ritual—it would be an unusual savory dish that didn't include a green salad. Britain in World War II was healthier than it has ever been before or since, due to an eating discipline imposed by food rationing that induced a less fatty diet and made healthy items more easily available.

More Americans eat out each week than go to the movies or ball games. Comparing the restaurant industry with the entertainment industry may seem, at first glance, rather odd. But understanding *restaurant theater* is crucial. Some successful restaurants prosper in spite of dreadful food, service, and prices. Absurdity must be recognized and indulged. Many restaurant customers are not there only for the food, but also for company, conversation, to see and be seen. People-watching and profiling have long been popular pastimes. *Restaurant presence,* whereby one's appearance and manner encourage the maitre d' to offer the best tables and waiters to strive for perfection is a quality prized by some.

The key word is *success.* "Nothing succeeds like success," as Field Marshal Montgomery said. Some restaurants succeed mightily through no fault of their own. There are accidents, there are consumer quirks, there is whimsy, there is a propitious moment for everything, and there is location, location, location. There is also a strong element of theater, which every successful restaurateur must embrace to a greater or lesser extent. Luck plays a part, as it does in everything else, and, while there's truth in the old adages about "creating your own luck," and "the harder you work, the luckier you get," the intelligent businessperson tries to apply common sense to his or her plans.

Much as the workaholic is revered in our society, the truth is that detachment and careful thought will often achieve more than toil alone. Probably the best mindset for the restaurateur (and any other businessperson) is total immersion in the business—doing every job from dishwasher to manager, then reading this book and achieving a magnificent overview as well as that precious commodity, detachment.

Detachment is the cool ability to assess and make decisions based simply on a common-sense view of the situation, thinking long-term, and refusing to be swayed by the emotions of the moment. The pathetic pattern of bending to every slight change in wind direction is what makes many restaurateurs so neurotic. Never mind today's tornado or flat calm. From where does the prevailing wind blow? So you have attracted the business of a small, quirky crowd who want fiercely hot curry on the menu, ice-cold beer from some obscure state, and medieval music on the jukebox. How many customers will you lose from neglect by catering to these eccentricities? And when the crowd moves on, how will you recover the customers you lost during their brief reign?

A restaurant should be run as one would order one's life. Be "master in your own house." Don't suffer fools gladly, but be flexible, and don't insist on trivial points simply for the sake of showing who's boss. Although there's no hope of being all things to all men, the ability to happily accommodate an amiable customer's mild eccentricities is a talent to which almost every diner and drinker responds positively. One should know how to deliver a firm no if necessary, yet be ready to grant a small request that might be taken care of in a brief, two-minute diversion.

London's Savoy Grill was recently successfully refurbished and modernized in every way. A regular customer of 20 years arrived as soon as the restaurant reopened. A new waiter offered him the menu. The customer said, "Thanks, but I know what I want—a piece of grilled turbot with some Hollandaise sauce, please." The waiter shortly returned with the news that "the chef isn't making Hollandaise sauce today." Apoplexy was averted when one of the old hands came over to say hello to the customer, and was able to produce the goods. Make them happy, and they'll come back for more.

The feel-good factor is crucial. Restaurant staff must smile a lot. That's why so many struggling actors make ends meet by working in restaurants while awaiting *the call*. In winter, many restaurants have fierce overhead heaters by the entrance, proclaiming a warm welcome. If the next experience is a smiling maitre d', the restaurant experience is off to a good start.

Success can be defined as operating one's own business at a profit that at least equals the amount one could earn by selling one's services for the same amount of time in the ordinary job market. One of the most exciting things about the consumer economy is that those who take risks can expect a greater reward than those who choose security.

Doomed-to-fail amateurs often fall into the trap of thinking that sheer charm and cuteness will bring in customers. Others think that the skill of the chef they've discovered will attract gourmets from afar. Perhaps the saddest losers of all are those who think that they have enough friends and acquaintances alone to enable them to run a successful restaurant. It is an old adage in the trade: "*Nobody* has enough friends to keep a restaurant in business."

Professionals who succeed will pay more attention to location, local competition, current trends, and efficient management. It is a question of carefully balancing all these factors. Everything must come together like choreography. Above all, the pros ensure that the people they hire perform as well when the boss is away as they do when he or she is around. In no other business do the mice dance quite as vigorously when the cat's away!

No restaurateur should set forth with the idea that he or she is embarking upon an extremely hazardous adventure. The failure rate of restaurants is lower than that of other retail businesses. It is in any case inflated by the unknown number (which may be considerable—how much cocaine did organized crime sell this year?) of restaurants that are never intended to succeed, but are spawned to fill some accounting or tax niche. Another factor that inflates the statistics for failure is that restaurants which have closed, not "failed," for any one of several reasons including divorce, ill-health, and, most commonly, what some call the "I had no idea" syndrome. Owners find they've bitten off more than they can chew, especially regarding the amount of time they have to put in.

If you've done your homework, if there is enough cash available to keep you afloat during the inevitable shakedown phase, and if your management is diligent and attentive without risking a heart attack because a customer complains, the chances of success are above average for business in general. A survey of opinion puts the new restaurant success rate at about 60 percent. A fuller discussion of this appears later.

These are tremendously encouraging odds. To put them in perspective, only 1 in 20 new consumer items ever finds a permanent place on the national store shelf. Factors mentioned in this introduction will be explored at greater length in the following chapters. Total immersion in this book, coupled with a measure of hands-on experience working in the industry in as many capacities as possible, will qualify the budding restaurateur for success. The target audience for this book is the would-be owner of a licensed restaurant seating 50 to 200 people.

CHAPTER 1

HOW IT ALL BEGAN

A BRIEF HISTORY OF THE RESTAURANT INDUSTRY

It's hard to believe that none of the 104 taverns in ancient Pompeii (population about 20,000) served food—they must have offered at least bread and olives. But there were no restaurants as we know them today. The classical world was a slavery-dominated economy. Slaves cooked the food at home, for their masters and themselves—though, judging from ancient shopping lists, the masters enjoyed a better menu. This is echoed in modern times in those restaurants—usually highly expensive gourmet establishments—where the help are fed rudimentary leftovers before they go on duty. A few years ago, *New York* magazine obtained this information from insiders in several famous restaurants and published it: Waiters and bartenders were fed meatballs and spaghetti before going out to dispense *foie gras* and lobster! Only a very few restaurants insist on their staff eating from the main menu so as to be able to describe dishes to customers.

Chaucer's fourteenth-century pilgrims were lucky to get a bite to eat at the Tabard Inn. Food was not always provided for travellers in those days. They often had to carry their own or buy from farmers and stores along the way. Salted pork was the most common meat, and even if April showers had been unusually sweet that year, the choice of vegetables would have been small. Neither tea, nor coffee, chocolate, or peanuts had yet arrived in Europe, and it would be nearly 300 years before Louis XIV examined his first potato (of which only the sparse foliage was eaten at that time) and sighed, "Always something new from America!"

Fortunately, Chaucer's crew was on a pilgrimage to Canterbury, which, like Santiago de Compostela and a score of other places on the Continent, drew thousands of religious visitors every year, just as Lourdes and Mecca do today. They were, in effect, early tourists, and their routes were as well marked as those from New York to Miami or London to Paris now. Naturally, the locals along the way soon cottoned on to the fact that there was money to be made from feeding the travellers.

At Chaucer's Tabard Inn, the pilgrims were doubly lucky. Often, the innkeeper would invite travellers to dine with him, at the "host's table," a phrase we still use today as *table d'hôte*—a set menu for a fixed price, as distinct from *à la carte,* where one selects separate dishes from a menu selection (which may or may not turn out to be more expensive). The host offered a free meal to the guest who told the most entertaining story. Is this the first recorded instance of using a gimmick to drum up business?

Travel was dangerous then. Finding a meal and a bed before nightfall so as not to be ignorant was a real problem. Highway robbery was common. Jaded modern tourists may opine that, in some respects, little has changed.

There are scarcely any references to any aspect of dining out in European or English literature up to the middle of the eighteenth century. There were always taverns, at which Falstaff and his cohorts could quaff vast quantities of *sack*—cheap, and probably rough, Spanish red wine. At the Globe Theatre you could buy oranges from the baskets of budding Nell Gwynnes. For the small middle class, there were clubs and coffeehouses in the major cities.

The rich usually ate well at home, judging by household records and menus. Even Roman villas well inland have been found to contain large quantities of oyster shells, presumably brought from the shore along those long, straight roads in carts with regular changes of horses. The exact manner of transportation is not known and is a subject of much conjecture. There may have been horse-drawn water tanks.

But there weren't any places where, for a few denarii, you could pop in, check your toga, order a medium rare dormouse with larks' tongues in aspic on the side, and inquire the way to the vomitorium. (Incidentally, at the risk of disappointing generations of schoolboys, a *vomitorium* is NOT where gourmands go to throw up what they've just eaten in order to eat more. No such room was to be found in a Roman house. A vomitorium is simply an exit, from an arena or theater, for instance.

Even for the affluent, foods were largely seasonal. Medical historians believe that the bleeding gums and other symptoms observed in late winter in medieval times were probably early signs of scurvy. There were no vitamin C–rich fruits or vegetables until spring broke through.

The problem of food storage was acute throughout the ages. All food (except salted or smoked meat and fish) had to be transported fresh, and was subject to swift wastage, which inevitably made the notion of restaurants as we know them today a highly risky and expensive business. In any case, there simply weren't enough people with disposable income to support an industry.

In 1795, Francois Appert invented heat sterilization of food, which led to canning. Although used by armies as early as the Napoleonic Wars, canned foods were expensive and not a common consumer item until the middle of the nineteenth century.

Ice was used at the ancient Roman and Chinese courts, and was brought at great expense from the Alps or the frozen Yangtze. It was often stored underground during winter, but was generally a luxury until the end of the nineteenth century when steam-driven refrigeration was invented. This created the massive meat industries of New Zealand and Australia.

In 1913 the Domelre electric refrigerator was invented in Chicago, followed by the English Electrolux silent electric refrigerator in 1927. In 1929,

Clarence Birdseye invented his eponymous freezing process, and by the early 1930s many grocery stores included a frozen food section. Interestingly enough, the first frozen vegetable was asparagus.

The repertoire of recipes was expanding continuously throughout history. Ancient corpses preserved in mud usually reveal a depressing diet of porridge and seeds. Someday, someone may write a paper relating the effect of increased protein in the diet to technological improvement. But useful accidents were happening, starting with the realization that meat tasted better and was easier to chew when burned a bit, and grain was more easily digested when cooked in hot water. Later fortuitous accidents produced such more elaborate delicacies as Peach Melba and Chicken Marengo.

Strasbourg geese were fed large quantities of walnuts to enlarge their livers for pâté. In the sixteenth century, the spice trade from the East was always lucrative, and the court of Louis XIV went wild when peas were imported from Italy.

Toward the end of the eighteenth century, the Industrial Revolution increased travel and created commuters and that indispensable element to the restaurateur—an affluent middle class. Gradually, supply and demand created the modern restaurant industry.

The first modern restaurant is believed to have been opened by A. Boulanger, a soup vendor who opened his business in Paris at the corner of Rue du Louvre in 1765. (There are other contenders, but this is the favorite.) At the entrance, one sign said "*Boulanger débite des restaurants divins,*" meaning "Boulanger provides divine sustenance," while another said, "*Venite ad me omnes qui stomacho laboratis et ego vos restauro*" ("Come to me those with empty stomachs and I will give you sustenance"). The word restaurant comes from the French verb *restorer*, meaning "to restore" (i.e., to improve the health), because that was Boulanger's original pitch. One could say that the first restaurant was a health food place. At first, Boulanger offered only one dish—sheep's feet simmered in a white sauce. What made the place new and different was that it focused on food and not alcohol. The two were shortly happily married as the industry developed. Boulanger's premises are now called Café du Musée.

America's first proper restaurant was Delmonico's, opened in 1836 in what is now the Battery area of downtown Manhattan. It was a purpose-built building, constructed to be a restaurant, three and a half stories high, with several dining rooms or saloons, and a wine cellar containing 16,000 bottles of French wine—the American wine industry not yet having been invented. There were inlaid floors, expensive décor, and an entrance that featured marble pillars from Pompeii. The clientele consisted mainly of European businessmen based in New York. By 1876, a few restaurants did a roaring trade in the major cities of the United States. The Bull's Head, Fraunces Tavern, and Mr. Little's were landmarks in New York. They laid on banquets with extensive menus, but the ordinary bill of fare was usually limited to beef, ham, and vegetables.

Restaurants had become commonplace in Paris by the time of the French Revolution. In 1814, an allied army of English, Dutch, Belgian, Prussian, Spanish, Russian, and Austrian troops occupied the city, having defeated Napoleon at the Battle of the Nations. The World War I song, "How Ya Gonna Keep 'em, Down on the Farm, after They've Seen Paree?" might equally well have been composed at this time. All ranks had a high old time in Paris. Those lucky enough to have received wages could spend their money at last. Officers' families paid long visits.

The troops took home the memory of the fun they'd had, and they spread the word. As society changed from agricultural to industrial, the demand for restaurants grew naturally. An increasing number of people needed to eat away from home. But growth was slow. Then, as now, the rituals of courtship and adultery provided restaurants with regular customers, mainly from the ranks of the rich and the newly rich. By the 1820s, strangers entering Stephen's Hotel in London would be stared down by the waiters and served with reluctance— an early example of what's now called the in crowd! At Crockfords, a gambling club where fortunes were lost, dinner was served from midnight to five in the morning by a named chef, Ude. There was no charge for the expensive delicacies and excellent wines. But the gamblers were encouraged to leave a £10 note on the green baize, if they chose.

Socializing, the privilege of the rich, took place mainly in private houses. In London in 1821, Lord Alvanley, a Regency character, had an apricot tart on his sideboard every day of the year, at a time when eight months' wages for a domestic servant would buy one bottle of champagne. The menus for the Prince Regent's feasts at his Brighton Pavilion by super chef Antonin Careme indicate the vast array of foods available for those who could afford them. The Prince Regent couldn't, as it happened, but he enjoyed them anyway.

As the century went on, restaurants boomed. Railway travel all over Europe increased. By 1880, Charles Dickens was complaining about the sandwiches at the railway buffet. In 1908, Edith Wharton mentioned four restaurant experiences in the same love letter: "The last course of luncheon was being served with due solemnity . . . our first luncheon at Duval's . . . our waiter at Montmorency . . . you . . . caring about the waitress's losing her tip if we moved our table. . . ." The theater of restaurants had arrived.

France, where gastronomy is a national passion, remained the fountainhead of the trade, and many elements of restaurant routine originated there, although Italophiles will insist that the French only stole ideas from the Italians! It is at this time that restaurants became common in America, but only in the major cities. The system of chefs, sous-chefs, sommeliers, and brigades adopted by Maxim's of Paris was widely imitated in the grander restaurants, and it still is.

THE MODERN INDUSTRY

Today, in the United States, there are more than 878,000 eating establishments. They range from coffee shops where an early bird special—orange juice, two eggs any style with bacon and toast, and coffee—costs as little as $5, through every type of ethnic cuisine from Tibetan to Thai, to the kind of restaurant where the white truffles are whisked in from the airport by special messenger, the soup water is flown in from China (or so the restaurateur's public relations firm would have you believe!), and the set menu, without wine or tips, costs $300 and up. There are about 100 restaurants in America where dinner for two can cost $400 with very little effort, and about 200 more where the same punishment can be exacted by insisting on outlandishly priced rare wines.

All restaurateurs are in the same business, bound by the same dynamics: supply and demand, competition, fashion, rent, the state of the economy, and the weather. Some restaurant chains include hot dog stands and luxury joints, taking the profit from each with equal pleasure. Whether it's preferable to sell 100 hamburgers at $5 each or 20 roast pheasants at $50 each is not merely a matter of taste, however. Different circumstances require different operations.

EDUCATION

An old military cliché states, "Time spent in reconnaissance is seldom wasted." The more you know about the restaurant business, the better. You must start observing when you go to restaurants. And thinking: Why is this place a success? What's it got? Why isn't this joint jumping in such a nice location with such great decor and marvelous food? What an unimaginative way to position the tables! Is there some structural reason why the restrooms are in that awkward spot, killing three tables stone dead? Why don't they partition off the entrance? Couldn't someone tell that busboy *not* to crash a load of dirty plates into the tray so noisily every two minutes? The maitre d' is handsome, but why does he look so sad? Why did that waitress suddenly burst into tears and rush off the floor? What a boring menu! Ah, but here's a good idea! And so on. Discussion will help, though there will come a time when the requirement is not for conjecture but for *action*.

Most restaurateurs work in the business and graduate to opening their own places. Starting young, they learn on the job and rarely undertake any formal study, confining themselves to occasionally checking out the competition. A long line of successful restaurateurs started as chefs, but they often employ front men as managers and maitre d's to cope with the fine art of handling the public and staff.

Reading is important. Advertisements, food critics' reports, and an enormous number of publications covering aspects of the industry will all yield useful information and ideas. The public library should have a copy of the *Small Business Source Book,* which lists publications pertinent to your business.

You should be aware of the ways in which you can learn about the business. Most major cities, though not all, have places where you can study. Since tuition is expensive, the cost of travel and board should be considered. If you live in, and plan to open your business in, an under-restauranted part of the country—a very smart idea—you'll have to travel to a city to study and get your first jobs.

COOKING SCHOOLS

There are cooking schools everywhere, but they don't all teach chefs how to prepare 300 dinners a night. The CIA (Culinary Institute of America) at New Hyde Park, New York, has a good reputation and offers a full training course.

An important aspect of restaurant school training is that the instructors get you out into functioning hotels and restaurants so that you can undergo your baptism by fire.

Many colleges also have courses, most notably Cornell, which has a Hotel and Restaurant Management School. In addition, there are wine courses at various colleges in New York and California that are part of their agriculture curriculum.

Most major cities now have bartender and waiter schools, which are not terribly expensive and offer short courses, sometimes lasting only two weeks. Many of them are no better than adequate, but they do orient a complete beginner in the basics. They'll teach you how to make a Bronx cocktail, which nobody orders anymore, and how to separate a locked shaker and mixing glass with a sharp blow from the heel of the hand instead of a bang, bang, bang against the bar. With a bit of luck, they'll teach their pupils not to slam cheap glassware into ice cubes so that it breaks, necessitating replacement of the ice and possibly a trip to the emergency room. Servers will be shown how to organize their orders and marry up half-empty ketchup bottles.

However, they don't teach charm, deportment, or the way to a customer's heart. These interpersonal skills have to be learned elsewhere. Restaurateurs seem to fall into three personality groups. There is, of course, Falstaff, ever ready to laugh and converse. Those little nips of white wine he has regularly throughout the working day preserve a gentle buzz to sustain this approach. Then there is Malvolio (or Lady Macbeth), who watches everything from afar, employing attractive young people to do the necessary smiling, and probably sneaks back to the restaurant after closing time to fill the Chivas Regal Scotch bottle with cheap plonk bottled in New Jersey. And last but best there is the well-trained, well-disposed person who brings genuine warmth to the workplace. Fortunately, there is something that protects against personality defects, and it's something most Americans possess: simple good manners.

Although some of the schools have a job placement service, most of them can't offer any public exposure. Only the better-established college schools can do that, and their training restaurants, which are open to the public, are a good bargain. (Because the students are willing and positive in their approach, the service and food are often better than you will find in many a "real" restaurant. They're good value and well worth checking out.)

All these establishments are a good source of staff, as well as places where you can learn the business. Students have to make the transition from the ideals of the classroom to the reality of business. Only real experience can teach you how to feed everyone at 8 P.M., how to lie convincingly, or how to compromise when you can't reach the standards you've set for yourself.

It's worth repeating that many—possibly a majority—of restaurateurs have no formal education at all. Many hardly speak English. They work in all the disciplines of the business until they have enough confidence, money, and initiative to go it alone. On the whole, they don't seem to do any worse than those who have expensive training, but this is a matter of some controversy.

One headwaiter decided it was time to teach his young son the ropes. He had him work as a busboy and general lackey for a while. Then one night he threw him in the deep end when a regular, friendly couple came in. Thrusting a pencil and a pad into the boy's hand he said, "Go over to that table and say 'Good evening, sir'—and we'll take it from there." Despite some trembling, there were no disasters. The young man knew he could do it, and he soon became an expert.

It doesn't much matter how you learn, as long as you learn. There's no proof that greater profits accrue to those who are expert chefs, scour the vineyards of the world, and know every fine restaurant in civilization. They probably enjoy life more, because knowing one's job and liking it usually means less stress and worry. But there appears to be no correlation between worth, merit, talent, and success.

In the process of learning the restaurant business, many people learn a lot about themselves. Occasionally, they may regret that greater self-knowledge.

So may their friends and loved ones. For better or for worse, it's a business that can change people.

THE RISKS

Many people will tell you that the restaurant business is *the* highest-risk business in the retail spectrum. This simply isn't true. The failure rate for eating places in general is below the average business failure rate nationwide. Camera, furniture, and apparel stores regularly top the failure list.

Some may doubt relevance of comparing apparel stores to restaurants. It may not be realistic. Apparel stores just sell clothes. Shirts don't rot, but lettuce does. Many restaurants don't just sell food. They sell service, convenience, atmosphere, escape, ambiance, theater, romance, adventure, excitement, love, therapy, and dreams. They offer their customers a unique playground. And they require a large capital investment—the single biggest roadblock to entering the business.

Perhaps a better comparison would be between Broadway musicals and restaurants, but market research hasn't gotten that far yet. However, some have managed to bring an intelligent eye to the subject.

H. G. Parsa, associate professor of Hospitality Management at the Ohio State University, carried out a longitudinal study of 2,439 restaurants in Columbus, Ohio, for the three-year period 1996 to 1999. He found the failure rate for restaurants was 57 to 61 percent. This figure may seem high, but it is in line with other businesses. First-year failures totaled 26 percent, second-year failures 19 percent, and third-year failures 14 percent. Parsa reviewed other studies and concluded that the failure rate after three to five years was no more than 60 percent.

We are currently living in more promising times as anyone who goes to restaurants can plainly see—franchise failure figures were at the 57 percent level, 4 percent below that of independent restaurants. The professor interviewed many "failed" restaurateurs and discovered that many of them had simply decided to do other things with their lives, or suffered from family disruption, or poor health. All complained of the immense time commitment a restaurant requires. People with well-managed families, single people, and divorcées seemed to cope best.

This could be optimistically interpreted to suggest that the true failure rate was actually lower than was finally concluded. Nor should one overlook the unknown percentage of restaurants never intended to succeed anyway, being used as tax shelters or for some convoluted accounting reason.

A recent reality TV show on NBC called *The Restaurant,* which many budding restaurateurs will no doubt have watched avidly, referred to a "90 percent failure rate." This grim, but actually fanciful, statistic was repeated in every episode. Such glib generalizations are very bad for the industry and for potential restaurateurs. Large amounts of money are often borrowed for start-up, and clearly if a bank manager or potential investor is imbued with such a dismal failure figure, it will be harder to raise cash.

The show involved a real restaurant, and, as it progressed, the main owner and the celebrity chef (described as "conceited and philandering") fell out. It emerged that the owner was a convicted felon with a long legal history behind him.

Dunn & Bradstreet's Business Failure Record (which ceased publication in 1998), cited an optimistic failure rate of only 106 per 10,000 units for "eating and drinking places," which is only 1.06 percent. However, it was using the most conservative definition of failure—which only includes those that went bankrupt, or closed with unpaid financial obligations. Also "eating and drinking places" covers everything from hot-dog stands to the Four Seasons. Unfortunately, no one has found a method of precisely refining the figures to the point where the failure rate for licensed restaurants seating 50 to 200 (the general focus of this book) can be calculated.

Alcohol licensing agencies can give no clue either, since the failure of a restaurant doesn't mean the cancellation of a license. Ten percent of the 5,000 (approximately) full liquor licenses in the five boroughs of New York City turn over every year, and the figure is just about constant. Turnover doesn't necessarily indicate failure; it indicates change—which might be due to sale, retirement, death, or expiration of lease.

In summary, the most cautious interpretation one can put on this discussion is that the restaurant failure rate is no higher than that of any other business.

REASONS FOR FAILURE

The stark reasons for business failure are worthy of study. Most retail businesses (68 percent) fail as a result of economic factors, some of which may be beyond their owners' control. These include loss of market and no consumer spending. A more significant figure, perhaps, is the next most common reason for failures (22 percent), grouped under "experience causes." These include incompetence, lack of line experience, lack of managerial experience and, quite important, unbalanced experience. Kitchen experts with no flair for handling the public, beware!

Most experienced restaurateurs agree on the two most common reasons for failure:

1. *Inadequate funds.* You run out of money before the restaurant attracts enough customers to go into profit.
2. *Poor management.* This is a catchall phrase, but should not be dismissed on those grounds.

Sometimes it becomes apparent soon after you open that a restaurant just isn't going to work. The chef, whose credentials were so impeccable, turns out to be a drunkard or incompetent, or both, when you actually commence operations. A replacement takes time to find, because the next two you try out are no better.

Poor security may mean that your takings are stolen. Food and alcohol may disappear, too. An unattractive crowd may monopolize the place, driving other customers away. A know-it-all manager may insist on loud rock music when the average age of the potential clientele is 50.

Then there are the ordinary accidents of life. Key personnel may drop dead on opening day or—as is common—just not show up. In an area where the only labor pool consisted of students, one tired manager complained, "I hire five people in the hope that three will show for work." A well-known and successful New York restaurateur decided to open a branch in Southampton, hoping to profit from the summer crowds. It proved almost impossible to recruit local labor in an area where the standard eighteenth birthday present was a Mercedes sports car. Employees had to be brought in from distant areas, and it was impossible to assemble a reliable staff. When workers fail to turn up, the owner or manager has a stark choice. He can close or do the job himself. In the Southampton example, the owner soon realized that the manager was worked to exhaustion and decided to close the establishment. Remember: Everyone dreads working in a new restaurant, and if a prospective employee finds a job in an established place before you put her on the payroll, you've lost her in a majority of cases. That is why you should always compile a list of prospective employees that is larger than your basic need.

Remember, also, that employees are likely to quit on the spot, day one, if their worst fears are confirmed. They will be particularly irked by managerial eccentricities that are not immediately matched by good earnings. Suddenly remembering a heavy, time-consuming task that absolutely must be done just as waiters are thinking of going home is a real morale killer. One owner insisted that every single movable item on the bar had to be sent down a long flight of steps and locked in a cellar, only to be brought up again at the commencement of the next day's business. It's simply no good saying, "They're there to work." "They" don't necessarily share your mystical conviction. Another owner insisted on examining the contents of employees' bags before they left—a common and highly degrading house rule in many places. Many businesses now insist on a drug test for employees—another highly demeaning process that, sadly, is generally accepted.

In time, everything can be perfected. But if the money runs out, you fail.

A sudden rerouting of traffic or the disappearance of a local parking facility can ruin a restaurant. And kitchen fires are extremely common.

Sabotage by rival restaurateurs is fairly common, too. They'll burn you down, report violations real or imaginary, or stage incidents in the restaurant.

In spite of the endless discussion of the subject, you rarely hear of a restaurant failing because of its lousy food. That's because, although finding the chef of your dreams isn't easy, it is feasible.

Some restaurants fail because they were never intended to succeed but only to launder money or provide some bigshot with a private supper club. No one can estimate the number of restaurants that are simply not intended to be anything but a money-laundering device. One bartender tells of an excellent job he once had where there was no tape in the cash register, and only a trickle of customers, invariably bedecked in diamond rings and yellow leather jackets, accompanied by beautiful women. They tipped lavishly, but laughed when they were presented with bills. "Don't gimme no tab, pal!" Excellent food and wine were served, but ordinary customers were positively discouraged from entering. After six months, the bartender went to work one day to find the place burned to the ground.

The bartender was understandably sad, but felt it'd been a good run for the money. Interestingly enough, he felt that, had the restaurant been operated with serious intentions, it would have been a roaring success.

There's a big "fools rush in" factor in the restaurant business, meaning that, as in any other business, efficient management is essential. It isn't a difficult business, but it isn't quite as simple as it looks to the casual eye. Many people are overwhelmed by it and can't get out fast enough.

The purpose of this book is to steer budding restaurateurs in intelligent directions, and to reduce that inevitable X factor—luck—to the smallest significance possible.

Fools often prosper where the wise fail in the restaurant business. There are also accidents. Many failures remain unrevealed, except to those who lost money in the process. No successful restaurateur is likely to bend the ears of her admirers with the story of her failures or of the businesses she owns that are losers and that she's dying to unload.

Loathsome establishments offering indifferent food and offhand service often make fortunes, even if nobody visits them twice. It is not too fanciful to suspect a *masochism factor* at work somewhere in the consumer psyche! In the

1970s, a restaurant in New York was called Coup de Fusil. That means *gunshot*, literally. But it's also French slang for *rip-off*. It would be nice to be able to say there are a few basic rules that can guarantee success, but it wouldn't be realistic to do so. In the end, you'll be on your own.

There's another business where fools often prosper and the wise fail. It's the business that has 82 percent of its union members out of work at all times. You guessed right—show business!

THE THEATER OF RESTAURANTS

Even if you don't have a proper kitchen, you can easily fix dinner for two at home for $10 or less, not including alcohol. A middle-class saloon, bar-and-grill, or bistro type of restaurant (which is the main target area of this book) will not feed you for that amount. If you feature a bowl of soup for $4.95, you'll occasionally get thrifty customers who'll order just that and no more, and eat all the bread in sight. If the place is busy enough, you'll hardly notice. If it isn't, you'll find that waiters and waitresses have a way of freezing out such people—or, if it becomes a standing routine, pocketing the money without making a check! In the words of the old song, "Ya git no bread with one meat ball!"

Since it's clearly possible to satisfy the basic human urge to eat for quite little, why are so many people prepared to pay the truly astronomical prices to be found at some restaurants? Note the precision of the question. The question is not, Why do restaurants charge such high prices? There are plenty of reasons for that, which will be discussed. The question is, why are people prepared to pay them?

Clearly, the desire to eat is only one of the reasons why people go to restaurants, because you don't have to go to a restaurant just because you're hungry. The worker too far from home to return for sustenance and the traveller obviously need to eat somewhere, although some people either pack a lunch or buy a sandwich and eat it on a park bench during the lunch hour.

Most people go to restaurants in order to socialize, talk about business, or happily mix both. The enormous affluent middle class, with 128 hours a week to spare after its 40 hours of labor, has both time and money on its hands. Restaurants could be said to form part of the leisure industry.

In the television age, some argue, conversation is a lost art. Cute one-liners are what most people give and seek. The alternative is the long, often repeated speech from the soapbox. Since entertaining at home *always* poses the threat of conversation, it's not surprising that so many people, who could easily afford it, avoid it like the plague. Even when people entertain at home, in cities it's quite common for them to take their guests out for dessert and espresso.

(This is often a social ploy for making sure your guests disperse at a reasonable hour.) Also, with spare money available, why shouldn't people avoid the labor of preparation and planning, especially if they have jobs?

Thus, the restaurant takes its place alongside the cinema, the theater, and things-to-do. It has become a modern ritual. The fact that business entertainment is tax-deductible assures many a restaurateur of a good night's sleep. As in the travel business, corporations are the knights in shining armor. Some estimate that 60 percent of U.S. city restaurants would close if all bills were paid from personal disposable income. Apart from business entertaining, it's brilliant if your restaurant can become the hang-out for a large firm or profession. The Wall Street area of New York has many such establishments, and London is particularly clubby. In the United Kingdom, the Conservative Party patronizes Wilton's, while the Laborites prefer The Gay Hussar. There are pubs for journalists, artists, lawyers, and doctors. A restaurant or a pub that becomes an unofficial club will do well to indulge its clientele, who are enjoying all the delights of a proper club without subscription.

Restaurants offer a useful service and solve a lot of problems, including what to eat and where to meet, for people who live at a distance from each other. The restaurant is also a heaven-sent compromise for the affluent but inarticulate person who nevertheless wishes to relate to someone, whether for business, sexual, family, or social reasons. It provides unthreatening neutral ground, as well as an arena offering opportunities to flatter and impress for any number of purposes. If conversation suggests itself, you can have conversation. If it doesn't, you can discuss the other customers, the food, the view, other joints you've been in, or the way mother used to make whatever it is you're having. "Whatever happened to mashed potatoes/chicken á la king/garlic bread?" you can wittily demand, often prompting a flood of responses. Many people visit restaurants as an exercise in itself, in search of escape, in the same spirit that they would go to the movies.

Other customers can be very important, as people watchers watch *other* people-watchers in a sort of built-in cabaret that doesn't have to be listed in the owner's overhead. Experienced maitre d's soon learn the art of "dressing the room" by putting the most beautiful and affluent people at the most prominent table. Regular customers sometimes reciprocate by always wanting the same table, and that is just one typical restaurant situation you have to learn to handle. Nine out of ten times, customers accept alternatives with good grace. Sometimes they'll sit at the bar for a while, and sometimes they'll take another table on a temporary basis, which can cause some gnashing of teeth if, while two tables are occupied, only one of them is consuming. Customers who don't conform to the happy, beautiful, glossy ideal and look as if they might talk or swear loudly are usually consigned safely to an out-of-the-way spot.

For some people, being greeted by name by a hostess or maitre d' is the very stuff of heaven. Magazines regularly show restaurant floor plans, indicating the *power tables,* where famous regular customers sit. At many restaurants, such as Smith & Wollensky's in New York, brass nameplates over some tables indicate the names of their favorite occupiers. "Abe Weinstein sat here." "The Irving Schwartz chair." Glory indeed!

How long will it take before a diner commits suicide after being forced to occupy a table of less power than usual or after being consigned to "Siberia" or "Lower Slobovia" instead of "Banquette Number Two" (the hot table at the old El Morocco)?

It's a form of theater and a form of escape. Often, newspapers accord more pages to the subjects of food and restaurants than they do to theater and cinema combined. Restaurant scenes are hard to do on stage, but it's unusual to see a movie without one, and at least one restaurant scene is *de rigueur* in the modern novel. Dramatic events occur in restaurants. People decide to get married, occasionally die, are murdered, or give birth. Both sexes have been known to remove their clothes. Customers walk in with lions or ocelots on a leash, parrots on their shoulders, and boa constrictors around their necks.

In the movies, fights are not uncommon. Tablecloths offer an irresistible target—usually for jealous lovers. One vicious tug and there's chaos! At the Hotel Lexington in New York, there used to be a plaque on the wall commemorating the occasion when a woman blew her brains out while sitting at the bar, though whether this was meant as a comment about the service or the prices isn't indicated.

Incidentally, what happens in restaurants when murders or suicides or fights occur is quite simple. Everybody leaves. They very sensible don't want to get involved. And they often never return. For a version of what happens in a restaurant when a diner drops dead, Tom Wolfe's *Bonfire of the Vanities* makes highly entertaining reading.

Thankfully, few customers are as eccentric as William Astor Chandler, who became impatient while lunching at Maxim's one day in the 1920s because he had a horse running that afternoon. He threw his artificial leg plus sock, shoe, and garter at the waiter's back and shouted, "Now may I have your attention?"

Budding restaurateurs will breathe a sigh of relief at the assertion that 99 percent of customers enter, sit, drink, eat, pay, and leave without any noticeable contretemps. Smiles are part of the ritual.

It's vitally important that restaurateurs be able to put themselves in the customers' shoes and sense what they're thinking. Here are two examples of people with strong views on restaurants. What they have to say should be taken with a pinch of salt, and it's unlikely that you'll recognize any of your friends. But what they say may be illuminating and interesting.

Here's what a woman who loves to lunch and dine and take afternoon tea—in other words, a woman who just lives to go to restaurants—has to say:

I simply love going out to restaurants. It's such a wonderful escape from the cares and woes of everyday life. I have my favorite places, but I like to explore new restaurants, too. One of the things that makes being a woman such fun is that I often get taken to quite expensive restaurants free, because my charming male escort pays. If I'm with a woman friend, or a guy who really can't afford it, I pay my share. I think you can learn a lot about people from watching the way they behave in restaurants. I don't just mean their table manners. I mean the way they handle waiters and the various little situations that occur. Some people are gracious, kind, understanding, and forgiving, even when things aren't quite perfect. Others are quick to complain. I always notice how much men tip, because that's a good indication of what they're really like. Undertipping indicates a mean streak. Overtipping indicates insecurity and a desire to impress, and that always leaves me cold. I always take an interest in the decor, and what people around me are wearing. I think fresh flowers can turn a restaurant into a fairyland.

If I have new clothes, I like to wear them to a restaurant and gauge the effect they have on people. Above all, I love the moment of entrance, when everyone looks up at you. Sometimes it can be a little intimidating, but it's exciting, too. You feel like a great actor stepping on stage and about to deliver a thrilling line. Of course, this sensation is heightened when there are real actors or celebrities in the restaurant! I do like good service, when the waiters really convince you that they want you to enjoy the whole experience, and try to satisfy your faintest whim. Good waiters know exactly when to take away your plate and when to serve the next course. They anticipate your needs. It's nice to be treated like a star. I especially like it when the help can answer your questions properly, like, "Do you use first pressing olive oil in the salad dressing?" or when they fall over themselves to get you something that isn't on the menu. I simply hate it when they get the orders mixed up and you suddenly find yourself looking at a Canard Rôti when you were expecting a veal chop. It's even worse when they interrupt important business conversation or intimate confessions by asking, "Who gets the steak?" In my favorite restaurant, the maitre d' always presents me with a carnation the minute I walk in, which makes me feel so wanted and cherished, and the waiters are so kind and sweet, they actually run when you ask for something, which shows they really care."

At the other end of the spectrum, a restaurant hater—by no means an uncommon species—says:

I loathe restaurants, and have done so since I was a child, when I could never believe the enormous amounts of money my father was paying for food which tasted funny and not at all like we ate at home. Although the people smiled at him a lot, I could tell they didn't really like us. Nowadays I notice the awful pain in the eyes of some of the restaurant help, particularly the hostesses. It can be quite heartrending, and is hardly conducive to a good time. That servile whipped-cur look. Am I their temporary jailer? The other customers are a real turn-off, too. All those phony voices and smiles. Restaurant customers always look faintly embarrassed, like children on strict orders to mind their manners. All that intense buttering of bread and dainty chewing!

One of the reasons I hate restaurants now is that I can't escape the ritual. I *have* to go to lunch and dinner as part of my business, and I resent it, even though it costs me nothing, because important discussion of business gets lost in discussion of restaurant trivia. I hate having to listen to long descriptions of the Daily Specials delivered with the solemnity of medieval High Mass, and loud-mouthed conversations from other diners, often sprinkled with four-letter words I can do without.

Nor do I like the sound of my own voice as I desperately try to get something to eat and drink that approximates to the way I'd have it if I were at home. "Rare, but not too rare," and all that sort of thing sounds so inane. No wonder the waiters sometimes look at me in an indulgent, pitying way, as though they knew I was just recovering from serious brain damage! At home I just cook things my way, and shrug it off if I get things a bit wrong. I sound so cantankerous, insisting on a fresh bottle of soda for my drink, with just so much ice and extra lime. I often suspect the server thinks I'm a jerk, and who's to say he's not right, temporarily, at least? But at home I make my drink like that automatically, with a huge piece of lime, and top it up with a little vodka or soda the split second I feel like it—not when I at last manage to catch the waiter's or the bartender's eye! The fact that the drink is costing me $7.50 plus tip, when I can buy a whole bottle of vodka for less than twice that amount, doesn't help. Sometimes I feel I'm locked with the waiters by mutual consent in a form of ritual imbecility! Banging kitchen doors, dishes crashing into bustrays. Nor do I like to be sneered at by a waiter or waitress who's obviously just doing a little social research while awaiting the release of the hit movie in which he or she has a starring role. I don't like seeing people grubbing for tips—it doesn't seem very American to me. And, although I tip a straight 15 percent or more in order to make sure I get out alive, I really don't see why I should pay the restaurateur's payroll as well as his entrepreneurial markup, not forgetting a dollar to hang up my coat! Mind you, I was in Russia once, where you're not allowed to tip, and the service was so bad I thought I was going to starve to death!

As to the food, it's not what I'm in a restaurant for, so it hardly matters. If I'm paying, I just have the smallest, cheapest thing on the menu, having fixed myself a sandwich at home before I go out. But I do notice that, unless you're in an expensive gourmet joint, there isn't a damn thing on the average menu that I couldn't fix myself at home in five minutes flat for $4. Bah! Humbug! There's no escape. I shall just have to grin and bear it. However, there's a bistro place not far from where I live that isn't too expensive and the food's okay. They have good value wine specials. The owner's a nice guy, and the waitresses are efficient and friendly. I go there pretty often.

Experienced restaurateurs would not be impressed by these comments. They know there's resentment out there, and they know how to bear it. They try to turn the most reluctant cynic into a paying customer. They also know that business people are, in fact, the best customers and the easiest to deal with. Prompt service, decent food, and good drinks in a pleasant atmosphere will send people home having had an agreeable experience. That's the way to make them come back.

WHO OPENS RESTAURANTS, AND WHY

If your objective is to be in business for yourself, there are lots of things you can do besides open a restaurant. To some budding entrepreneurs, the prospect is unattractive. For one thing, you need a large amount of start-up money. You might just get off the ground with a 50-seat bar and grill in the country with $200,000. In a major city, $1 million would be a more realistic figure, given current rents.

There's a lot to be said for sticking with the business you know, and a lot of restaurateurs are people who entered the industry young and can envision no other way of life. They're usually the ones who succeed, but good privates don't always make good sergeants.

Many restaurants are inherited. For instance, many immigrants into the United States have received the call from an ailing relative to begin learning how to hustle their way into the restaurant world. It's amazing how swiftly and easily most of them take to their new role in life.

Opening a restaurant is sometimes the only way of making an old, much-loved home viable. Many European aristocrats, notably Lord MacDonald and Sir Fitzroy MacLean in Scotland, have done this, and the syndrome exists in the United States. The success rate in such operations seems to be high, but the aristos invariably complain, both in public and private, about the hard work involved. They look forward to their vacations.

SACRED MONSTERS

Some of the most successful restaurants in the country are owned and run, often with an iron fist and a beady eye on the cash register 24/7, by highly un-attractive people with no personality whatsoever, who are delighted to proclaim their contempt for mankind in general and their customers in particular.

Many restaurateurs develop absurdly inflated egos, perhaps as a reaction against the essentially menial nature of the work. Small wonder, then, that some magazines when reviewing restaurants described the currently famous chefs as "Restaurant Gods"!

The late Henri Soulé made a great ceremony of tearing up the checks of customers who dared to query them, informing his foolishly impetuous ex-clients with a sneer that they had "dined as his guest, but that they needn't ex-pect ever to be served again." When anyone offered the slightest comment, he would bow sarcastically and say, "Je suis Simonizé, m'sieur!" (It's a labored joke in translation: "I'm Simonized"—in other words, "I'm waxed, impervious to your remarks.") It's difficult to imagine him ever smiling or even being re-motely polite to anyone. Yet Le Pavilion is often invoked with nostalgia by el-derly gourmets who remember the food as being outstanding. The place al-ways had the air of a funeral parlor, such was the profusion of flowers. The bill for flowers was supposed to be enormous. (One restaurant in New York today claims an annual flower bill of more than $100,000. Skeptics may reflect that every petal and every stalk must be paid for by the customer.) Bing Crosby was turned away after daring to enter without a tie. "An insult to my restaurant!" the owner cried, lacking the gumption to lend the crooner a tie for an hour. In today's aggressively casual times, most maitre d's have on hand a selection of ties and jackets for their underdressed patrons.

The late Italian war hero and socialite Gianni Agnelli's proudest moment was when he was allowed into "21" wearing blue jeans!

Another sacred monster is the woman who spends all night at the end of the bar and makes out all the checks herself, using a selection of very sharp pencils. She pads the checks shamelessly, and when, as regularly happens, her unseen, undelivered, and certainly unconsumed additional "2 Stuffed Mushrooms, $28.00" is discovered by an alert diner, and she is forced to erase the line from the check, her language would make a stevedore blush! The hapless waiter makes the necessary apologies. She never explains, often complains, and never apologizes.

This ploy may make some frown as they think about it and wonder how anyone would dare do such a thing. But we live in affluent times. One sees groups of diners, often bankers or traders, eating lavish meals and consuming bottles of expensive wine, yet *not even looking at the check* when it's presented in its neat leather-bound case (called a *check presenter*) with a little slot where a credit card can be inserted, remaining visible so that the waiter knows when to pick it up. They all put their credit cards on the table and sometimes have a little squabble about whose treat it is. This is the other end of the spectrum from the little old lady lunchers who examine the check minutely: "Let's see . . . you had the pecan pie . . ." and include pennies, nickles, and dimes in their tip.

Quixotically enough, apart from occasional foaming at the mouth, this woman doesn't bother her employees much, and they speak of her with wry smiles rather than contempt. They make good money working for her. Her employees are queasy allies. They are not the enemy! She has been known to physically attack customers who displease her. On one occasion, she insisted on levying a cover charge on an ambassador's bodyguards, who'd hoped to sit discreetly at an adjoining table while their employer dined. And when the ambassador declined to pay the sales tax on the bill, pleading diplomatic immunity, she socked him in the nose with the cry, "I pay sales tax in *your* country." (One restaurateur in the United Nations neighborhood in New York printed a little notice addressed to diplomats: "Due to the extensive paperwork generated by allowing diplomatic immunity from sales tax, we regret that we are unable to accommodate the privilege." He was incensed by their much-exploited immunity from parking tickets. Diplomats either went elsewhere or paid the full bill. The restaurateur may have been wrong in law, but nobody sued.)

Nevertheless, restaurants like this attract celebrities, and their public relations firms keep them appearing in the gossip columns even though their food and service are sometimes—mercifully—forgotten.

The probable reason for this joint's undoubted success is that it's always full, and there's always a buzz from the crowded diners, which helps to dampen the loneliness of the many lost souls who go to the restaurant not only to eat and socialize, but for some reassurance that there's life out there. Whether you like it or not, crowded restaurants are generally more attractive than empty ones.

Then there was the late Glenn Birnbaum's famous Mortimer's. The exhaberdasher millionaire restaurateur would sometimes manage a thin smile as he regaled his admiring customers with stories about the time he bought a large quantity of white wine of such poor quality that the customers actually noticed and kept sending it back. He had the bright idea of using it only to make spritzers (white wine with seltzer and a twist of lemon—what the Victorians called hock and seltzer). Lo and behold, he got away with it, and turned less than $1,000 into about $20,000.

The food, kept deliberately down-market by way of reverse snobbery, was sometimes not bad. It's boldest innovations were *twinburgers* (two hamburgers on the same plate—"two burgers 21" in kitchen jargon) and sherry trifle. Often, people were turned away from his restaurant even when there were tables available. Since reservations for *deuces* or couples were not taken, one can only assume that he was hoping someone a little more interesting or glamorous would come in. If they didn't, that was okay, too, because he was a multimillionaire. Good-looking or rich-looking people were usually sure of a table, and a European accent helped.

He would back people up at the bar, where a two-hour wait for a table was not uncommon. If anyone querulously asked whether his table was ready yet, he would pull out his waiting list and brandish his pen threateningly. "Oh, you're leaving?" he'd say with another thin smile. A 22-carat snob, he would invariably try to put well-known faces on the first table nearest the door so that arriving diners might be lucky enough to see Mick Jagger, Jerry Hall, Madonna, Jackie Collins, Joan Collins, Tom Collins, Elizabeth Taylor, Princess Margaret, the Dukes and Duchesses of Roxburghe and Westminster, the Earls of Erroll and Westmoreland, the Aga Khan (who employs at least three gourmet chefs of his own at home), the kings of Spain, Greece, Bulgaria, and Albania, and on and on.

Unlike our lady monster, this owner was not looked upon by his staff with wry fondness. On the contrary, one of them tried to put a contract on him!

Lots of society functions were held at his restaurant for great-grandmother socialites in instantly identifiable designer clothes hoping to be mistaken for debutantes: their incredibly distinguished, sensitive "walkers," as young escorts are called in gossip columns, foreigners desperately trying to be cool Americans; and often rich young men sitting out the time until they turned 28 and thus no longer risked being required to serve in the military of their home countries. The monster was easily distinguished at these black-tie gatherings: he was the one in the crumpled polyester business suit and the garish tie. The list of guests, which was always the same, was faithfully recorded in the gossip columns. If one called him and asked for the number of his public relations people, he'd snap, "I don't do public relations," and hang up.

But the truth is, his public relations effort was relentless and expensive.

After a while, the place became something of an icon, and journalists would write about it in ribald tones describing the place as a "Manolo Blahnik floor show" and its customers variously as "trust fund bums" and "rich widow hunters." Also, the location, on an Upper East Side corner, was superb. The place was easy to find and within strolling distance of where most of the regular customers lived. It was usually busy, and business begets business.

This is an excellent example of snob appeal. People will go to a restaurant because it's the place their crowd—or the crowd they aspire to join—goes to. Such restaurants work very well when they work. But groups are fickle, and it doesn't take much to make the flock suddenly switch its allegiance. Should its leaders start going elsewhere, if the food is *too* awful or overpriced, or if the staff become rude in a way that is merely offensive and tiresome, affording no grotesque, pseudo-baroque amusement and no masochistic delight, then death will come quickly. No restaurateur should assume that today's recipe for success will last forever.

THE MASOCHISM FACTOR

In the face of such success, it may not be too fanciful to suspect that a masochism factor exists and that some people really do like a little punishment. We all know the *fashion victim* syndrome, where people squeeze themselves into uncomfortable clothes that really don't flatter them at all, for the sake of being up to date. Some people want to go where they're told they can't go, in the same way that some cannot resist touching what is clearly marked as wet paint. Establishing *exclusivity,* or the illusion thereof, can pay. Some people don't care how they're insulted or ripped off as long as they can enjoy the warm conviction that they're in the right place, the hot spot where the action is and where the movers and shakers congregate. But most experienced restaurateurs feel it's a dangerous game. There's too much competition in most cities. Longevity is the reward for restaurants that are consistent in their standards of food and service.

But are people really that much into pain? It's more likely a slavish following of fashion, relentless PR, and the attraction of a restaurant that is known to draw celebrities or a certain group or profession. It is precisely the pleasant prospect of seeing either someone you know or someone you'd very much *like* to know, that brings affluent socialites, or would-be socialites, to a restaurant like moths to the flame and, credit where credit's due, these ghastly ogres deliver! Your hamburger might be like minced shoe leather, your wine reminiscent of a herbal concoction, and your cognac of dubious provenance and measured with a thimble at an exorbitant price. But the modest, unassuming fellow at the next table, should you be so lucky, really is Mick Jagger. You are temporarily part of his world. If you catch his eye, he might even give you the Famous Grin. With a little effort, you might almost arrange to surreptitiously touch the hem of his garment.

THINKING POSITIVE — THE FUN SIDE

There's no doubt that a successful restaurant is a wonderful thing to own. There are many restaurants that turn over several million dollars a year. In 2000, the Windows on the World restaurant at the World Trade Center, which had had a $25-million re-vamp after the 1993 bombing, grossed $37.5 million, at that time, the biggest in America. Needless to say, 9/11 changed all that. In June 2004, Smith & Wollensky, a New York steakhouse, was said to be the largest grossing à-la-carte restaurant in the United States. After opening in 1977, the company now has 17 restaurants nationwide.

Cash flow is immediate. The sight of new restaurateurs queuing at the local American Express office to get the cash for the day's slips is quite common. It's mostly cash on the barrelhead, and the restaurateur suffers less than other business people from the curse of credit and unpaid bills. Also, there are many attractive, perfectly legal tax and expense perks. And, although the initial work effort is enormous, once the thing is flying, you can put it on automatic to a certain extent and work on a normal, healthy schedule. A little bit of flair and personality can go a long way. After all, you're selling goods at the retail level to people who may be seeking entertainment and relaxation as well as simple sustenance. The ability to make easy small talk with customers is obviously no bad thing, and restaurants do exist where the owner is established as a figurehead—sometimes a charmer, sometimes a rogue, but almost always wise, warm, and welcoming. Such owners build a following that is great for business but sometimes a bit of a problem for the new incumbent if the restaurant changes hands. ("Joe here? No? He retired? Oh, well, give him my best if you see him. Er. . . . no, we don't have time for dinner, we just thought we'd look in.") Good manners and a ready smile are quite sufficient for success— there's no need to be a legendary figure. Ideally, you should be able to say, like the owner of Le Cirque, "Our foundation is so strong that the restaurant could function for quite a while without any given chef, or maitre d'hotel, or me."

An awful lot of people open restaurants for reasons that are not purely businesslike. There's a certain mystique about owning a restaurant. You create a world that others enter. Sometimes there's reciprocity and you're invited into their worlds, too! One might call this approach the Casablanca factor.

THE CASABLANCA FACTOR

Few cult movies enjoy a greater following than *Casablanca*. Most would agree that it's a good flick—Claude Raines and Ingrid Bergman help it along. It's set at a crossroads of time and circumstance, in the subtropical Moroccan city of Casablanca, just before America entered World War II. Vichy French view Nazis with suspicion. Rick is played by Humphrey Bogart, that ingratiating basset hound with the sibilant, distinctive voice. The owner of Rick's Café oversees his own microcosm of mankind through a sad but compassionate eye. Rick's Café is a white-tablecloth restaurant with a black singer pianist and is, very conveniently, the general rendezvous for the cast.

The truth is, Rick lives! While making a better-than-average living and calling his own shots, he is the catalyst and sometimes-supreme arbiter of people's lives. We never know quite where he comes from, whether he has brothers or sisters, or prefers fishing to football, or whether he's 30 or 60, but one thing's for sure: In Casablanca, he has stature, authority, and identity. He's a reference point of local life, and he knows all the "usual suspects" intimately. When people want to sing their national anthems, they do it in his place. No arena could be more appropriate. And Rick? Well, he's lonely and sad, but chances are, he would be no matter what he was doing. His white tuxedo never has sweat patches, it's unlikely that he pays for his cigarettes, and he eats three squares a day.

Many budding restaurateurs want to be Rick. All successful restaurateurs become Ricks, whether they like it or not. Their restaurants become the center of many people's lives, a reference point and arena for their employees and customers alike.

But in the movie, we only see Rick enjoying glamorous dramatic moments. True, the police close him down at one point, but we don't see him trying to find two waiters, a bartender, and a dishwasher who fail to show for work 20 minutes before 40 customers arrive, while the air conditioning's on the blink and not a loaf of bread is to be found because of the bakers' strike. The languages of Casablanca are French and Arabic. So why does everyone so conveniently speak English?

The escapist function of the movies wouldn't work if, instead of looking at the interesting bits of people's lives, we wallowed in their plumbing problems. But to enjoy the ephemeral delights of glamorous Rickdom, one must first suffer a little. As the old English motto has it, "Through mud and blood to the green fields beyond!"

CHAPTER 2

LOCATION

THE IMPORTANCE OF LOCATION

The oldest cliché in the retail business is "Location, location, location." Many restaurateurs believe location to be *the* most critical factor in the restaurant success formula. Those who don't agree with that will cite the example of restaurants in clearly less than ideal situations, that are successful anyway. There are ways and means of making some mediocre locations successful. But a bad location can be a heartbreaker. Some restaurateurs, who can afford to wait, will spot a changing residential trend and move in, in order to be in place when the unattractive neighborhood becomes fashionable. That takes shrewd judgment, patience, guts, and more money than the tyro restaurateur can usually raise.

Would-be restaurateurs are sometimes put off by the presence of other restaurants near premises they like. If you plan a steakhouse, and there are already two others on the block, you may be unwise to join the throng. But if *your* operation is only in general but not specific competition with the neighbors, there may be no reason to be put off. On the contrary, a conglomeration of restaurants is often a business booster. There are several adjoining Indian restaurants in New York's East Village, for instance. Restaurant Row on New York's West 46th Street consists entirely of restaurants, all of different style and quality. The suburb of Highgate, near London, supports a coffee shop, a Chinese restaurant, an Italian restaurant, and a steakhouse. All do well. If you look around, you'll see that restaurant grouping is quite common, as it is in other businesses. London's tailors crowd into Savile Row, New York's diamond merchants all seem to be on 48th Street, and so on.

Many, but by no means all, new restaurants simply replace ones that have failed, or whose owners want to retire or move on for some other reason. Sometimes a renewal of a lease and consequent rent hike may make the operation nonviable. To pay, the restaurant is going to have to take in more money, and the owners don't see how it can be done. Maybe these spaghetti and meatballs have to be replaced by Chateaubriands. In contemplating the failure of predecessors, clues to future success may often be discerned. Frequently, you can get it right by carefully noting how someone else got it hopelessly wrong.

Clearly, an ideal situation for a soda, coffee, and doughnut shop is across the street from the local high school or in the middle of a busy business or shopping district. A licensed, middle-priced bistro will do well either in a city residential area or, again, in a business or shopping area. For a successful restaurant you simply must have customers!

A really high-class gourmet restaurant may do better in an expensive city or suburban area. If you check the addresses of those restaurants listed in guides as expensive, you'll notice that the majority reside in high-rent areas. It is often the case that a restaurateur in possession of, or renting, a property in such a neighborhood, will opt for the top end of the market, for all its extra problems and the well-known fickle nature of such clientele. In the same way, if you inherit the premises opposite the high school, your ambitious escargots and white truffles may be cast like pearls before swine!

Of course there are exceptions to the rule, but square pegs just don't go in round holes. The location and the type of restaurant should complement each other. Nevertheless, there's some suspicion that the rich actually disdain the high-end restaurant market, and will welcome cheap and cheerful places. Bad Homburg is said to be the richest town in Germany. As a suburb of Frankfurt, it houses senior people in the banking industry. Its most popular restaurant is called *Kartoffelküche,* meaning *potato kitchen.* It serves potatoes in every imaginable style, along with pork, ham, sausages, and salad. The simplest German dishes are concocted from these basic items. There is little or no décor, and customers share bare tables reminiscent of an army mess hall. It's a cheerful, bustling, children-friendly place, with an excellent location in the center of town. One perhaps wouldn't take the chairman there to clinch the Big Deal. However, there is a huge desire nowadays for people to demonstrate how unpretentious they are, as though there were a threateningly huge population of monocle-wearing men in white-tie-and-tails and women in tiaras looking down their noses at the rest of the human race. Certainly casual is the modern style, and even smart, expensive restaurants rarely dare to insist on ties, slacks, and jackets. Older people may not necessarily applaud this. When you've bathed, shaved and put on a nice shirt, it's a bit galling to go for dinner at 9 P.M. to find a restaurant full of people in T-shirts, sneakers, and shorts, the men unshaven—or should one say *designer-stubbled?*

Some locations are obvious winners. Top floors of skyscrapers will place as much emphasis on the view in their advertising as they do on the food, service, reasonable prices, and general joy of it all. P. J. Clarke's in New York became famous after being used as a location in the movie *Lost Weekend* and now enjoys a quaint solitude on a corner, surrounded by towering skyscrapers. It refused to sell out to the developers. Sparks steakhouse saw its business boom after Gotti's henchmen dispatched two rivals outside the entrance. A front-page picture displayed two neat corpses, one in monogrammed socks.

Mystical Factors

But some locations just don't make it—ever. The owner of a corner restaurant that had changed owners frequently called in an exorcist to try and drum up business. It was a dead corner, and such apparently cursed locations do exist. They're the first ones you'll come across once you start looking for premises!

But how come the restaurant at the diagonally opposite corner was such a roaring success? It offered nothing that the haunted house didn't have, but it was always full. The simple truth must be that some corners are more inviting than others. There are exposed corners and there are inviting corners, warm ones and cold ones. If this sounds illogical, welcome to the wonderful world of restaurants! The reasons for it may be buried deep in the subconscious, but people do seem to make instinctive choices in these matters. Nine out of ten people, walking into a room where the reasons for going to the left are absolutely as good as those for going to the right, will move to the left. Lost in the desert, the explorer who doesn't know how to navigate by the stars will walk in a wide counterclockwise circle. So there *are* mysterious forces at work! Not for naught do perfectly rational businessmen pay vast sums for feng-shui.

"I do business charts for someone opening a business," astrologist Lynne Palmer told *The New York Times*. "If a person is starting a restaurant, I determine the best time to open it. Years ago, . . . there was a restaurant down the block from me. Good food, reasonable prices. And yet there was never anyone there. The owner gave me the date he opened. I looked it up in my book of planets. Sure enough, he opened at the wrong time. Within a few months he closed."

At the risk of appearing unromantic, sticking to the normal disciplines of business is more likely to achieve desired ends than stargazing. However, any experienced bartender will tell you that the public's behavior often becomes very strange at the time of the full moon! (Hence the word *lunatic*, of course, from the Latin *luna* for moon.)

A keen eye will be able to tell whether a location can be developed and improved. When Michael Wharton opened Oliver's in New York, he took a chance on a bar that formerly housed illegal gambling in the back room on a rather bleak block. Neighbors assured him that bodies had been carried out of the place on more than one occasion. Nevertheless, he sensed that, though it wasn't ideal, there was nothing basically wrong with the location, and he opened a moderately priced American restaurant that, after a few nail-biting months, soon became a great success. On acquiring the lease to the upstairs space, he even managed to make The Upstairs Room profitable, in spite of the dour restaurateur's maxim, "They won't go upstairs." The simple truth is that "They" *will* go upstairs if it's made inviting enough! If they see a nice room with a bar and an attentive crew who give every promise of prompt service, there'll be no resistance. But too often, the upstairs room is empty, cold, and forbidding, and patrons suspect the visits from the waiters are going to be intermittent at best.

Regrettably, this restaurant was eventually closed after encountering lease problems. This brings us to a worrisome aspect of the restaurant industry. In many cities, a thirty-year lease on restaurant premises used to be standard. Thus, the restaurateur had time to maneuver and make changes if necessary. Nowadays, it's often hard to get more than a three-year lease, and one can be sure that the rent will increase if the landlord sees a successful business operation. For many restaurateurs this is insufficient security to commence operations. Although many operations break even within a year, the average rule of thumb is three years, and some will say even five. There are many frustrated would-be restaurateurs as a result of this.

The sublime solution is to buy a property outright or "freehold," and either convert it from its existing use or continue the existing operation.

There are some happy stories in the country. People have bought large properties and converted them for restaurant, and often hotel, use. Local governments tend to be easy-going in rural areas, especially if they suspect a business will generate jobs and spending. One such highly successful operation divided a large premises into three operations—fine dining on one floor, a diner-style restaurant on another, and a bar with sports TV screen on another.

Real estate and the restaurant business are inextricably intertwined.

Country and Suburban Locations

The oft-quoted statistic that 70 percent of Americans live in cities can be a bit misleading. Some American cities—Los Angeles, New York, Dallas-Fort Worth, Boston, Chicago—are enormous and include large areas of rambling suburbs that are not quite country. Nor should one forget "the country" itself, although usually a restaurant will not do well in distant, wild country unless it's on a major highway, a landmark, or the kind of place with cult status. Few people in California or Connecticut live more than 10 minutes from a gas station, police station, general store, or village center.

Rents and property prices are, inevitably, much lower outside cities. Getting help can sometimes be a problem, but most manage. Some restaurants get around the problem by offering accommodations over the shop to their employees.

The automobile is what makes the country possible as a restaurant location. Americans will commonly drive 50 miles to a restaurant on weekends—or during the week if they're retired or on vacation. At the Hilltop Restaurant in Saugus, Massachusetts, four of the restaurant's 700 employees direct traffic to the parking lot. Opened in 1961 with a seating capacity of 125, the restaurant now seats 2,000 souls, summoned to their tables by public address system at the appointed hour. A visit is a *must* for any budding restaurateur who happens to find himself in the neighborhood. The location is excellent. It's easily reached by car, and there's a huge landmark cactus sign outside to reduce a driver's chance of overshooting the target.

Fortunes await restaurateurs who correctly gauge the point on the map that will serve as a catchment area for local residents living within a 50-mile radius. The country is full of such unexploited sites. When thinking in this area, it's important to determine whether there's a heavy weekend factor. You'll be lucky to get a table at any ocean resort restaurant on a Saturday night in July. You might have to wait until midnight. But on a Monday night, you can probably walk in, and the maitre d' will even have time to make zabaglione at your table and discuss the weather. The fact that so many country and suburban restaurants are closed on Mondays gives you the clue!

Rent

With commercial rents in New York now in excess of $400 per square foot per annum, it's clear that in any major city, rent is going to be the restaurateur's main and inescapable expense. Many restaurants are only viable as businesses because their owners also own the building. Thus, the restaurant business merges with the real estate business. A man who owns a large building will often find that the best thing to do with the ground-floor space is to turn it into a restaurant, especially if the owner has difficulty in renting it out for some other purpose. This emphasizes the attraction of finding an inexpensive location. But defining a catchment area and opening up in it takes judgment and courage.

HOW TO FIND PREMISES

Restaurants for sale are often advertised in newspapers. There are restaurant brokers who specialize in the handling of restaurant properties. They will supply you with a list, usually free. You pay a commission if a deal goes through. Some of these lists get pretty worn, with old dogs of restaurants sitting in the lists for months and years, waiting for a sucker!

The lists give you all the information you could desire except for the very information you need, such as the rent, the price of the lease, and the exact location. That's because they don't want you going behind their backs and doing a private deal that excludes their commission.

Up to a point, *all* restaurants are for sale if the price is right. Many in business specialize in *in-and-out* operations. They like to set up a restaurant, get it rolling, sell it quickly, and move on. There are few bargains to be had. Potential owners must decide what sort of operation they're going to have, and they must have at least a general idea how soon they'd like to recover their investment. The rule of thumb used to be five years. Many people now expect to cash in within one year.

The Neighborhood

It's important to know what's going on in the neighborhood, especially if you suspect that most of your customers are going to be local residents or workers, as distinct from distant commuters or bold adventurers from the other side of the town or country. If the main source of your business is the local hospital across the street, and suddenly half the work force is transferred to another location too far away to maintain customer loyalty, then you could have a problem. This is why you should never be complacent about your source of customers, but should always try to expand into other areas—which, of course, must be acceptable to and compatible with your regulars. You don't want a motorcycle gang forcing out your accountants and legal secretaries!

Equally, a sharp eye for future development may pay dividends. If you suspect that a street will not be the last ditch before the slums for long, but will soon be taken over by the beloved bourgeoisie (and this is fairly easy to assess), you may take a calculated risk and get a friendly price or rent. Similarly, if you have it on good authority that a nearby empty space will soon become a skyscraper housing 12,000 workers, and this is not generally known, you may be a winner.

Converting Premises

The easiest and most common method of finding premises is to take over an existing restaurant location and revamp it to your taste and plans. Frequently, a grossly inflated goodwill factor is built into the price. But sometimes you can convert another kind of premises—a shoe store or whatever—into a restaurant. This involves zoning permission from the local authorities. But converting a commercial premises into a licensed restaurant is sometimes the most difficult kind of zoning permission to obtain. Different states have all sorts of restrictions—a famous one in New York is that liquor may not be sold within a hundred yards of a school, for instance. There may be neighbor objections in a residential area because inhabitants fear fumes and late-night noise. These are not unreasonable fears, and they are often insuperable. When applying for change of user, it's wise not to build hopes. However, local governments do change, and politics can affect situations. What is not acceptable one year may be acceptable the next. Moreover, if you're totally immersed in the subject, as you should be when looking for a place, you should have a realistic view of local conditions. *Caveat emptor*—let the buyer beware!

Laws and trends vary greatly from place to place and need to be explored thoroughly. Bearing in mind the law's delay, it's *never* too soon to explore these matters. There's no necessity to spend money on professional advice, but City

Hall will want to see the plans for your proposed conversion, which may have to be prepared by a qualified architect. They'll tell you their legal requirements for conversion, should they decide that your character and proposal are sufficiently decent to deserve their permission.

Conversion costs can vary enormously. If you want plush carpets, spacious restrooms, and a modern, fully equipped kitchen, and if you have to install walk-in boxes and freezers, air conditioners, heaters, and so on, then the sky's the limit. You could easily spend $200,000 on assembling a 50-seat restaurant.

But there are ingenious means of getting around this. In France, the average restaurateur doesn't spend a penny more than necessary on furniture and décor. Plastic chairs and tables, paper tablecloths and napkins abound. If a local artist wants to exhibit landscapes on the walls, that's acceptable, and a small commission can be exacted in the event of a sale.

In this respect, the more you look, the more you'll see. Once you "get your eye in," you'll be amazed at the number of restaurants that have only two or three attractive tables, all the others being equally unattractive. But—another contradiction in a quirky industry—some of the least charming oblong rooms, with rows of deuces along the walls and fours and sixes in the middle, serve the best food.

CHAPTER 3

WHAT KIND OF RESTAURANT?

WHAT IS THE TARGET MARKET?

We live in an age of obsession with food. Almost every food known to mankind from sashimi to sushi to borlotti beans is available, at least in the cities. There is such a thing as fashion in food. Where, oh where, are the spinach salads with chopped bacon and warm smoked chicken salads of yesteryear? On their way back, quite possibly. People are becoming more adventurous, and hot, spicy dishes now meet little resistance. Nevertheless, despite the increasing willingness to experiment, the average American still eats three hamburgers per week. Because of the obsession with diet and obesity, smaller plates and portions are in vogue in many restaurants.

Most new restaurateurs have a good idea of the kind of food they want to serve. The most common notion is to offer middle-of-the-road American cuisine, with perhaps some European overtones and gestures. In this area, menu inspiration can vary from moderately expensive steaks, chops, fish, and chicken dishes; through the exciting "Russian Burger" (a hamburger topped with caviar); to the bleak "individual can of tuna" and "no substitutes." It is rare for an owner not to make a gesture in the direction of his or her ethnic origins, which usually adds a welcome, exotic touch that might include lasagna, moussaka, corned beef and cabbage, burritos, tofu, or chicken Tikka.

Often, the choice is limited by circumstances. Ideal premises may be found near a highly successful steakhouse, with a terrific seafood place nearby. It might be asking for trouble to seek head-on competition by opening the same kind of operation.

It's interesting to note that the steakhouse will almost certainly feature two or three fish dishes, including lobster, while the fish joint will probably offer a steak for those who either don't like or are allergic to fish. This is an example of striving to please everyone all the time that can make the business such very hard work. A typical result of this is the overcrowded menu where everything's equally dull, usually because the only way a large selection can be maintained is by keeping many items deep-frozen. The microwave may be a godsend to the hungry and to the hard-pressed cook, but it has added little to the restaurateur or the gourmet's pleasures, apart from swiftly heated pie and quiche.

A happy compromise can be achieved by having a set menu with *daily specials*. These can either genuinely be the chef's inspiration of the day—perhaps coinciding with an excess supply of, or special market prices on, some item or other—or be a regular routine: pot roast every Tuesday, lobster every Friday. This is a useful way of attracting regular customers.

Given a nation of experienced consumers, an advantage of precise ethnic identification of a restaurant is that the customers know what to expect. Few would have foreseen the day when red-blooded Americans would eat raw fish, but Japanese restaurants are now all the rage. Indeed, there are those who will tell you that the United States is a great place for sushi! However, some cantankerous American men, the sort who would aver that "real men don't eat quiche," or "lunch is for wimps" will turn up their noses at more adventurous food. *Risotto* ranks high on these men's hate list! (See Appendix II for a glossary of menu terms.)

The broad classifications of restaurants are American, English, Irish, German, Austrian, Greek, Turkish, French or Continental, Italian, Spanish, Mexican, Chinese, Japanese, Thai, and Indian. In the larger cities the choice is even larger, as the following list demonstrates:

Afghan	Italian
African	Japanese
American (New)	Korean
American (Traditional)	Kosher
Argentinian	Latin American
Australian	Mediterranean
Bagels	Mexican
Bar food	Middle Eastern
Barbecue	Pan-Asian and Pacific Rim
Bistro	Peruvian
Cajun and Creole	Pizza
Caribbean	Sandwiches
Chicken	Seafood
Chinese	South American
Czech	South African
Coffeehouses	Southern and soul
Colombian	Southwestern
Cuban	Steakhouses
Delis	Sushi
Desserts and bakeries	Tapas
Dim Sum	Thai
Diners and coffee shops	Tibetan
Ethiopian	Turkish
French	Vegetarian
Health	Vietnamese
Indian	Wings

Health food restaurants, catering to vegans, vegetarians, and diners who seek purer food are now an established genre. They often offer *organic food,* which is said to have been produced in absolutely natural conditions without use of chemicals. In other words, the eggs have been laid by free-range chickens eating a varied diet, and the chicken itself comes from the same source. Here is an area in which the difference is notable—the cheaper variety of chicken often tastes of fish, which should come as no surprise, since intensively farmed birds are often fed on fishmeal. There are a few wrinkled noses here and there, and some say organic food is often less tasty than the norm.

Many restaurants simply fall into a certain category by limiting their range of food to fish, steak, chili, pizza, or kebabs. Others reduce the menu to absolute simplicity, offering, for instance, cold or hot stone crabs with hash browns and salad, or steak. Such a limited choice makes the waiter's job easy and speeds up table turnover. The kitchen becomes a simple production line.

Every type of cuisine and menu poses its own problems and challenges. But cooks are an artful crowd, and that which looks difficult is often quite easy when you know how. Even rather fussy dishes, such as anything *en papillote* (fish or meat cooked in a paper envelope) or Chicken Kiev, where butter is inserted into a chicken breast which is then sewn together, can be very quickly prepared and delivered to the table once the kitchen is properly set up and organized. As long as the kitchen staff can cope, one can offer dishes from a variety of cuisines which makes for a lively and interesting menu.

Opening Hours

Some restaurants open only for lunch or dinner. French restaurants are commonly open for lunch and dinner six days, closing on Sunday and often for the whole month of August. If the amount of business missed by these closures is insignificant, then the free time enjoyed by owner and staff will be worthwhile. But the pressure to do business during the open period is naturally so much greater, since the rent has to be paid whether the restaurateur opens or not. Restaurants that are open continuously throughout the day and evening, seven days a week, serving the same menu, save their regular clients from wondering whether they're open, and indeed this is an important ingredient in establishing a regular clientele. Most of the 24-hour restaurants or coffee shops in the country are gold mines, but location is crucial, and the formula will not work everywhere.

Which End of the Market?

Restaurateurs pay their money and take their choice. If they try to appeal to a wealthy gourmet crowd, they'll need a highly trained chef who will require a high salary. Sometimes, of course, the restaurant owner *is* the chef, which helps enormously. A special problem of this genre of restaurant is the necessity of maintaining a high standard of cuisine and service that will stand up to the scrutiny of food critics, who can make or break such places. Restaurateurs with the ego, the confidence, the financial backing, and the courage to open a restaurant at this end of the market will need no instruction from anyone in the restaurant industry. As a rule, they don't ask for advice anyway.

The celebrity-chef-owned restaurant, often replete with Michelin stars as a tribute from the *Michelin Guide* to the excellence of their cuisine, is now very common. A major advantage of a chef/owner achieving celebrity is that free publicity will be generated, and with luck business will boom. The general obsession with celebrity, which brings rich rewards from TV success, management fees, and royalties, has spawned a new breed of PR consultant. In America, the best-known is Joseph Baum & Michael Whiteman Co. Inc., who claim to have created more three-star restaurants in New York than anyone, in addition to nationwide and global triumphs.

Chefs like Emeril (reportedly earning $7 million a year) Rocco, Boulud, and Vongerichten bestride the culinary stage like colossi. Alan Crompton-Batt, the doyen of restaurant public relations consultants in England, recently died. There had always been a few celebrity chefs such as Ude or Brillat-Savarin, but Crompton-Batt developed the notion, changing the image of the chef from a faintly comical figure in checked pants and a funny white hat (the *toque blanche*) into a glossy magazine and television idol. In England, the queen of TV chefs is Delia Smith, wife of a director of the enormous Sainsbury's chain of supermarkets, reputedly worth around $40 million. She is a sort of Oprah Winfrey of the world of food. Any endorsement of a product by her guarantees success. Fly-on-the-wall TV programs showing chefs to be sometimes the most appalling foul-mouthed bullies have not dimmed their fame. Their excuse for being so vulgar and domineering is the stress of striving for perfection, but there are some excellent chefs who are perfectly pleasant people.

Many celebrities who are not chefs have ventured into the restaurant business—including Michael Caine, Clint Eastwood, and Robert de Niro. Naturally, such restaurant operations draw fierce attention from the ever-growing army of food critics, and it has emerged that restaurants with a strong figurehead, especially a chef-owner who is unlikely to be short of ego or to underestimate his or her own importance, have one thing in common: they tend to have a cold, unpleasant atmosphere. Everything is taken so seriously, and there is so much intimidating stony-faced gravitas among the insecure and oppressed waiters and staff that it's hard to relax and have a good time. The neighborhood joint is likely to be much more fun.

The restaurant at the Dorchester Hotel in London employs 85 people in the kitchen, from apprenti to demi-chef, chef, saucier, and so on. The Hilltop Steak House employs more than 700 people. Bills for flowers, publicity, and laundry at this end of the market can be daunting. Even a neighborhood 50-seater will employ at least 15 people if it's open seven days a week. In the early days of a restaurant the owner himself might perform as bartender and host, thus saving on payroll. That's one of the reasons why the business is so time-consuming in the initial stages. Martyrdom and exhaustion, unfortunately, do not guarantee success. The presence of clearly exhausted and over-stretched restaurant workers can be very off-putting to customers, though a minority may enjoy sharing their pain!

Middle of the road is the safest path, as in so many businesses. There are some food items with which you can hardly go wrong. Every restaurant in America that serves hamburgers claims to serve the best hamburgers. Few hamburger oases are empty for long.

Italian restaurants are immensely popular, whether they serve cheap-and-cheerful spaghetti, meatballs, and pizza or more expensive *osso bucco*. The food is easy to prepare and leans heavily on safely familiar tastes, colors, and sensations. At one end of the market, the keyword is *al dente,* which means the pasta should be faintly resistant to the teeth. This is one of those odd dining quirks that have become fashionable. Let it be whispered that al *dente* pasta may be chic, but it's awfully hard to digest. At the other end of the market, it's "heavy on the tomayder sauce, and can we git some more bread?"

Because of their popularity, the competition is fierce. In many cities it's not uncommon to find four or more Italian restaurants on a single block, all doing a roaring trade.

The more distinctively ethnic food operations are best conducted by their native sons and daughters, and will often appeal more to customers of that background than to adventurous diners. But most people enjoy a change, and even purists will do well to make some concessions to those of mundane tastes by having some safe and easily recognizable items available on their otherwise exotic menus. Personal tastes should be accommodated, too. If customers want ketchup on their filet mignon, there's really no good reason why they shouldn't have it. In one of London's best and most popular restaurants, Wilton's, the French chef cooks game to perfection. But perfection to the French means slightly on the rare side, which is anathema to many. However, this is a pleasant establishment, and though there may be a bit of eye-rolling back-stage, no one has ever been thrown out for requesting his or her par-tridge to be well done. Let the servers snigger in the kitchen, but good man-ners dictate that *de gustibus non est disputandum*—there's no disputing taste. The French also eat pork chops medium rare—a condition generally frowned on by the medical profession.

In China they eat dogs and cats. In Belgium and France they eat horse. Goat is eaten throughout the Middle East. In areas plagued by locusts, chil-dren will pluck insects from the air when they swarm, tear off their legs and wings, and eat them raw. A Borneo tribesman who disturbs a log in the rain forest to reveal a glowing green slimy slug will beam with delight and either eat it himself or, if he's a gent, offer it to one of his wives.

THEME RESTAURANTS

Some successful restaurants rely for their attraction upon gimmicks that have nothing to do with food. This might include such theme decor as model car collections, bicycle wheels, or barnyard implements. The theme is often pursued to the nth degree, with varying degrees of success. Menus will rely on puns or far-fetched adjectives to describe items, such as "dawn-gathered wild mushrooms," and so on.

Experienced diners' hearts sink when they read such guff, usually on menus that have been composed by a publicity writer rather than the chef. It practically guarantees that the food will be tasteless. Generally speaking, the more elaborate the décor and the staff's costumes, the less likely they are to have a slice of lemon for your fish and the more likely it is that the whipped cream will come out of an aerosol can.

Other restaurants rely on such things as a wonderful view or singing waiters. Some restaurants are done up like 1920s speakeasies or as cabarets with a running talent show.

ENTERTAINMENT

The piano bar is a great favorite, but some restaurateurs grumble that they could seat several parties in the space occupied by the pianist, who is naturally on the payroll and gets a staff meal on the house. The question of whether to have entertainment is an old and harrowing one, and it's never easy to please everyone. One pianist will play a condensed version of a classical concerto to the delight of some but to the annoyance of those who would prefer to hear "Send in the Clowns." Another will delight with her own inspirations, such as a medley of popular jingles from current commercials. One pianist who knew the Finnish national anthem made a regular tip from a homesick old lady. In general, a pianist whose repertoire embraces "Happy Birthday to You," "Our Love Is Here to Stay," and "As Time Goes By" will be perfectly adequate, and if the fingering isn't quite right, few will notice.

Wandering guitarists and gypsy trios are not much in vogue these days. Perhaps they could be revived?

A popular trend is for Japanese-style karaoke restaurants, where diners sing to the accompaniment of records from which the solo voice (Elvis Presley or Britney Spears, etc.) has been erased.

Some budding stars are so fond of the sound of their own voices, and so eager to have an audience, that they'll perform free at your restaurant, and bring in paying friends, too. It would be unrealistic to expect any big spenders on such occasions, however. Established supper club singers can become irate if diners—or *guests,* as they are often called in the business, in spite of the fact that they get a bill before they leave—dare to talk while they're performing. The restaurant that features Woody Allen on clarinet undoubtedly pulls in a few curious customers who want to hear their multitalented hero. A restaurant that makes a feature of jazz groups can do well, as jazz lovers are a solid, gregarious crowd. But there's never room for many such establishments. Occasionally restaurants even flirt with chamber musical recitals and poetry readings. But go to any New York midtown steakhouse on a Friday night (if you can take it) for a glimpse of intense consumption, which, if they're honest, is what most restaurateurs would like to see. The customers are there for steaks, booze, and conversation. A poetry reading wouldn't be appropriate, since you can hardly hear yourself think, and the Muzak is inaudible.

Some restaurants revolve on top of skyscrapers so that the view changes constantly. Before World War II there was a popular restaurant in Berlin with telephones at each table, so that people could ring each other up—an early version of the singles bar!

Neighborhood restaurants often profit by having a big TV over the bar. This enables diners and drinkers to watch ball games as they consume. Sometimes consumption is inhibited by too much concentration on the silver screen, sometimes it's increased. Inevitably, some customers won't like the blaring TV and the occasional touchdown war whoops, but most will feel they're part of a living, warming experience. Restaurants that actually build themselves around huge TV screens showing ball games and so on seem to do well, but there is almost certainly a limit to the number of such operations any given consumer population will bear. If this formula doesn't work, it is but the work of a moment to remove the screen and revamp! Nothing is forever, least of all in the restaurant business.

Entrepreneurial decision is required. If that big stuffed bear delights the children, then its space is well used. If not, then perhaps it should be replaced by a cash-generating table.

Appealing to Different Age Groups

Demographically, there's no doubt that restaurants that aim to please an older clientele may do at least as well as those that solicit the business of the young! The vast majority of customers in expensive restaurants are over 35. Retired people have lots of time on their hands and many have lots of money to spend. There's a big hole where their jobs and children used to be, and regular trips to restaurants help pass the time. In music, they'll prefer quiet standards to heavy metal, and they will be quick to complain about hot or cold drafts from kitchen doors or entrances. They are often bullies, determined to exact due deference to their age, which the younger help may be reluctant to offer. Their loneliness can often make them garrulous, too. The restaurateur must be able to deal with people at all stages of the vale of tears and laughter!

The young have plenty of money to spend these days. They can be unpopular as customers, however, because they tend to be rude, larcenous, highly demanding (because it sounds so clever to ask for something special), noisy, and poor tippers. Television and fashion magazines assure them that today's youth own the world, and many of them have accepted this doctrine with pleasure. Junk food and carbohydrates are what they crave, not haute cuisine, and blasting music will attract them in droves.

Mixed Business

It's sometimes possible to combine two businesses in one. You can build a full-fledged boutique around an ice cream parlor so that, after finishing their meal, customers may be prevailed upon to part with a little more cash for an obscene T-shirt, a stuffed elephant, or a clever card. One restaurant featured a pepper-mill that gave off sparks when twisted. Naturally they were on sale, too.

These restaurants, on the whole, are best left to big groups who are in a better position to take risks and make mistakes. New restaurateurs would do well to consider such ventures carefully. Twenty years' work was wiped out in six months some years ago when, in a classic case of wildly speculative over-extension, a 12-unit chain went bankrupt with an expensive new operation near New York's Times Square. For reasons much debated, but never established, the new venture never showed a ghost of a chance of succeeding. A possible explanation, fanciful though it may seem, is that the chosen building was one of those black holes where nothing ever succeeds. Some locations just won't make it. But it's possible that the upscale "yuppie chic" ambiance, with beautiful young male models as waiters, was simply wrong for an area that was then largely populated by tourists and pornographers! No one can really afford to make mistakes, but some can afford it better than others.

ALCOHOL AND LICENSING

An important basic decision to be made is whether you intend to serve beer, wines, and spirits. You almost certainly will. You don't have to, but if you don't, you'll deny yourself enormous profits. If you do, you'll need a general liquor license, or a beer and wine license, from your state liquor-licensing agency.

Such licenses can take several months to obtain. The day you wonder whether you're ready to open a restaurant is the day you should check your local licensing situation and the required procedure for obtaining an alcohol license. Fortunately, most states' Liquor Licensing authorities have Web sites that give all the information you'll need—including how much it's going to cost you. Generally, you can download and print the necessary forms from these Web sites that, ominously, do not always offer a telephone number. If you go to a search engine such as Google, and type in "Arizona State Liquor Authority," for instance, you should be one click away from the site. They are worth an occasional browse, as they post changes in legislation. For instance, at www.abc.state .ny.us we learn that it is now legal in New York to take home an unfinished bottle of wine.

Broadly speaking, the cost of a license depends on the population of the area. Although there are some safe generalities, there are also some extraordinary exceptions, and you'd better be aware of them Day One! Some states have extremely quirky liquor laws. In liberal New York, getting a license is usually pretty easy if eligibility is swiftly established. In neighboring New Jersey, the number of licenses is limited to a certain number per capita. New licenses have to be approved not only by the state agency but also by city officials. A license will usually last a year, but there are many exceptions.

In New York City, at the time of writing, a full liquor license (i.e., one that allows you to sell beer, wine, and spirits on your premises), costs $4,352, with a $200 filing fee. In the less populated areas a license can be obtained for $1,792, with a filing fee of $200. A wine-and-beer-only license costs $480, with a $100 filing fee. Jurisdiction of the sale of alcohol is a matter for the state, not the federal, government. The license must be prominently displayed. Look for it near the entrance of the next licensed restaurant you visit. Liquor licenses are an important revenue—there are more than 70,000 license holders in New York state alone.

Liquor licenses are not granted automatically. Shady characters with police records wishing to open restaurants will often have to find a front man to be the license holder. This intense legal focus is, of course, a hangover from the days of Prohibition, a historical disaster that gave the modern Mafia its power base on a plate. All license applications are investigated to determine eligibility. There are three general areas of investigation: the principals (i.e., the owners), the premises (which must satisfy licensing regulations as regards safety, provision of restrooms, etc.), and the source of finances.

All states keep a close eye on liquor transactions, for obvious reasons, and any query or impediment to your application can cause a lengthy delay. In most states, liquor deliveries may *not* be paid for COD. An account must be opened, and payment must be made by check or money order. Also, certain structural conditions have to be met where alcohol is served, of which the most common, important, and expensive is the requirement for restrooms. A coffee shop need not have a restroom: on licensed premises, it's mandatory.

There are lawyers who specialize in obtaining licenses, and since most restaurateurs will need such services from time to time, this can be part of their duty *ab initio*—from the beginning. These lawyers can speed things up, but as is well known, it is often in the interests of a lawyer to slow things down, so that the lawyer can submit a larger bill. A price for the service should be agreed on in advance, whenever possible.

It should be emphasized that you don't have to have a lawyer to obtain a license, in the same way that you don't have to have a lawyer to handle probate when you buy a house. But once the decision is made to get into business, there is an urgent need to get going. Money will be going out or tied up, and you will want to move to the money-making stage as quickly as possible.

You'll also need a business license, again a state matter. This is simply a matter of getting the appropriate forms from your local city hall, filling them out, getting them notarized, and handing them in. It's unlikely to cost you more than $40 anywhere in the country. But, as in all such matters, if you don't get it absolutely right the first time, you may find yourself wasting a lot of time on getting the correct forms, deciding what kind of business you have, and all the rest of it. Eventually, you may wish to become a corporation. At that point, you really would do well to find a lawyer.

INSURANCE

By law, you are required to be insured against damage to your customers. A comprehensive agreement will cover this, as well as the risk of your being sued for damage related to alcohol consumption served on your premises. Many view the fact that a bar can be held responsible for damage caused by one of its customers getting drunk as a happy collusion between the insurance business and the law. It is a touchy business, because many alcoholics do not appear to be drunk—until they get behind the wheel. Bartenders need to be vigilant. The bartender who reported three pilots because of their alcohol consumption the night before they were due to fly might have felt a bit of a sneak, but there can be no doubt he did the right thing. A bartender also has the right to refuse to serve anyone he believes to be already the worse for wear. This can, of course, lead to unpleasantness. In the case of the pilots, the case attracted press attention because they pleaded not guilty, saying that because they were all alcoholics, they were still fit to fly! They were all fired.

Employees are generally covered by workers' compensation if you are correctly registered with the state authorities and have prominently displayed a notice to that effect. But occasional special suits from employees are not un-heard of, and you may wish to specially insure against them. A typical example is a waitress who decided to sue her boss because she broke a tooth on a pret-zel (by no means uncommon!). The matter was settled when the restaurateur agreed to settle her dentist's bill.

In the age of the $600 raincoat and the $50,000 fur, you may wish to in-sure against loss of such items. But if you don't want to, you don't have to. If you don't, you should prominently display a notice to this effect (Not respon-sible for goods, clothes, or chattels left in this restaurant, etc.). If you sell your cloakroom concession to an outsider (a not uncommon practice), you may find that the cloakroom attendant will refuse to accept furs. This may suit owners who are loath to check them, but such coats can take up a lot of space in a dining room. Some restaurants simply don't have cloakrooms. This works well sometimes, except that on rainy days, the dining room can be a sorry sight, with dripping coats and umbrellas everywhere. High-class restaurants have spacious, properly insured cloakrooms. The cost of this useful luxury, of course, finds its echoes in the menu prices, as well as in the more-or-less mandatory tip for the attendant.

TAXES

All businesses are liable to tax, but the system of collection varies from state to state. You are required by law to keep records, and you will be accorded an employer's number that validates the W2 forms you issue to your employees at the end of the tax year. This is such a potential source of time-consuming work that almost every restaurateur in the world employs an accountant to take care of it. The reason for this, quite simply, is that what looks to you like a solid weekend of ulcer-making grind is easy to accountants because they know what they're doing. They'll save you lots of ulcers, and are not terribly ex-pensive. Also, the tax authorities are happier talking to accountants. They have their jargon and their accepted rules of combat. Matters are simplified and completed faster by talking to professionals.

PRICING

Deciding the price range of your menu, bar, and wine list is important. Ini-tially, your prices will relate directly to the overheads and expenses you antici-pate. If your rent is $25,000 a month, and you only seat 50, you probably won't make it if your most expensive entree is a $10 chicken potpie. Despite the attractiveness of the price, you just haven't got the capacity to feed enough customers to cover your expenses and overheads.

Fortunately, pricing is one factor that is easily changeable. On one hand, a restaurateur might feel that the only way to attract business is to undercut the local competition, and there's a lot to be said for this. In a busy neighborhood that has three restaurants and draws its customers from one or two central sources, word gets around. It's amazing how even a small reduction in price can improve business, especially in young communities.

On the other hand, an ever-increasing number of consumers simply don't care what they spend if they get what they want. This small but happy band tends to congregate in the major cities, however, and many budding restaurateurs find themselves, willy-nilly, hoping to establish themselves in other areas, trimming their sails to the prevailing market wind.

Certainly, a close awareness of what other restaurants in the chosen category are charging and serving is essential to competitive operation. You will soon learn the true meaning of phrases like "what the traffic will bear" and "price resistance."

A restaurateur who is largely dependent upon neighborhood business will do well to establish a friendly atmosphere, maintain consistent standards, and offer good value. *Good value* is, of course, a relative term, since a diner who wants a steak doesn't have to pay $20 for it! But in the consumer society, everyone is trained to consume and has an idea of what to expect for prices in the context of restaurants.

Regular diners-out, especially those who are spending their own money as opposed to the company's, often like to have a rough idea of how much they're going to have to spend. A restaurant will register in their minds as a place where, say, lunch for two with a couple of drinks and the tip will cost about $50. It's a good idea to have a quick selection from the menu as a price guide to offer over the telephone as an example of what customers are in for, should they ask—which they often do. A testy "We have a large menu with all sorts of different prices. It depends on what you have" is not positive selling. A common complaint in many areas of retail is the difficulty of getting a simple response to the question, "How much?" Far better briefly to recite the price of an entrée, a cocktail, and a bottle of wine.

Some restaurants make things easier by having a wide range of prices, so that it's possible to have a light lunch for quite little or a slap-up dinner for rather more. A sad aspect of this civilized view of life is that servers can sometimes become disgruntled by customers who aren't spending enough as they take up valuable table space, especially during the busy two-hour lunch period, which suddenly ends, leaving an empty restaurant. It can be a bit daunting to see your best table, that cozy corner for four, occupied by three sharing a salad and a bowl of soup, and taking their time about it!

Since tips are figured on a percentage basis, one might see their point, but appearances are deceiving. As has been said, tips average out uncannily "rough with smooth" to 17 percent nationwide. Sometimes servers will administer a cold bum's rush to small spenders, and although it sounds rather mean, it's probably just as well.

There is something to be said, however, at the lower end of the price range of the restaurant business for making it quite clear to customers that they can spend as much or as little as they want and still get the same cheerful service. The person who regularly spends $5 will occasionally come in and spend $50.

Naturally, there will always be a few customers who exploit such tolerance. From a waiter's point of view, $5 trips to the kitchen can be as arduous as $20 trips, with the irritating prospect of small reward. Perhaps this is a situation where restaurateurs can turn a blind eye, when their servers administer the bum's rush to a time and money waster!

Occasionally, deranged people go to restaurants, order "the works" with a good bottle of wine, then calmly announce that they have no money. Calling the police is an option, but it's not much fun for your other diners having a jolly evening to see the boys in blue arrive. One restaurateur shrugged his shoulders, told the bum to leave, whimsically wrote "PR" on the check, and put it on the appropriate pile. Such operators should, of course, choose their operating neighborhoods carefully. In some the reaction might be very fierce indeed.

One of the luxuries of writing about the restaurant business is that one need never fear appearing somewhat contradictory. It's a contradictory business! As in French grammar, there are almost as many exceptions to the rules as there are rules. Indeed, learning the language of the restaurant business is mainly what it's all about, as in banking, aviation, or anything else. And every language student knows that there comes a time when the books just don't help you anymore. You have to get out there and talk.

WHO ARE THE CUSTOMERS?

It doesn't take computers or Harvard MBA market researchers to work out who the customers are for a restaurant. The location and nature of the neighborhood usually define the clientele. There is, however, the phenomenon of a restaurant that becomes an iconic *destination,* when customers may come from all walks of life and, indeed, from all over the world. A restaurant opposite a hospital will attract customers from it. The sheer presence of people, the coming and going of patients and visitors, provides a business opportunity. Average local income will affect prices. The strange hours worked by some shifts may provide an opportunity for very early or very late business. Meat and fish market workers, for example, are famous for their inverted lives. Because they work by night, they often feel like a drink and dinner at six in the morning, and there are usually restaurants to accommodate them.

In the suburbs or country, where customers drive to the restaurant, the specific attractions of the restaurant will determine the kind of crowd that comes. The parking arrangements will be as important as the kitchen! Spaghetti and meatballs at cheerful prices will bring in young families for an outing on weekends. But where's the Tuesday night business going to come from?

Many restaurants suffer from a feast-or-famine pattern of business. Some Wall Street restaurants boom at lunchtime, but die at night. Restaurants of all kinds will normally reckon to do most of their business on Fridays and Saturdays. When competition is fierce, and customers are limited in number, the restaurateur must twist and turn to bring customers in on the other five days and nights.

WHAT DO CUSTOMERS WANT?

Not all consumers are so articulate, but it is amazing how many regular restaurant patrons are quick to list their dislikes yet unsure about what they like. Friendly, gentle advice is often welcomed.

It must be understood absolutely that, except at the basic level of a diner or cafeteria, customers want more than a bite to eat and a drink. They want an experience.

If all they wanted was victuals, people could feed and water themselves far more cheaply at home or out of a brown bag on a park bench. But even the humble diner operator can increase her business by making her establishment as agreeable as possible. A very happy niche is filled by those inexpensive coffee shops that have a license for wine and beer and that contrive, by clever decor and a general smartness, to pose as "real" restaurants. People in business and those who want inexpensive social meetings will flock. Often, for youngsters especially, such places are less intimidating than "proper" restaurants, with their sometimes rather-too-serious staff and exorbitant prices. Even the average cafeteria manager will work hard to brighten the place up, sometimes laying on entertainment and varying the menu to offer as wide a choice as possible.

Basically, all customers want reasonable-quality food and thoughtful, prompt service at reasonable prices, with room to breathe and the ability to hold a conversation without raising their voices.

But it isn't quite that simple. It is becoming increasingly apparent that there is a whole new breed of human being that likes noise. They will actually leave perfectly nice restaurants because they're too quiet. People flock to the crowded joints that have no hope of offering decent service or food because they like the sensation afforded by noise and crowds. The vigorous crashing of dirty dishes into bus trays is as much music to some ears as it is anathema to others.

At the risk of being accused of reverse ageism or of stereotyping the chronologically challenged—or should one say underprivileged—the young are especially decibel-hungry. There is no need to name the well-known restaurants serving hamburgers, chili, apple pie, and noise; many of them are famous. It has been demonstrated that people eat and drink faster when there is a lot of noise. Many restaurateurs insist on a high noise level from piped music and will turn up the music more when the place gets busier, precisely in order to increase turnover.

One can be forgiven for suspecting that some restaurants are actually de-signed to be noisy, so pointedly bad are the acoustics of their tiled dining rooms. This is a matter of personal choice for the restaurateur.

A well-designed restaurant will have a quiet area at least. A scenario that can make some diners long to walk out (but if they're entertaining, maybe they can't) is the one where, after the waiter has agreed to turn down the music, an-other waiter comes along and thinks, "Gee, what happened to the music?" and turns it back up again. Experienced diners arriving at a restaurant they haven't visited before will cautiously check the noise level. If it's high, they'll about-turn and leave. However, a quiet dining room can suddenly become like a football stadium if 12 celebrating brokers or traders suddenly arrive.

There are certain things that people commonly dislike, one of which is the hustle. People dislike having their check thrown down on the table when they haven't asked for it. The correct procedure if you are busy and therefore gen-uinely losing revenue by continued occupation of a table marked by conspic-uous lack of consumption is to politely inquire whether the customers wish for anything more, and if not, may the check be presented? In a neighborhood restaurant, once in a while a manager or owner will approach a table of regu-lar customers and offer them a drink on the house at the bar because the table is sorely needed.

Glowering unpleasant service can ruin a business. Some servers are all too adept at putting on a marvelous performance when the boss is around, but as soon as her back is turned the scowls return and the insults fly. Awareness is important. Customers that do not pay a return visit or stop coming, will not usually go out of their way to tell the restaurateur why they stop coming to eat there. Of course, people get bored, their tastes change, they relocate, and they die. But outside of all that, there must be a reason. The restaurateur should try to ensure that it is not bad service.

The restaurateur must approach customers with the view that they are potential customers for life. Good commercial value is important, but the real secret ingredient is the human touch. You have to make people feel like people, not like consumers, and you do this mainly by remembering their names or, failing that, their jobs or their hometowns—whatever it may be. Thus, you create a sort of home away from home. "The best restaurant in town is the one that knows my name," said the late doyen of New York chefs, James Beard. The theme song of the TV show *Cheers* expounded similar sentiments.

Small gestures can promote intense customer loyalty. At an Audubon Society dinner at a Hilton Hotel, a hungry diner finished his plate in a short time. "You must be hungry," said a kindly waiter. "I'm not surprised—it's so cold out. Would you like a little more?" The astonished diner enjoyed another plateful of delicious beef.

It's possible that the "Executive Director of Portion Control" might go into instant cardiac arrest upon hearing such a story, but one doubts it, since at set dinners the prepared food is either eaten or thrown out—either way, it's been paid for.

An executive who regularly travels Air India, even when its schedules are not ideal for his purpose, gave the following explanation for doing so: "After an unavoidable flight delay I heard the cabin director say to one of the stewards in the galley 'Raji—serve your dinner as soon as you can after takeoff. I know the people will be hungry with this delay.'"

We can all think of airlines where such concern would be most unlikely.

CHAPTER 4

RAISING
THE MONEY

START-UP MONEY: HOW TO GET IT

Avid readers of business magazines—and every budding businessperson should be an avid reader—will often wonder as they read the exciting report of how some brilliant entrepreneur spotted a hole in the market, risked all, worked hard, and finally achieved success: Where did the successful entrepreneur get the start-up money? Buried in the text, this burning question is often answered with a glibness that helps no one. "With a million-dollar loan from her father-in-law," or "using the idle resources of his existing factories," are common phrases. This doesn't really help the person who wants to get started in business, except to illustrate that an awful lot of the competition is way ahead before he or she even starts. Some will go so far as to say that getting the start-up money is the hardest part of any enterprise, since the economy of the Western world is growing constantly, and all you have to do to run the business is not get it terribly wrong, as distinct from getting it absolutely right.

Inheritance

Most wealth is inherited. This is a simple fact of life, and it doesn't refer only to Rockefellers but to everybody. The single biggest purchase most people ever make is a home. After the death of parents, the proceeds from the subsequent sale of their house are usually the largest sum of money most people will ever see. The cash generated by this event is often enough to enable an inheritor to consider investing the money in a business.

The family is the most common resource for restaurant start-up money. Many restaurants are inherited—there are family hierarchies that do nothing else, especially in France. Sometimes the inheritors are totally ignorant of the restaurant business, but they know a gold mine when they see one and decide to continue with it. As employers, such people have an appalling reputation! Their amateur eye is never on the doughnut but always on the hole, and they rarely trust anyone—customers or employees. Where the inheritor has grown up in the business, however, happiness often reigns. Family-run restaurants, especially on the continent of Europe, enjoy the best reputations. Many neighborhoods are blessed with mom-and-pop places that usually confine themselves to a small, simple menu and enjoy a regular clientele.

Of course, there's nothing to stop anyone from marrying money—or marrying a restaurateur.

Savings

Since wages and tips in busy restaurants are good, many people are able to go into business on the strength of their savings, with perhaps some help from the bank or partners. A hard-working waitress in a busy restaurant can easily earn $700 a week at the age of 23. If she lives inexpensively, with parents or roommate, and has no costly hobby or interests outside her job—which is commonly the case—in 10 years she may have saved $150,000.

This may not be enough to open a 50-seat licensed restaurant, but it's certainly a respectable amount of money to show to a bank manager or to potential partners. If she then marries a waiter with equal savings and similar ambitions, and they take their joint savings to the bank, they will be in an excellent position for getting a loan, if they require one, in order to set up shop.

Many restaurants are started by such people. They're often well qualified. Sometimes their view of the world and getting on with people may be a bit stunted, and restaurant work isn't renowned for bringing out charm in people. But they'll have a deep-rooted feel for how a place should be run, and that's a bonus. If charisma is not their strong suit, they can always hire someone with personality to front the place.

Bank Loans

Bob Hope defined a bank as a place that will lend you money, as long as you can show them that you don't need it. Someone else compared a bank with a friend who lends you an umbrella, but wants it back as soon as it starts to rain.

In fact, the system by which banks lend money is pretty cut-and-dried, with only a small area in which bank officers can exercise judgment and advise superiors or the board that the entrepreneurial risks under consideration are worth taking.

Restaurants are considered a high-risk business—perhaps exaggeratedly so, as previously discussed. Even a proven track record of success in the industry will not always impress banks. They will require collateral, such as your house or any other asset you may have, before lending you money. One budding restaurateur was required to cash in stocks and shares to raise cash for the bank's approval. The restaurant foundered, while the stock went on to incredible heights.

Banks are sometimes reluctant to lend money to someone who is leasing a property. They see no security for their money in a lease. Also, they usually won't lend money for the purchase of secondhand or leased equipment. They're often amenable to lending money to buy new equipment, however, for obvious reasons—the stuff probably has resale value. The very best scenario is a freehold property, or long lease.

Small Business Administration

The Small Business Administration (SBA) regards restaurants as high risk. But it might act as security for a bank loan if you can impress it with your experience and chances of success. If you're a veteran or handicapped, the SBA will look upon you with an even kinder eye. It is federally funded.

Loan Sharks

In every major city there are quiet, sincere loan sharks who'll lend money at rather steep interest to budding restaurateurs, for little or no security. Their service can lead to deep waters, and they should be avoided.

BUSINESS PLAN

If you approach a bank, or banks, for a loan, they may well request a formal business plan. This is often a time-consuming exercise and often has a hollow ring. Some of the things you'll be required to predict are impossible to predict. A military axiom says, "No battle plan survives the first contact with the enemy." It isn't actually true, but one gets the message. You must play the game. Gravitas is very important when dealing with bankers—it's part of their stock-in-trade.

Such a plan can be as long or as short as you wish, but it should give an overview of what exactly you plan to accomplish, and demonstrate that you've thought things through and know what you're doing. It will also help you as you go along, like a daily to-do list.

Here is a partial list of subjects you should consider, and be prepared to discuss in detail.

Premises (the bank will inspect them)	Menu
	Hours of opening
Lease (or, as is ideal, the freehold)	Prices
Rent	Special services (take-out,
Staff	banquets?)
Payroll	Advertising and publicity
Target market—Who will be	Your timetable
your customers?	Your experience

If your proposal is viable then it's important to shop around the banks. The minute they hear you're in discussion with others they'll be more accommodating. Remember, the bank, and individual employees, make money from lending it to you.

THE PROS AND CONS OF PARTNERSHIPS

References to *owners* in press and advertising often disguise the truth. As often as not, the owner whose beaming face shines from the advertisements owns only a small percentage of the business, but is paid a salary in addition to receiving a share of the profits. This owner is a *working partner.*

Because the capital investment is so huge, and because life is so short, many would-be restaurateurs will contemplate going into business with a partner. It can be an embittering experience. It can also be a great success. A majority of restaurants are owned by more than one person, despite whatever impression may be given in advertising and press gossip.

Many restaurant workers want to own their own place. It's the obvious step at a certain point for an ambitious person. Very highly paid chefs or maitre d's might be content with their earnings, but if not, the ceiling they inevitably reach at some point may be frustrating. They'll want to go it alone, and may have acquired a following over the years. While having a following can obviously do no harm to a new restaurant, it doesn't guarantee success. Customers like a change, but they won't always be willing to trek to a new and inconvenient location.

One of the clichés of the business is, "Nobody has enough friends to make a restaurant successful!" The oft-heard cry, "I was in advertising for 20 years I know literally thousands of people, and they all know me!" is a common and sometimes wistful one. An abundance of friends, however, may well give a restaurateur a nucleus, and if she's smart, or if her friends give her restaurant a good report, she can build on that.

Restaurant employees with ambition should make sure they get around and talk a lot about their plans. Eventually, they're bound to have enough contacts to find partners and put a team together. Some leave with the blessing and a helpful loan from their employers—as long as there's no question of a swift transference of customer loyalty! It's not unknown for employees to have to sign an affidavit stipulating that they will not open a business within a certain distance of the one in which they are employed. One bartender was slightly disgruntled when he was suddenly saddled with a partner who had talked the boss into allowing him to work with no pay, simply in order to learn the ropes. He cheered up a little when he learned that his pupil wouldn't be taking a share of his tip cup. But, as it turned out, they got on well enough to proceed with a joint restaurant venture that was an enormous success.

Potential partners, perhaps more correctly referred to as investors, are often ignorant of the restaurant business. They will delude themselves that common sense is the best guide and that what they learned in Business 101 or Economics 102 will provide all the answers. But restaurants are quirky businesses.

However, potential partners can hardly be blamed for their nervousness, as they are being called upon to part with that to which it's hard to say goodbye. Bold planning often makes them nervous. If you propose a family restaurant, then you'd better show a plenitude of such consumers in the area.

Potential investors and partners are most frequently made nervous by what appears to them to be an unsuitable location. "You want to open a restaurant on that street? But there are already six restaurants on the block!" they'll whine. It's up to you to evaluate the case. Maybe it's a good thing, because the area has a reputation as being a place where you have a choice of places to eat. Or maybe the area's saturated, and you risk getting lost in the wash.

Another disincentive can be the lack of other restaurants in the area! "Who the heck's going to come here for dinner? There aren't any other restaurants. Do other restaurateurs know something we don't know? No theater, no movies, no businesses."

When seeking partners, you may find yourself caught in the age-old dilemma. Which comes first, the discovery of the acceptable location or the raising of the money? You'll often find that potential investors and partners will agree in principle to go into business with you when you find what they consider suitable premises. Sometimes, to your frustration, you'll find what you absolutely know to be a suitable location that, unfortunately, doesn't appeal to your potential backers.

But, in fact, the necessity of coldly evaluating the suitability of premises serves as a useful and protective exercise. You really will have to think it through and be able to present a solid case for opening a business. Not only will you have to convince yourself and your spouse, but you'll have to convince people who are highly suspicious of the scheme's viability.

Multi-Partner Restaurants

Some restaurants have 25 or more partners. Some are silent, while others operate the restaurant and draw a salary as well as a percentage of the overall profit. In California and New York, where show biz, restaurants, and real estate are almost merged, there are several restaurants owned by show biz people who come and go as workers, according to the vagaries of their careers. Such restaurants afford a lot of fun—to their owners, at least. Unfortunately, few have proved truly successful. There's a lack of focus and continuity. Faces change, and varying degrees of efficiency cause the service and quality to vary uncomfortably, too.

There are all sorts of platitudes to embrace the possible difficulties of partnerships. Too many cooks spoil the broth, too many chiefs and not enough Indians, and so on. Sometimes it's by no means clear who's in charge. There are often employees who will take advantage of this kind of situation in order to carve out their own little niche. This ensures that they make a profit, but will do no good to the business as a whole. That's the principle of divide and conquer.

A disagreeable aspect of the restaurant business for many is the use of authority. All businesses require figures of authority, but somehow this is more apparent in restaurants. Authority is only palatable when it is quite clear who's in charge, and that person exerts authority in a cheerful, acceptable manner. Partners need to be very careful as they plan their venture in order to be sure that there will be no ego trips or constant meddling. Nor should bad workers who just happen to be nephews or nieces be allowed to dilute efficiency. Horror stories abound. One restaurateur was given a large amount of money to start a restaurant by his mother. The only condition was that his wayward brother, the black sheep of the family, must be found a job. Since, unbeknownst to the family, the brother had a $200-a-day cocaine habit, the result was disastrous.

Partnership Disasters

Sadly, the worst partnership disaster is probably the most common: One partner runs away with the profits! It happens all the time, and such is the flux and anonymity of American life that the thieves usually get away with it. Some make a profession of it, moving from city to city and suburb to suburb for years, looking for suckers.

No matter how formally and precisely the agreements are drawn up with a lawyer, if the cash has disappeared, getting it back will always be a problem. Obviously, when you are choosing a partner, the lawyer who was a college classmate or the man who's owned the local gas station for the last 20 years is likely to prove a better bet than the nice character from California whose past is misty, but who is so obviously a regular guy that you can only assume he has a clean and happy history.

Con Artists

Don't think it can't happen to you. The restaurant business abounds with them. The con artists' usual props are good clothes, a ready smile, a deep compassion for the human race in general, and a ludicrously sentimental attachment (to which they will readily confess, wiping away an escaping tear) to kids and dogs. Not uncommonly, they'll actually *have* a spouse, two super kids, and a dog, which they'll trail around as zealously as a detective with a pipe in an old-fashioned mystery thriller. Without being the least bit sanctimonious or holier-than-thou, they'll reveal a deep moral commitment, coupled with a sad contempt for the cynical superficiality of most people today.

Nothing's ever overlooked. They'll work long hours, never be late, and never be too proud to bus a table when the place is busy. "Let's get some turnover here!" they'll say sharply. Occasionally, a faintly reproving, brief frown will appear as they insist on some minor but apparently important point. And you'll hear about the horror you've just been saved from. They're pros and have seen it all. With such figures at the helm, how can anything go wrong?

Then, suddenly, the money's gone, and they're gone, too—lock, stock, and barrel. A call to their mother in Seattle will get you nowhere. Her child hasn't been heard from in years.

Working and "Sleeping" Partners

Another part of the minefield features two partners who actually operate the restaurant, while the other partners hope for a return on their investment. The *sleeping partners* will come to the restaurant regularly, often bringing friends to show off the place and help build business. But then they realize that, though the place is a roaring success, they're not getting a very good dividend.

They demand to see the books. These are duly produced. Sometimes, it transpires that the working partners' expenses include season tickets to the opera, yacht and golf club subscriptions, and so on. These are all plausibly explained under the general heading of public relations. But the two Porsches? Well, you have to drive to work in the morning, right? And what about this extraordinary bill for uniforms? Well, yes, the working partner's tailored clothes are sort of buried in there, too, but heck, they have to look the part!

In other words, those who are actually handling the incoming cash are in the best position to use it. The only way to prevent this kind of exploitation is to have the agreements firmed up before the bonanza begins.

When this sort of confrontation comes to court, as is not uncommon, the IRS takes a friendly interest. In fact, all parties concerned can hope to be accorded a special little niche on the IRS computer that will ensure close attention at all times—forever.

Friendships

Relationships between former friends can deteriorate alarmingly. Sometimes the feuds between partners become public knowledge. Actor Michael Caine and restaurateur Peter Langan once owned a relentlessly advertised London restaurant for society swingers and would-be swingers (who naturally far out-number the truly qualified brethren). These two gentlemen publicly abused one another's reputations. According to the local gossip columns, these epithets went along the lines of "He's a mediocrity with halitosis" and "He's a 24-hour-a-day drunk"—all nice, grown-up stuff. Whether it increased business or not is a fact known only to their accountants. It is totally possible that a significant number of potential customers, alerted to the fact that a visit to the restaurant might enable them to touch the hem of Caine's jacket, would grab their wallets, call up their friends, and go over. With luck, the great men might condescend to start a verbal battle before their very eyes. But what any of this has to do with food is anybody's guess. Michael Caine went on to earn a knighthood and opened a restaurant in Miami.

Partnership Successes

Happily, success is by no means uncommon for restaurant partnerships if the participants have some experience of business generally, or of the restaurant business specifically, are keen to make money, and are prepared to work hard to get it. Partners often find each other from the rank and file of the industry. Servers marry bartenders, pool their savings, and go to it.

Sometimes matches are made in heaven, as when the owner of a successful flower shop, a butcher shop, and a laundry becomes friendly with a local actor who wants to put her earnings to commercial use. They dovetail blissfully. The practical business side is managed by one partner, while the mystical elements are provided by the other.

Those matches that are forged upon the anvil of necessity are less likely to result in wedded bliss. But as long as the partners are talking civilly, there's always hope.

The restaurant business particularly attracts people who are cursed with a burning certainty that, if only the management will do this, all problems will be resolved. In this context, there is only one problem under discussion—the need to bring in customers. When a convinced amateur meets a worried professional, the atmosphere can sour swiftly. And the injection of money into new formats and advertising may not solve the problem either.

Perhaps the best recipe for a successful partnership is the same as the traditional one for a happy marriage: "Before marriage you should keep your eyes wide open. After marriage, you should keep them half shut."

A group of waiters, cooks and kitchen staff plan to re-launch Windows on the World, the restaurant in which they all worked until 9/11—when 73 employees on the North Tower's 106th and 107th floors were killed. They hail from countries as far away as Indonesia, Nepal, and the Ivory Coast. A plan to exhibit mementos of what was the largest grossing restaurant in America has been shelved, but one waiter said, "This is a legacy to the people we lost." One can only wish them well.

An Ideal Marriage?

One well-known operator inherited a restaurant from his father, which he promptly destroyed through hopeless mismanagement. He then did the same to five more businesses. Even his father's reputation (they were a fine old Long Island Italian family) would no longer inspire people's confidence in him. At last, he got a couple of lawyers with money to burn, who decided they'd like a restaurant. At about the same time, Our Hero married the executive editor of a popular illustrated magazine. Four pages of luscious pictures and praise in the magazine, representing thousands of dollars worth of advertising space but presented as editorial feature material (as so much advertising is), soon saw him on the path to glory. Alas, the building had a short lease and was eventually demolished. The marriage lasted only a little while longer.

FINANCIAL PLANNING

Some restaurants are crowded from the day they open, but most need to acquire patronage over a period of time. The rule of thumb is that restaurateurs should have enough money to cover all overhead for a year, assuming no profits whatsoever. The business picture usually emerges a lot sooner than that, however, and it would be unusual to see a failing business taking a whole year before changing its operations or closing down! Few restaurateurs will undertake the risks involved unless they're pretty certain that there's business to be done.

A reminder: Running out of operating funds before the business goes into profit is one of the *prime reasons* for failure. It's simply no good trusting to luck—the competition is too fierce. The degree to which you're prepared to gamble your money and that of others must be finely gauged.

In observing the industry at large, it's apparent that the more a place twists and turns for new gimmicks to get people in, the shorter the time before it suddenly isn't there anymore. The business is fickle, and it isn't as easy as it looks. But ordinary rules of business common sense apply quite a lot of the time.

Certain expenses or overheads are inescapable and must be paid every month. These are often referred to as the *nut*. Once they're paid, some of the cash coming in will be profit. The number of weeks you calculate you can pay this nut, without any recourse to the income you may or may not have, is the number of weeks you have to make it.

Rent is usually the largest sum to be paid, except where the restaurateur is blessed with ownership of the building. The next biggest bill is usually the meat bill, followed by produce, alcoholic beverages, general groceries, and fish. The nice thing about these bills is that the bigger they get, the more you must be selling, so in one sense, the bigger the better!

Payroll is a regular overhead. The chef is usually the highest-paid employee in the operation, where the owner is also the manager. Where a general manager is employed, his or her salary will often approach that of the chef. If a figurehead hostess is employed, who might be a local celebrity with a following, she might be paid quite highly, depending on whether she receives tips. If she is supposed to be too much of an executive to accept tips, then she will need more salary. Porters, dishwashers, and chef's helpers usually get minimum wage, with a bit more if they help the chef to prepare food.

Waiters, waitresses, and busboys are generally paid the legal minimum, since the bulk of their income is from tips. Bartenders are usually paid a little more on the grounds that their tips are somewhat less than the others. Every restaurant has a different situation. In some, the bartenders do little but prepare the drinks—they're more a *service bar* than a *front bar*. Sometimes they get a kickback, sometimes the house pays them a bit extra.

Some cities have strong restaurant employee unions that guarantee minimum wages and conditions. There is no need for a restaurateur to engage with them as long as his employees are as well treated as union members. This means set hours and paid vacations, above all. Staff can be increased or decreased at will. Few employees in the restaurant industry have any kind of contract, except occasionally the chef; some are protected by unions.

When tax is withheld, paychecks for employees who must declare their tips are often very small. So the fact that a restaurateur employs, say, 10 people may seem a bit daunting at first, but when you consider the minimal paychecks most of them are getting, it doesn't look so bad!

Bills

Some of the bills the restaurateur may have to pay after actually opening for business are as follows:

Accountant	Cleaning materials
Advertising, publicity, promotion	Computer equipment and
Bank loan interest	software
Bathroom supplies	Cutlery
Beer	Electricity
Cheese, cakes, desserts	Equipment repairs and mainte-
China and glassware	nance

Exterminator
Fish
Flowers and plants
Garbage pickup
Gas
General groceries
Insurance (several kinds)
Knife sharpener
Lawyer
Light bulbs
Linen (or paper equivalent)
Liquor
Liquor license, business license
Matches
Meat

Mortgage payments
Office supplies and expenses
Payroll and taxes
Printer (menus, etc.)
Produce and fruit
Rent of premises
Rent of some equipment
Sodas
Stationery
Straws, sipsticks, cocktail
    napkins, etc.
Telephone
TV, musicians, entertainment
Uniforms
Wine

The Go Position

"More haste, less speed" sometimes applies, but for the restaurateur with limited funds, it's *essential* to get into business as soon as the means are available. "We opened too soon" is a common accusatory cry. But most restaurateurs will agree that about five minutes after you are able to serve a hot hamburger and a cold beer, your welcoming doors should be wide open.

You are in the position of an advancing unit that *must* secure a certain landing field before it has any hope of resupply. Your money is going out from Day One. Your customers are your resupply.

Foreclosure

In the unhappy event that the operation fails, or even if "the operation is a success but the patient dies," it's possible the following notice will be prominently posted in the window.

MARSHALL'S NOTICE OF IMPENDING LEVY AND SALE
Civil Court of the County of Turkeyburger.

J. X. Doe, Marshall
Plaintiff
v.
Outtaluck Inc.

By virtue of an Execution issued out of the above Court to me directed and delivered: PLEASE TAKE NOTICE that I have this day

LEVIED upon and will expose for SALE at PUBLIC AUCTION, all the right, title, and interest, which the defendant had on this day, or at any time thereafter, in and to the following described chattels, sufficient to satisfy the execution together with the Marshall's fees and expenses.

INVENTORY

Entire contents of restaurant, bar, disco, club, including all kitchen equipment, refrigerators, stoves, tables, chairs, glassware, bar counters, piano, electronic equipment, workbenches, ice machines, bar stools, cash registers, speakers, videos, desks, cabinets, washbasins, vacuum cleaners, racks, and lighting systems.

Pay in full 48 hours before sale. Date of sale will be advertised at your expense. Execution and fees: $99,999 plus expenses and interest.

A further sad note may say:

The landlord has possession of these premises pursuant to a Warrant of Eviction issued by one of the judges of the Civil Court. For information, contact landlord.

You may come across such notices in the boarded-up windows of failed restaurants as you search for premises. Some premises seem to spend as much time boarded up as they spend open for business! In one such building on New York's Columbus Avenue, where no less than four restaurants had failed within 12 months, the new owner put up a notice saying:

REWARD

$250 reward for the person who comes up with a name for the new neighborhood restaurant.

Underneath, a cruel wag had scrawled "How about Ad Nauseam?"

Columbus Avenue is to the restaurant industry what the battlefield of the Somme was to the British Army in World War I—a graveyard of ambition and hope. Notices in its bombed-out premises should be seen as fair warning but taken in stride, like corpses seen by infantrymen as they make their way up the line to battle. Business is a form of war, and there are casualties.

"The wise can learn from a fool, but a fool learns from nobody." There is a certain amount of wisdom to be obtained by studying losers. But you'll do better to study the winners, like the Smith & Wollensky group, or the 125-seater restaurant that became a 2,000-seater grossing nearly $40 million a year.

BUYING A FRANCHISE

In the business section of your local library, you should be able to find a book called *Franchise Opportunities*. A section of it deals with eating establishments. Most franchise operations have Web sites. If you go to a search engine such as Google and simply type in the name of a company, you will be on your way. Often, you can request information by e-mail. There are more than 200 restaurant franchise companies in the United States. **WARNING:** Not all of them are licensed to operate in all states. So don't start fantasizing about your business until you've ascertained that it can be operated in the area in which you wish to do business.

When you buy a franchise, you buy identity. In the privacy of your soul, this may be what you truly seek in opening a business of your own. Whose identity do you want? If you find your brow puckering, welcome to the club. Franchise does have that effect. Some franchises work tremendously well. Some are disasters.

But, while franchise may not immediately appeal to your Rick-like dreams, it is certainly worth considering. After all, you could cut your teeth on a franchise and then go on to greater things. There's no reason why you shouldn't imbue your business with your own inimitable touch. The parent company may supply you with fluorescent salad dressing, and insist that it is served. There is wisdom in this. That fluorescent salad dressing may be the one thing your patrons seek, after having encountered it on a blissful Miami vacation, so all the franchise's "signature dishes" must be retained. Consistency, the certainty of what will be available in a restaurant, is a real strength. The Hilton Hotel chain prospered when the post–World War II world travel escalated quickly both for business and pleasure. Certain things that Americans took for granted at home often simply weren't readily available abroad. Europeans mocked this with jokes like, "And Hilton said 'Let there be iced water,' and lo, it came to pass, there was iced water . . . ," but in the end they got the message and became Americanized, to everyone's benefit.

Why are there such things as franchises? Let's say a clever cook invents a machine that makes hot, crisp mango-bangos, which sell at a terrific rate and profit, especially to the background of tango music and Walt Disney designs on the walls. Unfortunately, the inventor can't be everywhere, so others are allowed to spread the gospel. They must find their own premises and pay the rent, and in return, they are allowed to imitate the inventor's brilliance. Also in return, they receive up to 10 weeks of training, advice, and possibly some equipment, with regular counseling from corporate managers.

It will come as no surprise to learn that McDonald's, founded in 1955, is the biggest food service retailer in the world, with more than 30,000 outlets in 119 countries serving more than 47 million customers a day. Not everyone can become a franchisee—the selection process is quite rigorous. The minimum investment is $75,000, and this must be provided by the individual, not partners, corporations, or passive investors. This is only the beginning, however. More cash will have to be found to equip and decorate. Potential franchisees can discuss this during their assessment process. (An Arthur Treacher's franchise is only $30,000, but the total investment will exceed $200,000.) McDonald's doesn't provide financing. It often develops locations, buying the site and reconstructing or building a restaurant, and it may offer locations to its trainees, who will, of course, have to pay for all equipment and décor. Individuals must demonstrate "common business sense," a history of business success, an entrepreneurial spirit, and a strong desire to succeed. They must show their ability to motivate and train people, to manage finances, and be prepared to devote full time to the day-to-day operation. Training in all aspects of the restaurant business is given, and this can be part-time. Minorities and women currently represent 34 percent of franchisees, and 70 percent of all applicants in training.

Some companies are less rigorous than others. Most franchise companies are at the fast-food end of the business, which will not always appeal to a budding restaurateur.

A warning note is struck by the fact that few franchise companies offer any financial assistance. "Never spend your own money" is a favorite maxim for some entrepreneurs, and while its wisdom is obvious, so are its limitations. Some will offer you advice, such as how to prepare the proposal to take to the bank when you apply for a loan. They want your money. You are in the position of someone who buys a secondhand car that may prove to be unsound. The dealer may put a few things right and observe the warranty, if any. But, one thing the dealer won't do is buy the critter back.

Any business requires careful thought, and franchising can be very dangerous. There have been some casualties lately, especially at the cheaper end of the business. You'll do well to talk, observe, and, above all, read the fine print of the contract until you understand every word.

However, there have been some wild successes. One Pizza Hut franchisee started delivering pizzas at age 16, and by the time he was 30 owned no less than seven outlets.

There is a good case for considering a franchise if:

- You have some restaurant experience and have always wanted to have your own place.

- You are a restaurant manager who wants to be in business for yourself, but you cannot raise the capital required to open an independent operation. You know you could with a strong franchise relationship behind you, however.
- You are a real estate developer who wants a restaurant as part of your project, and you are willing to hire the right person to manage the business for you.

CHAPTER 5

EQUIPMENT AND DECOR

EQUIPMENT – OLD OR INHERITED

If you take over an existing restaurant, as is likely, you may inherit an amount of basic equipment. It isn't free; you paid for it. You may reject it, of course, in favor of new equipment of your own preference. But you'll have to pay for it. There are considerable savings to be made from using inherited equipment, even though it may sometimes look depressingly old and decrepit and quite out of sympathy with your brave new hopes.

Many a restaurant boasts a shiny espresso machine bought secondhand 10 years ago, still going strong, having paid for itself several times over and yielding a handsome profit ever since. This is increasingly a good-profit item, even though making espresso, cappuccino, and the various combinations currently in vogue is a time-consuming job, unpopular with waiters and waitresses. Brand-new machines can be expensive.

A practical eye is required. A freezer is a freezer as long as it works, whether it's new or 20 years old. A refrigerated storage room called the *walk-in box* is a standard requirement, and, if it's serviceable, why replace it at considerable expense? In this age of disposable items, where there's always pressure from suppliers to replace existing equipment with new, a lot of bargains are overlooked.

Any old refrigeration equipment that proves unreliable and beyond cheap local repair, however, should be promptly replaced. A breakdown on Friday night could result in a great deal of wasted food—including expensive items such as shrimp, lobster, and fish—by the time the mechanic arrives on Monday morning. You may discover that the comforting words *24-hour service* don't really mean much after all, as you encounter the voice on the answering machine, or the harassed manager who isn't quite sure where the repairperson is. Service people don't come cheap, either.

The standard gas range with its large oven, gas burners, and grill is another item often inherited, and science has done little to improve the basic design since it was invented in the 1880s. Gas cookers were a tremendous breakthrough. Before their invention, two hours a day might be spent just getting the fires going, and in summer the heat was very stressful. Ranges can get very dirty, but that's just about their only problem, and if they're cleaned daily it's a minor chore. Even if a really dirty old range is inherited, a thorough, painstaking cleaning with bicarbonate of soda and lots of hot water should restore it to usability. Some would say the older the better, because they're made more solidly. There's a French proverb, *"On fait de bonne soupe dans une vieille marmite"* (You can make good soup in an old pot), but this proverb is rarely used in connection with culinary matters!

The budding restaurateur with no flair for mechanics or machinery should try to have a friend who really understands refrigerators, air conditioners, pipes, toilets, stoves, gas, and electronics. Salvaging dilapidated equipment is part of the folklore of the restaurant business. "I took one look at that beat-up old refrigerator and my heart sank. Then Joe looked at it, and poked around. He discovered that all it needed was a new part and a good cleaning, and it worked perfectly."

Your equipment must relate to the kind of business you envisage. A new owner on New York's famed Columbus Avenue, where restaurants are many but satisfied diners are few, solemnly hoped to feed a seating capacity of 80 people from a three-ring stove. A really sharp chef with a limited menu designed for speed could do it, but this place couldn't. Its menu featured items that simply take time to cook, such as duck, and fish *en papillotte* (fish cooked in paper), utterly absurd menu choices. When chefs are limited to such equipment, they often resort to unspeakable practices in the name of fast production, such as putting ducks and chops into the deep-fry.

Customers would often wait half an hour for their main courses to emerge. They sometimes walked out, and few returned. The restaurant flopped, in spite of its brilliant corner location, and soon became a French sweater store.

EQUIPMENT — NEW

Brand-new equipment is the most expensive kind. The bank will be more inclined to lend you money for new equipment, but you'll pay top price. Sometimes equipment can be leased. Any of the dozens of restaurant-industry newspapers will tell you where equipment can be obtained. Companies are also listed in the phone book.

If you obtain permission to convert premises for restaurant use, you'll have to start from scratch, and the cost can be daunting. But if you are prepared to put in time searching, there are restaurant equipment bargains galore to be obtained. As we saw in the grim example of the foreclosure notice at the end of Chapter 4, restaurants do sometimes go out of busines, and their equipment is often sold. "It's an ill wind that blows nobody any good!"

By telephoning around and checking local newspapers, you can soon discover the local situation. The newspaper's advertising department can steer you in the right direction, and you may be amazed by the low prices. Available equipment can range from a complete carved wooden bar to enough cutlery to feed a small army.

Remember that there's constant wastage through breakage and souvenir stealing, so that a bargain price on 100 salt and pepper sets may be a good deal, even if your restaurant only needs 30 to cover every table and the bar. You'll use them all eventually.

A word to the wise: When an interesting sale of restaurant equipment is in the offing, the word goes out way ahead of time. If you live in a major city, you must understand that there's a whole network of people with ears permanently close to the ground. They live to open restaurants. They have no other plans in life. So the sales are often rigged, or the best items are siphoned off discreetly before the advertised day of the sale.

Another small point—which can be a nightmare—is that the purchaser is responsible for the prompt removal of the goods. This means a truck and helpers to carry the stuff. It also means you'll need some place to store it. Storage can be expensive, as can truck rental. And if you think you can get a garage in the suburbs at short notice, you may be in for a shock.

Again, we are back to the importance of planning ahead. Ideally, the painting and refurbishing of your premises should be finished on the day of the sale. Thus, one stage of setting up the restaurant dovetails into the next, with minimum loss of time and minimum expenditure. Sometimes you'll be lucky!

If you're not, and you have to store your newly acquired bargain equipment at your premises, you'll just have to work around it until you get to the point where you can put it where it belongs.

A lot of ingenuity goes into making cheap things look quite expensive, and, except in deluxe restaurants, most people don't expect to dine off classic china using heavy silver cutlery. The bent fork is a common sight in many restaurants. But, if you propose to charge $5 or more for a glass of white wine, the glass shouldn't look too cheap. And there is currently a heavy emphasis on visual presentation of food. As the current wisecrack has it, "When I looked at the food on my plate, I didn't know whether to eat it or frame it!"

THE WONDERFUL
WORLD OF LAUNDRY

Many restaurateurs are inclined to wax lyrical and mystical on the subject of laundry costs. Why this bill should hurt any more than the others is a mystery, but it seems to. It can be an irritatingly large weekly bill. There are laundry services that supply everything from cooks' aprons, pants, jackets, and white hats to tablecloths, dish mops, napkins, and towels. A cliché of the industry is the sight of the owner solemnly leaving with a bag of restaurant laundry to wash at home.

The Art of a Well-Set Table

A clean, white tablecloth does have a nice appeal, as does a colored and checkered one. Linen napkins add a touch of luxury. Humbert Humbert, the main character of Nabokov's *Lolita,* a bit of a snob who'd been brought up in a luxury hotel, pined for the "cool, rich linens of the Mirana Hotel" as he wiped his lips with pink paper! The bottom-of-the-range paper napkins normally found in fast-food restaurants and diners are simply inadequate for proper restaurants, especially those serving hearty fare or the sort of dishes that tempt diners to use their fingers. If the napkin provided is of high-quality, absorbent paper, and if it's emblazoned with the restaurant's name and/or logo, this can be effectively attractive and inexpensive, too. Heavier-quality paper napkins will usually satisfy all but the most demanding. Using cork or paper coasters for wet-bottomed glasses can often give a tablecloth a sporting chance of being used again, as can an adroitly placed flower arrangement. It can be a little dispiriting for customers, though, when a slight shift of the table arrangement reveals a nasty stain.

In expensive restaurants, you will notice that the waiters or waitresses often have an elaborate drill for changing tablecloths and setting up the table again in an amazingly short time. The tablecloths are folded just so, for swift deployment, and the napkins are in place, too. If they don't do this quickly, they'll get a frown from the boss, and (this is what really spurs them) if a new party arrives without a reservation, the hostess looks round the room and seats the people at the table that's ready. It's called table turnover.

Sometimes customers are happy to wait until a table they prefer is made ready. Some tables are more attractive than others. Servers are inclined to get the sulks when customers sit at dirty tables, as they are sometimes wont to do, because this makes the task of setting up more difficult. They adore disciplinarian maitre d's who ask the customers to wait to one side until their preparation is complete. Many customers enjoy this, too. It's all part of the ritual choreography of the joyous experience. It gives them an opportunity to show how incredibly gracious and understanding they are, and it also provides an opportunity for them to gaze round the dining room to see if there's anyone there they know or would like to know.

Laundry Alternatives

Restaurateurs twist and turn to reduce their laundry bills. It's not unusual to find expensive fresh flowers in abundance with paper tablecloths and napkins. There's something inelegant about having great swathes of noisy paper unraveled before your very eyes, however. Many people will never notice this. But some will, and if these happen to be the kind of people whose business you seek, then you'll do well to think long and hard about linen versus paper.

For casual dining, a happy compromise is often reached by having plastic, wood, or even marble tops, which can be easily wiped clean—often with the help of a little discreet and judicious spillage from a water glass by the busperson. For full effect, a flower in a Coca-Cola or Perrier bottle will do the trick.

All of these considerations are reflected in the restaurant's prices. Any potential diner knows perfectly well that if, on pressing her nose to the windowpane, she sees dazzling white tablecloths, then she'd better be ready to dig deep into her pocket. City dwellers are often driven crazy when out-of-town friends ask to be directed to a "not-too-expensive white tablecloth restaurant."

DECOR

For the modest fee of $200,000, Gigi de Frabazonia will fly in from Rome and design for you a unique restaurant that may, or may not, be so enchanting that people will come just to see it, and to heck with the food. However, it's possible to put together a perfectly acceptable restaurant without spending too much money on décor.

A simple theme is fun and can add charm to a place. There's no doubt that a chilled glass of dry sherry will taste better in a Spanish courtyard than in a chrome and plastic diner, just as a fine brandy tastes better from a snifter than from a Styrofoam cup. With a little flair, miracles can be achieved.

There's nothing wrong with lining the dining room with Topolski originals, as at the Carlton Tower restaurant in London, or with Hollywood studio memorabilia, as at the now defunct Maxwell's Plum in New York. It definitely adds to the pleasure of the dining experience, but it has to be paid for.

Some cynical diners believe that the difficulty of getting a slice of lemon for their fish or a large spoon for their soup is directly proportional to the emphasis placed on décor—and who's to say they're wrong? It is certainly irritating to a customer to note that, although the theme, logo, and ambiance have been carried through to the nth degree by a designer who has long since departed the premises, your white wine is warm and there's no mustard in the house.

Most food critics grade the restaurants they review in terms of food, ambiance, and service. Decor obviously affects ambiance. Design also affects service.

DESIGN

The object of all design in restaurants must be to provide the maximum delight to the customers, while efficiently serving as many customers as possible.

All restaurateurs juggle these two factors constantly. Some emphasize efficient service, others are big on ambiance, and others just crowd people in wherever they'll fit.

Hard though it may be to believe, many people like being crowded. Perhaps it gives them an illusion of being involved in some kind of group experience. It's common to see people standing in line to get into a crowded restaurant while disdaining the empty one next door, which is apparently just as attractive. It seems at least possible that many people prefer crowds to space. The higher up the market you go, in general, the more space the customer is allowed to occupy for the duration of his or her meal.

There's something to be said for every method. A red tablecloth, dimmed lights, and a candle in a bottle can seem very atmospheric when you're young, in love, and have had a glass of wine or two. A single flower in a coke bottle can add an inexpensive whimsical touch. Despite its banality, this favorite scheme hasn't stopped working yet. Why rack your brains for new ideas when old ones still work well?

A word to the wise: Some people detest candles and simply will not dine by candlelight, in spite of their flattering effect. Sometimes customers snuff them out, and the diligent waiter solemnly relights them. The objection is to the smell and the fumes. It shouldn't be too much of a stretch for a waitress to query, with a smile, "Are you happy with the candle?" This will also demonstrate concern for the customer's comfort. Serious restaurants almost never have candles, though they may have some form of electric light that gives the same effect.

As you study various restaurants, you'll soon begin to notice how some manage to make every table reasonably attractive. Some offer a good view, others offer privacy. Kitchen and restroom entrances are discreetly situated around corners, and so on. Ideally, there should be no bad tables in a restaurant. The problem areas in a small restaurant are invariably the tables in the space near the kitchen and the restrooms. Constant to-ing and fro-ing, banging of doors and odors from food destined for other diners can be aggravating. In bigger, smarter restaurants this problem is often resolved by total separation of these areas. The kitchen and restrooms may not even be on the same floor. But unless you have this kind of space availability, you may have to compromise. Double doors that don't bang and floor surfaces that muffle footsteps will help.

In some restaurants, of course, notably those aimed at the young, the noise and the bustle are part of the entertainment, and won't present a problem.

Many restaurants are unattractively stark, especially when you find yourself looking at an oblong room, with square tables lining three and a half walls, three or four round ones in the middle, and a bar occupying what's left of the wall space. This starkness can be broken up inexpensively. It can be done by partly partitioning some of the tables or putting potted plants here and there. Thus, the effect is coy, inviting, and gives a sense of offering more value for the money. McDonald's is ideal for some circumstances, but for social or business intimacy, a more confined space, perhaps with lower lights, is often a better idea.

Starkness shouldn't be confused with minimalism. For many, Formica-and-leatherette establishments with easy-wipe surfaces and gaudy tiles have their charms. Some premises offer roofs or courtyards, and very little needs to be done to cheer these areas up. The main enemy here is usually the pipes and other functional bits and pieces that have to go somewhere and are, unfortunately, clearly visible to diners. For some restaurateurs, a happy solution has been simply to paint the pipes or other offending obstacles in gay colors, defiantly suggesting some obscure school of art. A very real danger is the sudden release of unfortunate odors in the dining area, and this must be prevented.

In cities, it's sometimes possible to obtain permission to extend premises onto the sidewalk to form a sidewalk cafe. The sight in winter of some masochists eating omelets that haven't a hope of staying hot for more than 30 seconds, while the traffic roars by, is a wondrous one. But when glassed in, such extensions may have a charm, because diners can stay warm or cool and be spared traffic noise. Such extensions are not cheap, and many require our old friend, the disciplinarian maitre d', to tell incoming customers "Dinner Only!" to avoid the occupation of an expensive piece of real estate by people who will not consume more than $10 worth of food or drink during four long and happy hours of people watching.

Clever design can actually exploit bare walls, at no great expense. By placing lights adroitly, for instance, you can give the appearance of being on a film set, which many will find agreeable.

Allowing your restaurant to be used as an art gallery can solve decorating problems and be fun, too. Artists display their work, which is for sale. Sometimes the restaurateurs will charge a commission, sometimes not, depending on their commitment to art. The changing scene will give regular customers something to talk about.

Empty space is decorative in itself at times. However, Frank Lloyd Wright's concept of *powerful emptiness* should not be taken too much to heart by restaurateurs. Any space not occupied by people eating or drinking is losing you money. Most restaurateurs will admit that their dining rooms are a little cramped, but they excuse this on the grounds that to sacrifice even one table, they'd have to increase prices. They will usually diplomatically fail to add that it's been scientifically proved that diners who are crowded and subjected to noise will eat faster, thus enabling tables to be turned over more rapidly.

Somewhere between the tourist cabin of an airplane and the spacious baronial hall, an acceptable compromise must be found. As a rule of thumb, it's generally figured that people are optimally accommodated at three to the square yard. That's how to work out your seating capacity. Don't forget there must be at least some space between tables to permit access by customers and waiters.

CHAPTER 6

THE BAR

PROS AND CONS

There is no law that requires you to have a bar of any kind in your restaurant. Nor are you obliged to serve alcoholic drinks. Some restaurants, often stuffy and expensive, have only a token bar to oblige the occasional customer who might like a drink while waiting for others to arrive or while the table is being prepared. In this kind of restaurant, which tends to have strict reservation systems, delays are usually short. The token bar will usually not have more than four stools, if indeed any at all, and either the maitre d' or one of the servers will serve the occasional drinks required. Designer breweries often offer only a minimum selection of drinks other than the beer brewed on the premises. It isn't uncommon to find a restaurant with no bar at all. Those owners often do not want a *bar crowd,* and they may feel they're not missing any trade because their customers drink heartily enough at the tables.

It must be understood that the profit on alcoholic drinks is enormous. The current price of a glass of house white wine is about $7. That is not much less than the price of a gallon jug of one of the most popular table white wines in the United States, and 25 to 30 glasses of wine can be poured from one bottle. This is a profit markup to make even importers of Italian shoes envious! A Beefeater martini in the Oakroom Bar of New York's Plaza is currently about $13, a price that includes local sales tax. A liter bottle of Beefeater's gin costs about $24.99 in a New York liquor store. That's the *retail* price; wholesale prices are much lower. Liquor prices vary from state to state.

A mean bartender who mixes a martini with lots of ice and gives it a good long stir, thus creating lots of *meltage,* can easily squeeze 30 martinis from a liter bottle. Thirty times $13 is $390. Even with generous free pouring, a bottle of vodka, gin, or any spirit will yield a huge profit. The American insistence on ice in drinks is good news for bar owners. Most people who ever drink in bars and wouldn't dream of fixing themselves a cocktail at home are happy to accept huge amounts of ice and tiny amounts of liquor. Those who don't like so much ice will order their drinks saying, "Very little ice, please," but, because such a subtlety often falls on deaf ears, it's common for such customers to ask for "ice on the side."

The enormous profit on drinks sometimes leads restaurateurs to whine, "I don't make any money on the food, only on the alcohol," which is arrant nonsense.

Fancy drinks such as piña coladas and strawberry daiquiris are excellent profit items. You can charge a lot for them, but they require no more hard liquor than any other cocktail. Customers don't care. They enjoy the theater of preparation. Fancy drinks are popular with bartenders who aren't too busy because they provide an opportunity for a song and dance that can bump up the tip. Noisy blenders are good conversation killers, too, and sometimes an order for six piña coladas will be welcome, since it will interrupt the extended first chapter of some customer's life story on its third re-run.

The absence of consumer price resistance at a bar can be surprising. One busy Sunday afternoon, two bartenders decided to experiment. They selected a rather chic nonalcoholic fizzy water (which shall be nameless, though at one point its producers informed the world that it was "made from natural rain") and started off by charging $5 per bottle, the regular price. Then they raised it to $6. At $14.50, without a quibble, they told the owner what they were doing. He turned pale. "Stop it—you'll get me shot," he cried.

But on another occasion in a summer resort, a customer who ordered two daiquiris and was charged $20, balked. "Utterly ridiculous," he foamed, "This isn't the Plaza. I'm leaving."

Rising to the occasion, the bartender said, "I agree our prices are a bit steep. But I can't do anything with the drinks I've made, so why not have them on the house?" The customer stayed, guilt kicked in, he spent some money anyway, and the bartender got a decent tip—a subtle kind of chutzpah.

FOOD AT THE BAR

You can also serve food at the bar. Many newly opening restaurants start offering the full menu at the bar, only to find that this stretches waiters, waitresses, and bartenders too much. "Suzy, could you check on that steak for the bar, please?" the bartender will plead helplessly, "And could you bring me a setup? Dressing on the side for the salad, by the way. Did I write that? Sorry."

In the end, they usually get organized and offer a bar menu of simple items that are least prone to complication and most quickly delivered. If the bartender has a small supply of knives, forks, napkins, salts and peppers, and condiments such as mustard and ketchup handy, it can work very easily. People dining alone often prefer to eat at the bar rather than sit at a table. Of course, flexibility is all, and if the place isn't busy, there's no reason why the full menu shouldn't be offered. This is a matter for trial and error, where one simply has to see what works best.

Hot snacks and appetizers at the bar can be a welcome little money-spinner and attract regular customers who really don't want the full restaurant treatment. In an age when everyone's on a diet and trying to eat less, Spanish *tapas* restaurants are doing well. *Tapas* are simple, small dishes originally designed as appetizers, such as *gambas al ajillo*, a small dish of shrimps fried in wine, onions, and garlic. Such a dish is ideal as a bar snack. But, for no very good reason, providing bar food often causes resentment in the kitchen. "They're paid to do the job, and you can only do a day's work in a day," you may retort. But a sulking chef can do terrible harm—turning out lousy food, losing customers, and causing your most efficient servers to quit before you get the message. Owners sometimes need to display diplomacy in these matters.

The practice of putting out nuts and dubious bits of cheese and crackers on the bar is a much-debated one. Customers usually love it. But it has its drawbacks. It's unhygienic, though most of the hands that dive in and out are probably clean. Cockroaches and mice simply love bar nibbles. There's always plenty dropped for them!

People who can eat things for free are likely to spend less. If that little corner that might be nicely filled by a $6 slice of chocolate cake has already been filled by cheese nibbles, you've lost a sale. When waiters are setting up the restaurant, you'll often hear a veteran instructing a novice not to put out too much bread, as it may reduce the customer's appetite.

Every bar that puts out a generous selection of nuts and cheese nibbles and hot hors d'oeuvres at cocktail time will attract some customers who eat everything in sight but drink little. In some places, it's possible to have dinner for the price of one drink, though meatballs every night will not appeal to everyone. Some owners have fits of guilt about drink prices, and feel they must show a little mercy by offering their drinking customers something to nibble. Cheese, nuts, and nibbles are surprisingly expensive and rapidly consumed. Cheap compromises both look and taste unappetizing.

The theory that salty tidbits will induce thirst doesn't work for some reason—perhaps it has something to do with the fact that sodium intake is essential for the proper absorption of water. Too *little* salt in the system is more likely to induce thirst than too much, as anyone who's suffered even the mildest level of heat exhaustion can testify.

Some diners will resent the drinkers' laughter or applause at sporting events on television wafting over the dining room from the bar; others will love it and enjoy people watching. It is entirely a matter of choice. Sometimes the best of both worlds can be achieved by having separate rooms, or at least a separating wall or rail—well disguised by potted plants, of course.

THE SERVICE BAR

In the average 50- to 200-seat restaurant, one end of the bar is called the "service bar." From it, waiters pick up the drinks to be served at the tables. In larger establishments it's often a separate bar, possibly out of the dining area.

Sometimes, to cover busy periods, you'll need an extra bartender to handle service. In really busy bars, with 10 stools or more, you may need two bartenders all the time.

Often the cash register on the bar is the main register for the tables, too, so that the bar is an important focal point of operations. A common bar problem is that of "too much work for one, not enough for two." But that's the name of the game. Most bartenders would rather sweat a little than split their tip cup down the middle! One solution is to employ a part-time bartender to work the service end during busy periods. Overstretched bartenders must be discreetly supervised, as they tend to cut corners and sometimes become downright sloppy. The night bartender is normally supposed to leave the bar ready to roll for the day shift. But old hands arriving for the day shift know perfectly well that they should check to see the bar is correctly supplied. Glasses must be thoroughly clean and lipstick free.

The emphasis at the service bar is on speed, getting the drinks made, so the servers can move on to other tasks. It's now common practice for the waiters or waitresses to pour glasses of white wine themselves, since this is the single most commonly requested tipple in any bar not catering exclusively to a beer-drinking crowd. They may pour house red wine too, though this is less frequently requested. Occasionally, waiters or waitresses will abuse this practice, either by drinking too much wine themselves or by selling it in a private transaction and pocketing the money received. Owners, beware.

You will do very well to sacrifice a small amount of profit and give your customers a decent glass of table wine. Many notice, even if they don't always mention it.

Since the service bar is often hidden from view, it's possible to get away with murder by serving cheap substitutes for what has been ordered. This is a shortsighted policy that will win no friends. Although it may be cute to give the cheaper MacDickensian's Old Malt instead of the rather more expensive Famous Grouse and to feel superior when the customer doesn't notice, it's a small victory and an unworthy one.

Having said that, at really busy restaurants where the customers seem to relish being treated like cattle, bartenders are often instructed to pour cheap brands, no matter what is ordered. They get away with it most of the time. Some owners fill expensive brand bottles with cheaper liquor in the dead of night for the extra small profit involved. Sometimes a bartender who simply cannot find anyone to go downstairs for a bottle of a popular brand-name vodka will simply fill the bottle from another source. Vodka, of course, is the drink where subterfuge is the easiest, since they all taste much the same, in spite of the huge variance in prices.

A few years ago, a magazine surveyed several bars to find out how much vodka they were putting in their Bloody Mary cocktails. In some well-known restaurants, they found that no vodka whatsoever was put in the cocktails from the service bar.

Amusingly, there was no speculation as to why this should be so. Presumably most people thought it was just a straightforward rip-off. Now, mean though many of them are, few owners would instruct their bartenders to omit vodka from a popular cocktail entirely. The decision to deprive customers of alcohol does not derive from a concern for their health. Omitting vodka from the drink, while charging full price for it, helps to make up for drinks given away "on the house." The Bloody Mary is tailor-made for this deception since, with tomato juice, Tabasco, Worcestershire sauce, salt, pepper, horseradish, and sticks of celery all vying for attention, the shot of bland liquor isn't greatly missed—until the drinker is suddenly surprised to find himself remarkably sober after several drinks!

On weekends, Bloody Mary's are much in demand at lunchtime. To speed up service, many bartenders pre-mix the tomato juice, and add the vodka when the drink is ordered. Some owners deprecate this method saying solemnly, "We build our Bloody Mary's individually from scratch." It's hot air. Premixing and storing the spiced juice in its original container ensures consistency and quality—as well as fast service. Bloody Mary mix can be used, and some owners despise that, too. But in a comparative tasting, the commercial canned mix will almost invariably be voted the most tasty, the only exceptions being those drinkers who like extra Tabasco to give the drink more oomph.

Incidentally, Bloody Mary's can be given a twist by using aquavit (a Danish spirit) instead of vodka. This is called a Danish Mary. And some prefer V8 juice to tomato juice.

STOCKING THE BAR

Your liquor suppliers will provide you with lists, order forms, free pens, sponges, water jugs, and all sorts of useful bits and pieces. You will need more than one supplier, unfortunately, because not every company has every brand of liquor available. You get your Beefeater's Gin from one house, and your Dewars Scotch from another. This is yet another legal artifice to avoid monopoly and maintain as much government control as possible over the industry. Occasionally, winking liquor delivery drivers will approach you with bargain offers— a case of vodka for a mere $50, perhaps. An accomplice at the warehouse will have sneaked on board the truck an extra, unlisted, case of liquor. Food suppliers and amateur fishermen will also make these under-the-counter offers. Let conscience be your guide.

In the United States, as in many countries, the liquor lobby is a powerful one. They control huge fortunes. Producers of alcohol enjoy household names in their own countries and worldwide. In France, everyone knows Hennessey, Chateau Rothschild, and Moet & Chandon. Gonzalez Byass, Riscal, and Domecq are famous in Spain.

The English are well represented, too, with their scotches, gins, and beers. In England, a true vertical monopoly exists in the wine and spirit trade. The huge corporations own the breweries, the vineyards in Europe, the bottling plants and warehouses, the liquor stores, the pubs, the restaurants, and, increasingly, the hotels. *Free houses*—independently owned pubs that owe no allegiance to a brewery and can therefore carry a larger selection of beers and spirits—are rare indeed, mainly because the powerful brewery groups offer unrefusable prices to buy them out. The last free-house pub in London was sold in about 1955. It would serve no great purpose to try to alter the system. Capitalism tends toward monopoly, whichever way you shake the kaleidoscope. However, legislation required the British brewery conglomerates to reduce the number of pubs they owned to no more than 2,000. Consequently, the least profitable pubs could be bought for a song. Many restaurateurs have seized the opportunity to convert these establishments, invest them with some character, and turn them into thriving businesses.

This experience, though not directly relevant to the U.S. scene, underscores the worldwide importance of the property market and its close relationship to the restaurant industry. Also, every restaurant is a retail point of sale. The regular attentions of salespeople are something the restaurateur has to get used to. Once in a while, among the blandishments to buy a tenth delicious gin for the bar or a phone system that will net you a big fat $50 in savings a month, you will discern bargains—but they are few and far between.

If, in the United States, all wholesale suppliers were allowed to carry all liquor brands, there would soon be a vertical monopoly that would violate antitrust law and a dangerous increase in the already enormous economic power of certain dubious elements of society.

Bar Inventory

Here is a partial list of what a well-stocked bar might carry:

Rye or American whisky: Seagrams 7, VO, Crown Royal, Canadian
   Club, Southern Comfort, house
Bourbon: Wild Turkey, Maker's Mark, Jack Daniels (more correctly, a
   "Tennessee whisky")
Scotch whisky: Dewar's, JB, Cutty Sark, Johnny Walker (Red and

Black), Chivas Regal, house. Also very expensive single malts like Glenlivet and The Macallan.

Rum: Bacardi (light and dark), Black, Gold, Myers, Mount Gay, house

Gin: Beefeaters, Gordon's, Tanqueray, house

Vodka: Smirnoff, Finlandia, Absolut, house

Sherry: Tio Pepe (dry) Harvey's Bristol Cream (sweet)

Tequila: Cuervo

Irish whisky: Bushmill's

Cognac and brandy: Rémy Martin, Courvoisier, apricot, cherry, Armagnac, house

Cordials and liqueurs: Campari, Grand Marnier, Calvados, Bailey's Irish Cream, White Mint, Green Mint, Chartreuse, Kummel, Jagermeister (sweet, and wildly popular with the young)

Vermouth and wine cocktails: Lillet, Dubonnet, Cinzano, sweet and dry Vermouth

Champagne: Moet, Taittinger, Cristal, Dom Perignon, Korbel, etc.

California white: Chardonnay

California red: Cabernet Sauvignon, Zinfandel

German white: Moselle, Riesling

French red: Beaujolais, Pommard

French white: Chablis, Pouilly Fumé

Italian red: Valpolicella, Chianti

Italian white: Soave Bolla, Pinot Grigio

Rosé: Tavel, Anjou, Mateus (or house white with a splash of house red in it . . .)

House wine: red and white in half-gallon jugs

Beer, bottled: Heineken, Budweiser, Amstel, Amstel Light, Miller

Beer, keg: Budweiser, Watney's, Bass, New Amsterdam, Coors

Beer, nonalcoholic: Buckler, Kaliber

Soda: Coca-Cola, Diet Coke, Seven-Up, ginger ale, tonic, seltzer

Juices and bottled waters: Perrier, orange, grapefruit, tomato, cranberry, pineapple

Miscellaneous supplies: Worcestershire sauce, Tabasco sauce, horseradish, bouillon, salt, pepper, cherries, olives, onions, lemons, limes, lime juice, oranges, milk, cream, coffee beans, coconut cream, sugar, nutmeg, straws, stirrers, napkins

The full list of possibilities would require a separate volume, as you'll discover when you start getting suppliers' brochures. *House* means the brand selected for general pouring when no specific brand is requested (e.g., scotch and soda), as distinct from Grouse and Soda. It's usually the cheapest available, but it doesn't need to be. Experienced diners and drinkers will note with approval the use of a popular brand such as Dewar's scotch or Gordon's gin for general issue at no extra charge.

When you look at a well-stocked bar, the array of bottles may be bewildering. Be assured, however, that the contents are basically the same. Ethyl alcohol is the common ingredient in all intoxicating beverages. It should not be confused with the industrial methyl alcohol that sometimes finds its way into Christmas party punches, killing a few and blinding others, or into backstreet brands of Italian *grappa*. The other ingredients—the juniper berry flavoring in gin, the caramel coloring in scotch, whisky, rum, and brandy, and the hundreds of chemicals—give each liquor its individual flavor and, some say, its individual effect. Some say that scotch is calming, gin is depressing, and so on.

Alcohol is a depressant. That is the whole point of alcohol. It first affects the brain in a positive way, by depressing pessimistic thoughts and making one cheerful. But too much alcohol means too much depression, hence the cartoon character, the maudlin drunk. Fizzy drinks such as champagne or scotch-and-soda, especially on an empty stomach, are faster in their effect because the alcohol goes more swiftly to the brain via the stomach wall. Experienced party hostesses know that if guests are offered bubbly champagne on arrival, the room will soon be buzzing with conviviality.

It might be observed that, unlike the tobacco industry, currently much beleaguered in the west, its product being banned in many public places (but which remains unperturbed as it targets enormous oriental markets) the alcohol industry on the whole does not seek to create addicts but, on the contrary, preaches moderation, and steady, beneficial, responsible consumption. Nevertheless there are irresponsible elements at large, and certain companies specifically target the young and stupid in the marketing of their invariably supersweet alcoholic beverages.

Cocktails

You may ask yourself whether some of the more obscure brands of liquor are used much. The truth is, they're not. When did you last enjoy a Chartreuse (yellow or green)? So what are they for?

The answer is simple. There is an occasional demand for most of them. The first two drinks served from any bottle on a bar usually pay for the whole bottle! All subsequent pourings are profit. While awaiting its next customer, and its debut as a profit item, that dusty bottle of Old Czechoslovakian Boar's Brandy will take up little space, be decorative if dusted from time to time (or not, according to the preferred ambiance), and give barflies with uneventful lives something exciting to discuss. But obscure products are sometimes foisted on gullible owners by unscrupulous salespeople.

Also, from time to time a liquor company will mount a huge advertising drive featuring some kind of cocktail: Horse's Neck, Long Island Iced Tea, Pink Squirrel, Fuzzy Navel, and so on. If demand is sufficient, you might as well buy the ingredients and serve it.

Most of the cocktails in the *Bartender's Guide* belong to a dim and distant past. The chances of being asked for a French 75, a Sazerac, or a Bronx cocktail are slim. Some cocktails, such as Banzai or a Long Island Iced Tea, are aimed at the young and are dangerous because their sweet taste conceals a large amount of alcohol. Sometimes, when a bartender finds an excuse not to make these kinds of drinks for a bunch of giggling young adults, she's not being old and boring. She's avoiding the problem of vomit all over the bar and the restrooms, the need to talk some taxi driver into taking the kids home, and, most important of all, the responsibility for putting a poorly controlled high-speed projectile—a car—into orbit.

Opinions differ as to how cocktails came into existence. Some say it was to disguise the appalling taste of moonshine liquor during Prohibition, and there may be something to that. But the basic reason is to disguise the fairly horrible taste of alcohol by adding something fruity, bubbly, sweet, or all three. Alcohol is very much an acquired taste. Ask a child to taste whisky, and you'll get groans and splutters—a reaction far removed from the adult's glow of satisfaction as the first martini slips into place (i.e., into the bloodstream).

But there's also an element of theater. There used to be what were derisively called Hollywood bartenders, who would make a tremendous show of juggling with the cocktail mixer, often throwing it from hand to hand or over and over in the air. And bar customers love the sound of their own voices as they specify a brand for their martinis, give silly instructions like "shaken, not stirred," "in and out" (put a drop of vermouth in the glass, then throw it out), "in a chilled glass," "with olives" (plural), or "Face east, hold up the glass and whisper Vermouth."

It's all a bit pathetic, but the restaurant industry invented this claptrap with one purpose in mind: to increase sales. And it works. Movie buffs will recognize Tom Cruise's acrobatics with bottles in the movie *Cocktail*.

Mercifully, the current repertoire of cocktails is comparatively small. Drinking habits seem to be centralizing throughout the Western world, and hard drinking is getting a very bad press in the age of jogging and bottled water. In some circles, the consumption of alcohol has been more or less eschewed completely. An English actor lunching in Hollywood with new friends set off for the restroom, saying as he departed, "If you see the waiter, would you please order me a glass of white wine?" He'd already had one, so one of the group turned to another with a frown and said, "Does he have an alcohol problem?" A bank vice-president who enjoys a scotch-and-soda equally enjoys watching people's jaws drop when she orders one.

Liquor salespeople will do their best to load you up with every bottle they can sell. "Sale or return!" they'll say with those warm smiles that make you shiver. "Tell you what; just put a bottle of this new product on the bar and see how it goes, huh?" When a public holiday or strike is imminent, they'll exhort you to back yourself up with enough supplies to survive a siege. They are to be pitied, but they must be resisted.

RESTRICTING INVENTORY

The busier you are, the more space you need and the less time you have to talk to salespeople and do book work. Of course, at the expensive end of the market, where prices are irrelevant and the customers compete to see how much they can spend, a huge wine cellar with necessary staff may be appropriate.

There are hundreds of beers on the market, with newcomers all the time. One popular, inexpensive restaurant on New York's Lexington Avenue carries two beers only, Heineken and Budweiser. This not only reduces storage problems but narrows the area for discussion in a busy joint. Other luxury restaurants only offer Lowenbrau, in spite of enormous advertising pressure from nonalcoholic and lite beers.

The frenzy to find a wine from a huge list, which happened to run out weeks ago but was not replaced by any of the assistant managers, can generate a lot of stress. Other tasks are held up while the search goes on and the frowns and curses mount. It is not unknown for frustrated servers to start screaming like wounded animals at the tops of their voices at the thought of having to tell a customer they don't have the wine ordered, thus, endangering the tip.

Computers are a godsend for keeping inventory records—but they must be carefully kept up to date. As many people as possible should be familiar with the program. Unfortunately, some obsessive owners deliberately obstruct too much familiarity with the computer by their employees, for fear that they may use it to their own dishonest advantage.

The daily liquor list—the list of bottles that need to be replaced at the bar before commencement of business to bring it up to par—consists largely of white wine, vodka, rum, gin, and scotch in swiftly descending order of magnitude. Eight bottles or jars of white wine, four bottles of vodka, and only one of everything else ought to do it. *Par* is simply the regular inventory for the bar (see more under the Liquor Control section).

No matter how large the wine list, the same old favorites will sell day after day, while the obscure or more expensive ones are often ignored. Choosing the second least expensive wine on the list has become a standard joke. Inevitably, a backlog of some wines will accumulate, and eventually they can be used for pouring as house wine, or offered as "Specials." Sometimes, a wine that simply won't move for $10 will fly from the racks at $18, and there's enormous fun to be had with this kind of price juggling.

Storage space is always at a premium in restaurants. Beer and white wine take up precious refrigerated space. Bottles that don't have to be refrigerated must be stored securely in a room that locks. Two things that have an uncanny attraction for light fingers are cash and liquor.

Beer on Tap

If the apparatus for keg or tap beer is in place, it may be wise to continue its use. The profit on keg beers is huge. Some think the sight of pump handles on a bar is a little down-market or unchic, however. Again, it's the boss's decision.

It really isn't that much bother. Once in a while you'll have to pay to have the pipes cleaned out. It's many years since, in a freak accident, a metal spigot blew from the keg and killed a poor bartender stone dead. The apparatus is now much simpler, but the keg must be connected to the pipes properly. All that hissing can be a bit unnerving, but if you follow the instructions, which should be prominently posted in your beer cellar, there's no problem. Make sure your supplier shows you exactly how to connect it, and pass the information on to as many others as you can.

Make sure you understand exactly what delivery entails. The keg should be delivered inside the building right down to the place where it's connected. If it isn't, you're in trouble, because those kegs are dangerously heavy. Just to cover yourself against occasional hitches, you should be assured, also, that any difficulties in tapping or connection will be attended to by the beer suppliers. In the majority of cases, the delivery person will take care of everything without a murmur, have a drink on the house (possibly one of many in the course of a day), and depart in peace. But sometimes they're neglectful. Don't get the kegs mixed up. Trying to tap a keg with a line designed for a different attachment can be messy, particularly if you achieve a halfway fit, which will mean endless leaking and hissing.

Sodas and Mixers

Many restaurants now use a *soda gun* instead of storing cases of bottled sodas. The line comes up from tanks in the cellar, through a little hole in the floor, and into a plastic nozzle that emerges at the bar. On a larger bar there'll be a nozzle at each bar station, including the service area where the servers will usually add the required mix to the liquor provided by the bartender. The syrup combines with carbonated water and is piped upstairs to the bar. On the nozzle are little buttons marked S for soda, T for Tab or tonic, Q for quinine (tonic water), G for ginger, W for water, and L (lemon) for Seven-up—or some variation on this essential and highly profitable theme. You press the button and out squirts the required soda. This is a good profit item, though the quality is possibly not as high as that of bottled sodas. The sweet drinks are too sweet, and they are often insufficiently effervescent (i.e., not bubbly enough). The tanks in the cellar are likely to run out at a busy time, Murphy's Law being a fixture of restaurant life. All the more reason, then, to make sure that just about anyone can connect the lines to a fresh keg or a new container of soda in a couple of minutes without fuss.

If you have a regular crowd of sophisticated drinkers, it's a good idea to have a supply of bottled sodas as well as the soda gun. Serious drinkers sometimes have to resort to what sounds like cantankerous pomposity to get the drink of their dreams. Ordering a scotch-and-soda will result in an ounce of inferior scotch going into a glass chock full of ice, with a dribble of not-very-fizzy soda from the gun. Therefore, you'll sometimes hear drinkers asking for "A double shot of Grouse, straight up, neat, no ice; ice on the side, and a bottle of chilled Perrier." This ensures a decent drink, though at a hefty price.

LIQUOR CONTROL

Liquor control is easy. You keep a record of everything delivered, possibly by entering it into your computer. You decide your bar and wine rack par, in other words, the amounts and kinds of bottles you want instantly available at the bar. For instance, you'll probably have two bottles of vodka in the well or *ready rack,* which is suspended for easy grabbing by the bartender at about knee level, with six backups in the cupboard. Your par for vodka, then, is eight bottles.

As the day progresses, emptied bottles are not thrown away, but put in a container such as an old beer crate. Every day, either at close of business or before the beginning of business, the bartender or manager counts and lists all the empty bottles, which have been neatly arrayed on the bar for easy counting. This is the liquor list. A full bottle is then issued against every empty. Sometimes the bartender gets the liquor room keys and does this herself. If the owner is paranoid about theft, a not uncommon state, as we shall see, a manager issues the booze.

Since liquor is, or should be, rung on its own special key on the cash register, you can easily compare the money you took in for liquor with the amount you issued to the bar. This enables you to work out your percentage profit, or PC. Usually this will soon strike a level from which it will not deviate much in the course of a year. Although the level of business may vary, from New Year's Eve at one extreme to New Year's Day at the other, the percentage profit should be fairly constant. When there is a sudden large difference from the norm, something is probably wrong. This could be the result of overgenerous pouring, stealing, too many drinks being given on the house to encourage generous tipping, consumption by alcoholic employees, or an unhappy combination of all of the above.

However, neat though this sounds, it sometimes breaks down. The liquor list will call for the issue of a bottle of Old Dickens Gin, but the delivery has been delayed, and there isn't any in the cellar. A solemn note is made, but it gets lost. Such OD as remains on the bar is used up, then, six weeks down the line, the delivery is made. So the bartender asks for six bottles, though he has no empties to show. Thus, that week, an unusual amount of OD gin has been issued for no noticeable return in the cash register. Yes, it balances out over the months, but it looks a bit funny if you take a weekly reading. Multiply this by 100 brands and you'll see that it makes sense to keep a close eye on inventory.

Sometimes a bartender will neglect to *marry up* bottles so that the next-day bartender starts with three bottles, each of which contains a tablespoon of vodka. When that bartender counts her empties, she'll have three more than usual. There are also bottles that get broken and stolen, and bottles of wine that have to be poured down the sink for one reason or another. There's a trickle of alcohol to the kitchen, too, for cooking and refreshment.

Large establishments employ a wine steward or even a food and beverage manager to take care of inventory. But what happens at the 50- to 200-seat restaurant under discussion, in practice, is that the owner develops an instinctive idea of just what's going on, what's being issued, and how much cash is coming in. Of course, even if the inventory goes haywire, the amount of cash paid out for liquor is recorded so that if an owner wants to know the story of every nickel and dime, and has the time and patience to work it out, it can be done.

Initially, while business is building, one hopes to see an ever-increasing pile of *dupes* (kitchen orders) and truckloads of empties. But at some point, most restaurants rise to a level of business from which they don't vary much. This can be a blessing, because it's only by constant comparison of income figures that the restaurateur can tell whether the business is on course. A steady increase calls for little action, beyond hiring more help, until it reaches a point where expansion can be considered. But a downward trend on the sales graph, which persists even after considerations of weather, taxes, stock market disasters, holidays, and new competition have been made, calls for action.

Types of Liquors

Owners don't have to be experienced bartenders, but it certainly won't hurt. It will help them to supervise the bar better and reduce dependency on the expert knowledge of the bartender. At the very least, they should know what drinks are all about. If they knew how to shake cocktails, once in a while they can take off their coat and step behind the bar at rush hour. Then both customers and help will join in an admiring chorus of, "What a boss! Doesn't mind lending a hand when it's busy!" This is the stuff of which Rick's dreams are made.

Grain Spirits. Whisky, gin, and vodka are grain spirits. Their different characters stem from the type of grain used and various additives, such as coloring for all whiskies and juniper berries (among other fruits and herbs) for gin. In the case of scotch, aging plays a part. At the distillery where the grain spirit is produced, some of it is bottled as vodka, while the rest is flavored and becomes gin. Of all spirits, vodka is quite the purest, closely followed by gin, and this undoubtedly accounts, in part, for its immense popularity. It's a "clean" drink, so they say, and less likely to give you a headache because of its lack of *congeners* (the technical name under which ingredients other than alcohol spirits are grouped). Some believe it has less of a telltale smell than other drinks, another social plus. Vodka is sometimes made from distilled potato juice, and there is a mounting interest in flavored vodkas from Russia and Eastern Europe.

Wine Derivatives and Liqueurs. Campari, Vermouth, Cinzano, Dubonnet, and several other brands are flavored wines. Most liqueurs are simply flavored brandies, in spite of the arcane nonsense about secret recipes known only to the abbot himself, to be divulged to his successor with his dying breath. Inevitably, cheaper versions of the most expensive liqueurs have been devised, notably orange flavor. Grand Marnier and Cointreau are tops, but Curacao, Triple Sec, and several others will do for cocktails.

Brandy. Brandy, cognac, Armagnac, Marc—all generally referred to as brandy—are made from the distilled juice of grapes, not grain. When stored in wood (for up to 40 years, after which it tastes too "woody") cognac matures, acquiring a deeper and more complex taste. Once bottled, cognac doesn't change. Caramel is added to deepen the color and keep it constant, as it is in whiskey. An "old" and expensive brandy may actually contain a very small amount of really old brandy in a generally much younger blend. Calvados is the distillation of apple juice, sometimes called applejack or apple brandy. It can be made legally at home in France, and is very strong.

Fortified Wines. Port, Sherry, Madeira, and Marsala are *fortified* wines. They've had brandy added to them. Originally, this was done to maintain stability during transit, but now it's just part of the style. Spanish Manzanilla sherry is probably the driest (least sweet) drink in the spectrum. It's actually a bit too dry for American tastes. Sherry sales have slumped in recent years, even in England, which used to take 70 percent of the product. Recently, it was admitted that the whole range of sherries had been considerably sweetened in the hope of improving sales.

Though delightful and generally of high quality, fortified wines have been crowded out by the heavy advertising of other products and changing drinking habits. Very few offices offer visitors a glass of sherry or Madeira and a slice of seedcake at eleven in the morning these days, and port after dinner puts a considerable strain on a liver that has to accompany its owner to work the next morning.

Wine

As with restaurants themselves, an elaborate theater and folklore have been built around the subject of wine. Up to 10 years ago, wine consumption in the United States was increasing dramatically. It is now declining, for a host of reasons, of which general obsession with health is probably the most important factor.

Wine needs to be stored at a cool, consistent temperature. Ideally, the bottles should be on their side so that wine and cork are in contact. Lots of wines are sometimes available at discount prices, but lack of storage space can be a problem.

Wine production in the United States is at an all-time high, principally in California and New York. Domestic wines are often of good quality, a fact reflected in their surprisingly high cost. After an outbreak of a vine disease called phylloxera damaged the vines of Europe, they were replenished with vines brought in from California, in a classic example of the New World being brought in to redress the balance of the Old.

There are literally thousands of names of wines. But they're all made from the juice of grapes that have been allowed to ferment, not infrequently with a little scientific encouragement. To produce white wine, the grape skins are removed from the vat immediately; for rosé, they're removed at a certain stage of fermentation; and for red, they stay to the end.

Champagne is white wine that has been made to ferment a second time, producing fizzy bubbles. Tradition has it that the monk Dom Perignon created champagne accidentally. It's traditionally served at celebratory events. It should be chilled, but most people agree that it tastes better when it's been in the glass a while and not quite so cold. When opening it, great care should be exercised. If some ignorant handler has agitated the fizzy wine the cork may be discharged like a bullet. Eye injuries from champagne corks average 400 a year in the United States. (This is one of those uncannily consistent statistics, such as 400 people dying from snakebite every year in India, and 40 people being struck by lightning every year in South Africa.) A napkin should be wrapped around the cork as it is gently pried from the bottle with gentle circular motions. In some circles the loud pop is considered vulgar, in others festive. If the wine starts foaming, this can be controlled by simply putting the neck of the bottle into a glass.

Most wine improves with age, either in bottle or cask, but only up to a point, and some wines are best drunk young. Red wine is usually drunk at room temperature, which improves its flavor. But even the French often drink red wine chilled, especially the young Beaujolais. White wine is best drunk chilled, as is rosé. Drinking some of the white wines warm will sometimes expose unattractive tastes, and there is no doubt that chilling can cover a multitude of sins.

An endless number of books are written on the subject, and it is possible to study wine at some colleges in New York and California. The University of Bristol in England awards a degree called Master of Wine. In this book there is only space for some basic information.

The science of wine, or *oenology,* is undoubtedly a fascinating one. It attracts a fair number of know-it-alls, bores, and pundits who are ever anxious to impart their greater understanding at great length, even to people who aren't desperately interested in the subject.

In Burgundy in the fall, mortars are fired to break up rain clouds as the selected grapes are left on the vine until the last minute in order to increase their fruit sugar content, until they achieve something called *pourriture noble,* or noble rottenness. In Germany, the best and latest grapes are called *Trockenbeerenauslese.* Sherry gets its unique flavor from a yeast called *saccharomyces elipsoideus beticus,* and the *solera* system, whereby young sherry is continuously added to old so that the combination assumes the characteristics of the older wine, is a fascinating showpiece of the vineyards at Jerez, Spain—along with the drunken mice who love to get their snouts into the sherry!

If you are interested, there is a whole world to explore. Some vineyards are open to the public on occasion, and many magazines and radio stations have their own wine correspondents. The best way to get to know wine is to drink it and reach your own conclusions.

The broad classifications of wine are red, white, rosé, and fortified. Most restaurants feature a selection of French wines such as Burgundy reds (Chateauneuf du Pape, Pommard, etc.), Burgundy whites (Chablis, Puligny Montrachet, etc.), Bordeaux reds or clarets (Mouton Cadet, Chateau Lafite—very expensive), and Bordeaux whites, of which some, like Graves, are dryish and others, like Sauternes, very sweet. Chateau Yquem is the most heralded and the most expensive of the Sauternes. The design of the bottles used for Burgundy and Bordeaux wines is slightly different, which can be helpful.

Then there are the Italian wines—reds such as Chianti and Valpolicella and whites such as Soave Bolla and Pinot Grigio.

Most German wine is white, much of it sweet and loaded with chemicals. Some, such as Bernkasteler Doktor, is sublime and therefore expensive. German wines fall into two groups, those from the River Rhine valley, and those from the valley of the River Moselle. Both come in traditionally shaped tall, tapered bottles. They can easily be distinguished, however, because Rhine wine comes in brown bottles, while Moselle bottles come in green. Remember that the word *green,* has two e's, like the word *Moselle.*

Spanish wines are common, as are wines from Yugoslavia, Hungary, Morocco, Argentina, and Chile. A very impressive quality has been reached by the Australian wine industry. Younger countries' wine industries are blessed with the wisdom of the old.

However, American wines, especially the California whites, win prizes all the time, and the French certainly don't disdain them. Indeed, several French firms, notably Moet Chandon, have bought interests in the California wine industry, to everyone's benefit. An oft-heard national complaint is, "Why are our domestic wines so darned expensive?"

Wine Mystique. The enormous folklore of wine was created by the English in the eighteenth century, as part of that robustness that accompanied the burgeoning wealth of the newly industrialized society. Some of it corresponds to those absurd French phrases used by the Victorians, which no Frenchman ever heard, such as *nostalgie de la boue,* meaning a longing for mud or the low life. However, if the "milords" liked to play, the French were far too good-humored to stop them or interfere with trade.

One of James Thurber's cartoons for *The New Yorker* shows a man pouring wine and remarking: "It's just a charming little domestic Burgundy with little or no breeding, but I think you'll be amused by its presumption!" The vocabulary has increased since then, to include such descriptions as flowery, foxy, fruity, and so on. Wine buffs call a wine's aftertaste its *finish,* and often describe a wine as having a blackberry or black currant finish. This isn't surprising, since black currant wine, called Cassis, is commonly added to red wine to cheer it up. It's also added to white wine to make a cocktail called a Kir, after a Burgundy mayor who devised the mixture to make some of the local wine more palatable.

Such is the enormous proliferation of wines that it would be naive not to suspect a tiny element of flimflam here and there in the vast industry. Although wine names are strictly controlled in Europe and elsewhere (*appellation controlée*), those vast tankers full of Spanish and Moroccan undistinguished wine that roll through the French countryside at night are all going somewhere.

Chemicals. The wine industry will fight to the last round to prevent legislation requiring that ingredients be listed on labels. For obvious reasons, they don't want to spoil the image of healthy naturalness and laughing peasants joyfully treading the grapes.

An increasing number of bottles can now be seen bearing the words "Contains Sulfites." This is only half the story. The average bottle of wine contains more than 1,000 organic compounds, some in miniscule amounts. The main ingredients are alcohol (about 12 percent, but some are 15 percent), water (85 percent), and sulfites (3 percent), as well as very small amounts of urethanes (a carcinogen) and histamines.

Glycol and methanol are sometimes used, with occasional deadly effect, by unscrupulous manufacturers. Because the resulting mix tastes so awful and is so cheap, only the poor are at risk from these concoctions. American soldiers are said to make cocktails from aftershave and antifreeze, which contains glycol (its sweet taste can confirm suspected radiator leaks), but it's hard to understand why they should.

Most wine is routinely filtered through sulfur to stop it from rotting. Red wine is brightened with potassium and white wine with cyanide.

If you consider what happens to grapes when they're left out of the refrigerator, it's easy to understand that wine is fundamentally unstable, and it wouldn't be very good business not to use the wonders of science to help it along. Apart from anything else, it wouldn't travel.

The purpose of these revelations is not to deflate the mystique of wine but to get the subject into perspective. Wine manufacturers may be shooting themselves in the foot by encouraging snobbery and superiority. Many potential consumers are intimidated by the whole business, as is shown by the acute embarrassment felt by some people in a restaurant when they're given a great leather-bound wine list and invited to choose.

If wine is ever to be made a mass-market item, it will have to be reduced to the folksy level of beer. For the moment, it remains an almost exclusively bourgeois product, which, fortunately, is the main area of appeal of most restaurants.

Most restaurateurs try to keep a small list of wines that are simply described (e.g., Sanfrandino Puligny Montrachet—a light, dry white wine with a hint of fruit, ideal with fish, chicken, and veal or for casual drinking).

In general, restaurateurs will do well to *demystify* all aspects of wine and food, except at the $150-a-head end of the market, where baloney seems to be best appreciated. Most Americans out to dine want to have fun, and while they may have a healthy interest in the new and unusual, they don't want to be lectured.

Once the average wine-loving customer has gotten over the shock of the price, the delights of Bernkasteler Doktor '78 or Chateau Lafite '73 will be so apparent as to defy verbal description. To a wine lover, the old story of the man who kept a vintage bottle of Tokay specifically to be administered at his deathbed isn't a bit ridiculous!

Selling Wine. It must be remembered that the wine list is a sales *tool,* as well as an inventory of wines. Therefore, it must be clear and simple. It should name its wines, describe them briefly, and perhaps mention which foods they will complement best. It's a good idea to have some very reasonably priced selections for customers on a budget, and for the prices to be sensibly spaced. Offered the choice between a $40 bottle of wine and a $10 bottle, a majority of customers—yes, even in the most chic and expensive restaurants—are going to select the cheaper alternative.

If there are *no* reasonably priced wines, the customers are likely to settle for beer, or nothing, and become rather nervous about what sort of a final bill they are going to receive. But they might have happily paid $20–you'll never know.

A general awareness on the part of the staff will help here, too.

"I'm having steak and my wife's having scrod. Which wine should we have?"

"We have a light claret, number 14, which should be ideal for you both."

"Red wine with fish?"

"Maybe not with a delicate fish like sole, but a lot of people enjoy red wine with a fish like scrod, especially with a robust sauce."

Sold.

But if not sold, why not a half-bottle of red and a half of white, or wine by the glass?

This counsel is admittedly a bit glib, because outside "serious," expensive restaurants, the help may be intimidated by having to immerse themselves in wine facts, especially if they are not restaurant professionals, which, whether you like it or not, will often be the case. But they can be coaxed to learn about wine and even, with luck, may become interested in the subject and derive pleasure from it for themselves, as well as bump up your sales.

Many restaurants have a bottle of wine sitting on the table as part of the standard setup. This is often the bargain special of the week. Sometimes they have two wines, a red and a white. Many customers are happy to have their minds made up for them. This isn't necessarily because they are weak-minded or out of their depth. They may have romance or business on their minds and not wish heavy digressions on the routine and simple question of what to eat and drink.

It's a good idea and good business to prompt diners in a friendly and knowledgeable way. Customers who trust the establishments in which they regularly wine and dine are the easiest of all and often the most fun.

Here is a guide to what sort of wine goes with what sort of food:

Appetizers	Champagne, dry white wine, sherry
Beef	Hearty red
Lamb	Hearty red
Veal	Dry or medium white, rosé
Chicken	Dry or medium white, rosé
Fish / seafood	Dry or medium white, rosé
Dessert	Sweet wine, port, Madeira

The ground rule is simply red wine with red meat and white wine with white meat, fish, or seafood. National wines often complement national cuisine, so that a good choice with Spaghetti Bolognese, for instance, would be a red Chianti or Bardolino. Greek wine such as retsina really only comes into its own alongside Greek food.

Serious wine will be wasted alongside highly spiced food. With Indian curry, for instance, beer is by far the best accompaniment.

These rules are based on long experience of what goes best, but there's plenty of room for personal preference, scrod with red wine being a good example. It's fun experimenting. The customer who regularly sits at the bar and orders a plate of clams on the half shell and a glass of Cointreau may cause a raised eyebrow or two, but it's a free country.

Some restaurants keep track of which server sells the most wine and pay a small bonus, say, a dollar a bottle. This is harmless enough, and the regular winners will have something to brag about.

Occasionally, diners will wish to bring their own wine. If they do so, they can legally be charged *corkage*—an amount of money to cover the profit the restaurateur is losing. This need not be too punitive. In the case of a regular customer, it could be waived. It doesn't happen often enough to pose a threat or a problem.

Some very successful restaurants are BYOs (bring your own), where you bring your own wine or beer or perhaps buy it from the liquor store across the street. Such restaurants don't have an alcohol or wine license, usually through some tedious technicality of the law having to do with location or the building. In this case, no corkage may be charged.

THE EFFECTS OF ALCOHOL

Many restaurants feature a bar, and it is important for owners, who may have no experience of, or liking for, alcohol to understand what it is that they're selling. What is alcohol, and what does it actually do?

All alcoholic beverages share two common ingredients. The first is water, and the second is ethyl alcohol, sometimes called ethanol. Ethyl alcohol occurs in unfermented orange and tomato juice and, as a solvent, finds a home in lacquers, varnishes, stains, and perfumes.

The coloring in most drinks is just vegetable dye. The flavor is achieved by other additives.

There are other sorts of alcohol such as ethylene glycol, used in antifreeze, and isopropanol, which is rubbing alcohol. Methyl alcohol occasionally gets put by mistake into a student party punch. The kids see the word *alcohol* and don't understand that it isn't booze. This mistake often results in blinding, because the chemical causes the optic nerve to swell, or death.

The strength of alcohol is expressed as degrees of *proof,* for example, 86 proof, and this can be confusing. In the United States, proof is twice the alcohol content in the bottle by volume. Thus, a bottle of spirits marked 86 proof indicates 43 percent of alcohol by volume—the rest is water, coloring, flavoring, and chemicals. There are rums at 120 proof, bourbons such as Wild Turkey at 101 proof, and vodkas at 100 proof. The French simply give the percentage volume of alcohol in a system known as the *Gay Lussac* scale. In Britain yet another system is used. If you look at a label on a gin bottled in England, it may very well say 86 proof, but would only be labeled 75.25 had it been bottled under the U.S. system. Some actually find this lesser strength adds to the delights of certain British spirits.

American spirits are now often labeled thus: "Alcohol 40 percent by volume, 80 proof."

All the restaurateur needs to know is that the higher the proof indicated on the bottle, the stronger the liquor.

It is sad that any discussion of alcohol must almost immediately concern itself with the abuse thereof. But considering the dangers, it is probably just as well. When used in moderation, alcohol may well be good for the health, and by depressing social inhibitions it makes for conviviality.

A whole bottle, that is, a fifth, of regular-strength whisky, vodka, or other spirit, drunk as one dose, will kill the average healthy young man within 24 hours. The reason two-bottle-a-day alcoholics survive is that they drink small amounts throughout the day, and are saved by the regular excretion of alcohol.

The danger line is narrow. When the blood alcohol content (BAC) is between 0.4 percent and 0.6 percent, respiratory failure can occur, followed by death from asphyxiation. To put this in perspective, in most countries where motorists are breathalized to check their alcohol intake, 0.05 percent BAC is the upper limit tolerated by law. In some countries, the faintest trace of alcohol above the tiny amount naturally present in the blood means prosecution.

What gives each brand of liquor its essential character is the *congeners* that accompany the basic mix of alcohol and water. These might be as mystical as the yeasty taste of the enzyme *saccharomyces ellipsoideus beticus,* which gives sherry its unique tang, or as simple as peppermint or fruit syrup, or the juniper berries and fruit flavorings that are added to vodka to turn it into gin.

Although generally reckoned to be a "clean" drink, gin has 13 other components besides water and alcohol. Vodka has the least number of congeners of any drink available. Some believe they are sparing their systems the worst ravages of alcohol by drinking only wine and beer. But wine can contain up to 1,000 separate chemicals, and many a heavy tippler's liver would welcome a dose of uncomplicated vodka as a pleasant change from nonvintage "Chateau de Plonk."

Different drinks have various reputations in alcohol folklore. Gin is supposed to be rather depressing, but all alcohol is. Alcohol first depresses mental inhibitions, which is relaxing and helps conversation, but it then starts depressing everything else, which is when overindulgence starts to rear its ugly head. Instant character changes can occur. The shy person becomes forward, the quiet person looks for a fight, and so on.

Scotch is thought by many to have a very comforting effect, and champagne has the reputation of swiftly inducing good cheer. This is simply because the champagne bubbles whisk the alcohol through the stomach wall and into the bloodstream efficiently so that the effects are felt in the brain almost immediately. Any liquor drunk with carbonated water (scotch and soda, gin or vodka and tonic) will have the same effect. Runners who do their brisk three miles of an evening, take a shower, then relax with a gin and tonic, or scotch and soda, will achieve instant inebriation, so should avoid such consumption.

Alcohol doesn't linger long in the stomach, but goes quickly to the small intestine, from which it continues to enter the bloodstream. The presence of food at this point in the works can inhibit this transference and help delay inebriation—the polite word for the effects of alcohol, or drunkenness. Pills containing Phosphatidylserine are said to keep one sober, and prevent hangovers.

Everyone knows that one shouldn't drink on an empty stomach because this will accelerate the effects of alcohol. Some drink milk before drinking or delay their drinking until after a meal. Still others have been known to drink a spoonful of olive oil before imbibing.

Eventually, most alcohol is metabolized (processed out, deconstructed, or broken down) in the liver, where busy enzymes convert it into acetaldehyde, then acetate, carbon dioxide, and water. The entire blood supply of the human body circulates through the liver every four minutes or so.

Some alcohol is excreted through urine, sweat and, notoriously, breath. The liver processes alcohol rather slowly—three hours for an ounce of pure alcohol, which means about an hour for a martini or a glass of wine.

Volume is really the bottom line of drinking. Once the broad definition of *moderation* is exceeded, chaos breaks loose, as anyone who has ever had a hangover can testify.

The human liver will take enormous punishment. It's the only organ that regenerates. If you drank a bottle of whiskey every day for 20 years, your chances of getting cirrhosis of the liver would only be 50 percent. This surprising statistic grimly underlines just how much you have to drink to damage your liver. Oddly enough, while almost all those who develop cirrhosis are alcoholics, two-thirds of alcoholics never develop this disease.

However, this is entirely an academic consideration, because long before the liver and health generally are threatened, the effects of alcohol on the nervous system render the drinker incapable of driving, flying, sailing, riding a bike, thinking rationally, functioning sexually (in the case of the men), or operating machinery. A few minutes after a pregnant woman takes a drink, her fetus is drinking it, too. It's believed that a quite small intake of alcohol can cause fetal alcohol syndrome, so many expectant mothers these days go on the wagon for the duration of their pregnancy.

The heart can be dangerously enlarged by excessive alcohol intake. Alcohol also affects the brain function that governs urine retention. Hence, the heavy traffic in the restrooms.

Many drinkers worry about their drinking. Are they indulging in a harmful way? The only definitive way to assess alcohol damage is to have a liver biopsy, in which a needle is inserted in the lower half of the rib cage and a sliver of the organ is removed for examination. An easier but slightly less accurate method is to have a straightforward blood test called a liver function test. If the gamma GT cell count is elevated, then this is suggestive of liver damage. Alcohol also increases the size of the red blood cells, and this can be detected by the same test.

The world's heaviest drinkers are the French. By cutting their alcohol intake by a third, they have reduced their alcoholism deaths by 60 percent. At the same time, it appears that the French are less prone to heart attacks than other nationalities, and the reason for this may be red wine, of which much is consumed.

While one cannot ignore the salad-and-olive-oil-intensive French diet, plus the fact that the French are not an overweight people, much credence is given to the possibility that moderate alcohol—especially wine—intake can be good for you. Some American wine producers are lobbying for permission to post a reference to this on their labels—perhaps to balance those depressing warnings about sulfites and the dangers of drinking during pregnancy, which are now mandatory.

It appears that something in alcohol generally—not just in red wine, though that is the established favorite in this area—increases the level of fats other than cholesterol, called HDLs, in the blood. HDLs may protect the heart.

Modern people do not consume as much potassium as their ancestors did. This trace element is necessary for the health of the heart and nerves, and a high level of it is found in wine, where it is used as a brightening agent. Iron, calcium, and vitamins are also present. Some less welcome ingredients are histidine, histamines, and tyramine, which are suspected by some of causing the headaches that ruin the pleasure of even small wine consumption for many. Burgundy wines from the Pinot Noir grape are the least offensive in this context. Urethanes, which are carcinogenic, are found in negligible quantities, and most wine is routinely filtered through sulfur to stop it rotting. Wine is grape juice, so why should it be any less prone to rotting than the hapless tomato left thoughtlessly on top of the refrigerator, after all?

White wine gets a lot of its quintessential sparkle from potassium ferrocyanide. This shocking revelation should be taken with a pinch of salt—after all, a commonly dispensed modern anti-coagulant medicine started life as rat poison.

We have a good idea of how "moderate drinking" can be defined. The U.S. government (FDA, HHS) defines "moderate" as two drinks per day for men and one drink per day for women. The discrepancy does not represent some chauvinistic conspiracy, but rather the simple fact that women tend to be smaller.

Restaurateurs must remain alert to the risks of alcohol, cutting off over-imbibers firmly, despite the loss of profit. A drunken scene in a restaurant can empty it very quickly.

HELPFUL HINTS FOR BARTENDERS

Handling Drunks

Bartenders must beware the sweetly smiling person who comes in, sits down in a civilized manner, orders a drink, and then starts shouting the place down. When a customer walks into a restaurant, it's not always easy for an inexperienced bartender to ascertain how many drinks he or she has had on the way. The first martini in your establishment may be the critical fifth of the day that pushes the drinker over the limit into drunkenness.

The drill is quite simple. When you realize the customer is drunk, you hand back the money and pour away the drink. You offer no discussion or conversation. The matter is instantly resolved. Almost invariably, a stony silence and a stonier look will penetrate even the most drink-sodden brain, and the customer will go quietly into the night. Sometimes a little gentle assistance may be necessary. All male staff must be instantly on call to assist in these situations. A circle of glowering employees will usually get the message across, removing the need for any physical contact whatsoever. It's important that managers and owners back up the bartender's authority, even if, later, they may suggest ways in which situations might have been better handled.

Turning Away Unwanted Guests

Unkind though it may seem, there is sometimes a case for giving a customer the cold shoulder. One risks being thought rude, but there it is. Construction guys in filthy work clothes who are thoughtless enough, or ignorant enough, to come in for their Budweisers at the cocktail hour when the smart office crowd is expected any minute should be politely dissuaded. Remember, "A soft answer turneth away wrath," and one must beware the danger of arousing anger in dismissed customers. No good can come of making a rejected customer so angry he wishes he had a shotgun—and, perhaps, knows where to get one.

Some owners may regard this as un-American discrimination, and if their principles in this regard are more important than the business, they are doubtless to be deeply and reverentially admired. But they won't stay in business long. Apart from anything else, no one will work for them.

Situations can be wryly amusing.

A ghastly, scruffy-looking young nerd shambled into a bar at the cocktail hour.

"Say," he whined, eyeing the big TV over the bar. "You guys showing the game tonight?"

"Nah," the bartender, recognizing a loser, frowned frostily, "Bleeping TV broke down and we can't fix it."

The sprightly young manageress passing by heard this. As it happened she didn't much like this particular bartender. "What are you talking about?" she interpolated. "Of course we're showing the game! I'll put the TV on right now." Which she did.

The nerd sat at 1 of the 10 barstools and said, "What's the cheapest drink in the house?"

"A cup of coffee, $1.50."
"D'ja get a re-fill?"
"One."
"An' a glass of water?"
"Sure."
"I'll take a cup of coffee, please."

Hours later, the nerd was still sitting nursing his water and having a whale of a time in the crowded bar. "Holy ****!" he'd cry, every time someone scored, "Did you see that?"

The manageress proved to herself what a really nice person she was. The house lost not less than $200, and the bartender lost at least $40 in tips. True story!

Organizing the Bar

Such is the obsession with drinks being chilled within an inch of their lives that it's often a good idea to keep a selection of beers immersed in ice. Martini glasses can be displayed stuck into a little mountain of crushed ice—a bit fussy, but it warms the cockles of some drinkers' hearts.

Cocktails containing lemon juice will benefit from a dash of Cointreau, Triple Sec, or Curaçao. You can confidently charge a little extra for this.

Everything on the bar must have its designated position—fruit, fruit-cutting knife, salts and peppers, mixing glass, shaker, strainer and bar spoon, and every individual bottle. When a bar gets busy, as one hopes it will, there's no time for, "Oh dear, where on earth is that pesky bar spoon?" or, "Do we have any Chivas Regal?" Obsessive though it may sound, a very good drill for bartenders is to solemnly put their hands on every bottle displayed so that they can go right to it when it's requested. Group bottles together for convenience—scotches, gins, bourbons, cordials, etc.

Dealing with Personal Issues

Bartenders must stand a lot, and this can be a strain. There are certain defensive steps one can take. Sit down whenever you can (i.e., when there are no customers at the bar). When standing, always try to elevate one foot, perhaps on a discreetly positioned beer crate. If there are no bouncy wooden duck boards on the bar floor, you'll need to take all protective precautions. Support socks or stockings may sound nerdy, but they help. Thick-soled shoes with laces are the most comfortable, even if they're not very chic. Rockports offer a great selection. Slip-on shoes and loafers are disastrous. Trainers give excellent support but are a bit hot, and the house may not approve of garish red and yellow footwear. Plain black examples can be found. All this may sound rather uncool, but there's nothing cool about aching backs, hemorrhoids, or varicose veins.

A bartender's hands are very much on display and must always be clean so that it's fine for him or her to squeeze lemon peels or limes into drinks. If, as is common, glasses are washed at the bar, then great care must be taken with the hands. The best method is to allow a few dirty glasses to accumulate, then put on rubber gloves and wash a batch. This might draw a few hoots of derision from the macho element. However, two weeks off work and a course of steroid injections is the price some have paid for damaging their hands by refusing to wear gloves when they regularly washed glasses in fierce hot, soapy water. Apart from anything else, dishpan hands look like hell.

Where glasses are taken to a remote washing machine, it mustn't be assumed that they are ready for service when they return. Some lipsticks are extraordinarily tenacious. "Not my shade!" the customer will wearily reply as he rejects a lipsticked glass.

The price of efficiency is eternal vigilance.

After mixing a cocktail involving cream (Brandy Alexander, Grasshopper—not very common these days), wash the mixing glass and shaker in the kitchen, not at the bar, in order to avoid greasing up the washing-up sinks.

Back problems are very common in the restaurant industry, caused by prolonged standing and lifting heavy weights. The bartender who sets up the bar for the day's business will often be saddled with the job of bringing heavy bottles from a distant cellar or storage point. It's better to make several journeys than to carry heavy cases. The reason for this is that back problems are often caused by cumulative strain. One trip with a heavy case may not hurt, but 10 in a week may very well. The straw that broke the camel's back, and all that.

Where lockers and changing rooms are provided, bartenders, and indeed all staff, should have some back-up clothing, especially a spare shirt. If there are no lockers, there's probably room in the bar drawer or somewhere to store it. Disasters happen, and the effect of an exploding bottle of fermented ketchup has to be seen to be believed.

Individuals have their own quirks for quick refreshment. President Reagan would insist on fresh socks and shoes if he didn't have time to shower and change on busy days. President Johnson liked a change of shirt. Many bartenders like to freshen up for the cocktail hour. This is good, but make sure your hands are free of perfume or cologne when you return to the bar. If you make a drink with perfumed hands, the drink will be unmistakably tainted, especially martinis.

Protecting Against Dangers—of All Sorts

Pick up tips promptly and put them in the tip cup, which should ideally be opaque, and placed so that it's inaccessible to the casual grab-and-run thief.

If you are the victim of armed robbery, hand over the money instantly and without question. Say nothing. If there's a police panic button and you can discreetly press it, do so. But no heroics! After a certain hour, many bars lock their doors and admit only known, regular customers. One of the most famous armed robberies, at Mortimer's in New York, was carried out by a group of smart-looking young men in dinner jackets!

Warn departing customers to be careful. Certain robbers stake out bars, waiting for slightly befuddled customers to leave. Some restaurants employ armed plainclothes security people, usually moonlighting cops—an excellent deterrent, but a considerable expense.

It's not uncommon for regular drinkers who have cars to hand over their keys to a bartender if they feel they may have exceeded the limit. A good bartender will have a taxi service on speed dial.

Bartenders of both sexes will often find themselves propositioned by customers. This may be welcome, of course, but if it is unwelcome, the best defense is a wedding band (for both sexes) and the light reference to the existence of a spouse (e.g., "Gee, I hope my husband/wife doesn't get caught in this rain.") Meeting members of the opposite sex is a well-recognized and prized perk of the job for those who aren't already attached.

A lady once asked the bartender whether a certain sherry was sweet or dry. "I don't know, lady," he drawled, "I don't drink." Whether or not a bartender drinks is nobody's business but his, but he should know about the goods he's selling. Or at least say, "I'm not sure, but let me ask Suzie, she's the wine expert round here."

Serving the Drinks

One of the worst things a bartender can do is to jam mixing glass and shaker while preparing a cocktail, and then proceed to achieve separation by banging them against the edge of the bar. The simple solution is to hold the glass at face level and hit it briskly with the heel of the hand just below the rim of the metal shaker. It works every time.

Always use the scoop when putting ice in a glass. Never use the glass itself as a scoop. If the glass breaks, then all the ice in the bin or sink must be disposed of, and fresh ice brought up—a chore if the restaurant is busy. Ill-trained waiters who are seen doing this should be corrected.

If a glass breaks on the bar itself, after the obvious pieces have been brushed into the dustpan, the whole area should be mopped with a damp dishcloth, which should then be discarded, not recycled. Tiny, scarcely visible bits of glass can stick to idle fingers that may touch the bar. If someone then unwittingly touches his or her face, or worse, an eye, serious damage can be done. Lawyers are always poised for attack.

Many people under 50 or so are impervious to noise. On the contrary, they're unnerved by silence. But one sound nobody likes is the distracting and alarming breaking of glass. While empty liquor and wine bottles must be kept in order to be counted before they're re-cycled, beer bottles are often discarded. Some bartenders have the horrible habit of deliberately dropping them into the garbage can so hard that they break noisily. This is irritating and unprofessional.

A custom that seems to be here to stay is the drinking of beer direct from the bottle. To anyone over 50 this is the height of bad manners and is considered uncouth. Traditionally, when a guest orders a beer, the glass is put in front of him and a token amount of beer is poured, in much the same way as the *sommelier* or wine waiter will pour a little wine for the drinker to taste. Of course, this is still the case in "smart" places. There is a small rationale offered. Some who like their beer ultra-cold will say that pouring it into a glass reduces the chill. Sometimes you'll hear a bartender ask, "Do you need a glass?" and the drinker will wittily reply, "Nah —it's already in a glass." One advantage of this lugubrious custom is that beer can be served quickly, and there's less washing-up.

Some owners and managers have little or no experience of bar customs and traditions, such as drinks on the house in neighborhood restaurants that have become part of the local community, attracting a regular crowd. If they're not aware of the custom of giving big-spending customers a drink on the house, they should be. Some ingénues react with horror when they see a bartender dispensing free liquor. "He's giving the joint away!" they'll cry. Of course, an owner is perfectly entitled to take the view that he's in business and shouldn't be expected to give his merchandise away. He may make the point that if you buy two shirts you don't get one free—but, actually, sometimes you do. Because offering drinks on the house bumps up tips, some bartenders get carried away, and then the boss has every right to step in. Experienced bartenders will know what the traffic will bear, but it's best to have an idea of what the owner's policy is on this.

CHAPTER 7

THE KITCHEN

PROFIT MARGINS

Kitchens can be terrifying to the uninitiated. When fully in action at the height of the lunch or dinner hour, the business can be so intense that it blurs. "If you can't stand the heat, get out of the kitchen" is an old line. But for the restaurateur who is not actually a trained chef, better advice would be to observe and learn, so as not to be intimidated and, most importantly, given the run-around by a power-seeking chef. The kitchen is undoubtedly the hub of most restaurants, despite the common heartfelt cry from amateur restaurateurs: "I don't make any money on the food, only on the bar!" How anyone can say this is mystifying, when a salad sold for $6 often contains only 50 cents worth of material, even at retail prices. But it is a common cliché of the trade and perhaps a symptom of the amateurishness of many of its practitioners.

The wise words of the executive who once replied to a writer's complaint that, although the world price of coffee had gone down, the price of coffee in the supermarket had gone up, may be significant in this context. "If coffee beans suddenly cost nothing," he said, "the price of a jar of instant coffee would remain the same." No matter how cheaply you buy your food supplies, you still won't escape the overhead that must be financed from your income.

True, the kitchen overhead in terms of payroll and materials alone is heavier than overhead expenses of the bar. Also, some food items are much better profit items than others. But the restaurateur must take the overall view. After all, even though food profits may not be in themselves tremendous, if you don't serve food, you don't have a restaurant!

The two biggest bills you'll ever have to pay, after your rent, are the meat and/or fish bill and the liquor bill. Selling cooked food at a profit takes a certain skill. But the steak priced at $20 on the menu has usually cost the restaurateur no more than $4. Many steakhouses are actually owned by butchers, in order to provide a heavily marked-up retail outlet for their goods.

At the more expensive end of the menu, in the area of carefully and expertly prepared special dishes, the profit margin is just as healthy. If you serve Chicken Kiev, for instance (that's the one where, at the prick of a knife, melted butter spurts from a sewn-up chicken breast), there's preparation time involved, and the people who do the work command full salaries—that is, their income isn't subsidized by tips. In other words, there's a labor cost. The profit level should be assessed carefully on a regular basis. An average 2 percent profit is generally considered the minimum. But, remember, November and December are almost invariably busier and more profitable than, say, January.

CHEF POWER

For some reason, the area of food intimidates restaurant owners who are not, themselves, trained chefs. Apart from the general lack of control and confidence this attitude creates, it often leads to a dangerous psychological imbalance in the running of the business: The owner is in awe of the chef. An owner who can't do the chef's job can succumb to a ludicrous dependency. To an extent, this isn't unreasonable. If this important end of the business is well taken care of, no one can be blamed for wanting to keep a key employee happy, even if this means that the employee gets away with murder, as many chefs do.

With one telephone call, any member of staff can usually be replaced within the hour—except the chef. The new waiter, busboy, hostess, maitre d', manager, cloakroom attendant, car valet, porter, or dishwasher may not be the employee of one's dreams, but they'll help to muddle through a shift. Finding and replacing a chef can be a nightmare. "Better the devil you know . . . ," the boss will say with a sigh. "At least the chef's *fast* and can get the orders out promptly." Sadly, speed of production is often a better qualification than quality.

All too often, these factors result in chefs being able to rule the roost. They'll come in drunk, go home drunker, insult the staff with dirty talk far beyond the usual harmless badinage, make enough smoke to cover a divisional river crossing, and generate enough noise to drown out even the loudest pianist or juke box. Few customers are ever likely to return for a repeat experience.

Once in a while, though, most chefs are steady, conservative people, just one will go berserk and actually attack someone. Anyone will do, no particular employee is at risk, unless it's a waiter who insists, on the customer's behalf, on getting what was ordered, or a waitress who's kept silent in the face of his filthy insults. A dreadful murder case in California some years ago involving the chef of a famous restaurant raised a few eyebrows, and had a few people wondering what kind of people lurked behind that swinging kitchen door. (It was a revelation that this prince of the skillets, who was often invited to come out and discuss the recently consumed meal with the customers, had very little money in the bank, despite a high salary, and didn't even have a driver's license.)

Bearing in mind the profusion of deadly weapons in the average kitchen, from meat cleaver to frying pan, the dangers are obvious. The optimum freakout point for most chefs is when a dish is returned to the kitchen, either as a reject or requiring further treatment, or when an order arrives just as the chef is about to start closing up the kitchen. Many owners will insist that late arrivers be served, even though they lack the courage to go into the kitchen and smooth the chef's feelings. Some owners have rigid last-order times, but many can't resist the opportunity to take in a bit more cash. It's what they're there for, after all. When owners are chefs, they'll sometimes volunteer to do the cooking themselves, and, if in the process they build up a clientele who insist on arriving late for that special treatment, well, it serves them right.

Ironically, the unshaven short-order cook with the bleary eye—thank goodness no longer equipped with the drooping cigarette dropping ash into the food—is just as likely to be temperamental as the brilliant young chef whose picture is in society magazines and who studied under the great prince of the kitchen, Coglioni di Medici, and is being paid $100,000 a year plus bonuses.

The question arises, would a nasty chef be easier to deal with if tipped by the waiters and waitresses? The answer is, probably yes. But how many people are they supposed to take care of? They've already got to tip the bartender, the busperson, and possibly the captain. Although it's no longer common, the old hands used to tip the chef quite routinely for getting their orders out promptly and not giving them too much of a hard time. Nowadays, a bottle of beer snitched from the bar as a peace offering is more usual. On Cunard ships at one time, a waiter could not put in an order unless he first tipped the kitchen. Management looked the other way, as it continually must in the union-dominated Merchant Marine.

Although the management skills required of the restaurateur do not exceed those required of the most junior NCO in the army, few restaurateurs seem to possess them. What is worse, they don't seem to learn them. There can be no doubt that the best and most successful restaurants are run either by well-educated people who've learned the relevant skills or by people steeped in the business who just happen to have natural management ability. It's a shame, because there's rarely a requirement for more than routine common sense and diplomacy.

In order to maintain the edge of authority and reduce stressful dependency, restaurateurs, if they are to accumulate any specialist knowledge at all, would do well to address their training time to food, more than any other area of the business. Many owners will freely criticize every aspect of their operations except the sacrosanct domain of the kitchen. In comparison, everything else is easy. Some restaurateurs find dealing with people difficult. But attractive young people who can work as hosts and hostesses are easy to come by in cities, if this is the case. They tend to burn out fast in the least attractive job in a restaurant, but they're as easy to replace as a Napoleonic army after a disastrous battle.

For obvious reasons, it's not in the interests of highly paid chefs to reveal just how easy cookery is, once one becomes aware of how food is supposed to look and taste when it's done right. The trade guards its secrets jealously, but it doesn't take much working out. With a little practice, you'll find you can even open clams.

This is not to put down the art of cookery. However, chefs themselves are notoriously skeptical about their "art" and often cite, as their favorite meal, fried eggs and french fries or a nice juicy hamburger. Some of this is probably a bit tongue in cheek, of course—they might mean farm eggs and french fries double fried in goose fat.

But too many owners are totally intimidated by kitchen problems. If they get into the subject seriously, they'll soon learn the ropes, and they'll get better results in the kitchen, too.

Bakery is a branch of cooking that takes knowledge and practice. Amateur flair and beginner's luck will get you nowhere in this department. You have to practice and get it wrong a few times before you eventually get it right. But in the end, you'll find you can do it.

It is extremely unusual for employees to be allowed to sample the whole menu in restaurants, even though they're solemnly expected to be able to describe dishes and advise customers. People who work in good-quality gourmet restaurants, and are allowed to eat what they want (which would be highly unusual), find everything tastes the same after a while.

This demonstrates the consistency of the chef's work, and is in fact to be encouraged. Regular customers will know what to expect. If you think about it, although all the tastes of home cooking are well known in most families, you really wouldn't want it any different.

Finding a reliable chef who isn't too much of a prima donna can take forever. Many restaurateurs do not embark upon their business project until and unless they have first secured the services of such a person, knowing the pitfalls awaiting them. That's another reason why you should get around, meet people, and make friends in the business. When the chef is a partner—capable, pleasant, and not too neurotic—things often go a lot better. The waiters and waitresses have to be a bit more on their toes, but they often get treated better and are less subject to stress, which makes them a better sales staff.

When hiring a chef, it's important to stress that they are only employed on probation. Some are better at job interviews than they are in the kitchen. Attitude, background, and experience should be assessed. Formal training is always a big plus.

Incidentally, one of the best chefs you can hire is an ex-serviceman. An army cook sergeant will have attended a long and rigorous course, and will be used to feeding 600 soldiers three times a day, often in adversarial conditions. True, services kitchens are well equipped and fully staffed, with extra labor on call (KP duties), but these chefs can usually take everything in stride. Nor should it be feared that such a chef will be deficient in the chic gourmet haute-cuisine department. Inside most army chefs there's an Escoffier struggling to get out! The mundane tastes of the military are often frustrating. One sergeant shook his head wearily as he contemplated his elaborate salad bar, largely ignored, and said, "I sometimes think that if I gave them hamburgers, fried eggs and french fries three times a day, they wouldn't complain." Because of their high civilian employability, this trade is one of the most sought-after in the services.

Sadly, it must be mentioned that famous and expensive restaurants owned by the chef get mixed reports from food-writers. While often (though by no means always) praising the food and decor, they report a cold and frigid atmosphere created by unsmiling absurdly grave staff. The reason for this is almost certainly the coldly obsessive demands of the chef-owners. Recent fly-on-the-wall TV shows filmed in restaurant kitchens reveal character far removed from the genial, smiling, all-things-to-all-men celebrity chef interviewed on the late-night chat shows. In some places, the pictures of dreaded food writers and restaurant reviewers are displayed. Sometimes they may not be served. But more often, they serve the purpose of warning the staff that they're being assessed.

It can be an unhappy business, full of petty hatred and jealousy. This is almost invariably a result of personality deficiencies in the owner or manager. The brutal truth is that some unhappy restaurants do excellent business anyway. But if an owner wants to stay happy and reduce stress, then putting together an efficient crew motivated by more than the ordinary need to do a job isn't a bad idea. Also, there can be no doubt that when staff morale descends below a certain level, the effect on business can be disastrous. Customers will pick up the vibes, and they often won't endure them. Remember, customers can be prima donnas, too, and they certainly don't want to be surrounded by misery when they're out relaxing and enjoying themselves. Personality and powers of leadership are real strengths in creating restaurants that are pleasant to visit and efficient providers of food.

A somewhat over-effusive writer recently said of the Paris family-owned restaurant (or *bouchon*) Le Moissonneur, "To eat here every Saturday for the rest of your life wouldn't just make for a happy marriage—it would make mortality bearable." The chef seemed like a "heroic paragon," his children were "sweet and beautiful," and his wife "all that is best in French womanhood." Few will evoke such praise, but one can try.

One of the most dramatic true stories from the history of food is that of the seventeenth-century steward to the Prince de Condé, Francois Vatel. Though never a full-fledged chef, Vatel had once been apprenticed to a pastry cook. However, he made a name for himself as a general manager of great estates. His employer was the Treasury of France, but he was borrowed by other employers to supervise or put their households in order.

At the Prince de Condé's chateau near Chantilly, where the dessert dish

Pear Condé (pear cooked in red wine and port and served with rice) and Chantilly (sweetened whipped cream) were created, Vatel had his own apartments and servants and was allowed to wear a sword and jewels. Unfortunately, he found the chateau in a state of neglect, and the task of restoring grounds, chateau, and servants to some sort of order was enormous. He did a magnificent job, but although only in his thirties, he began to suffer from the stress. He complained that he couldn't sleep and that his head was spinning. Others thought he seemed ill.

In April of 1671, King Louis XIV came to Chantilly with his vast entourage, and Vatel had to ensure accommodation and catering. Throughout history, one reads of the dubious honor befalling those visited by kings and queens—it was often a ruinous business. Cromwell's father, for instance, was almost ruined by a royal visit, and this may have colored his future politics.

There were too many guests to be accommodated in the chateau, and they had to be housed in the neighborhood. On the first evening of the visit, the roast meat ran out and two tables received none. The elaborate and expensive fireworks display was a dismal failure.

Next day, a small order of fish arrived, and Vatel nearly had a fit when he was told that was all he'd ordered. The thought of another fiasco was intolerable. He went upstairs and stabbed himself to death with his sword.

Too late, one of his staff arrived to remind him that he had, in fact, ordered more fish from another supplier, and that it was safely on its way. As a suicide, he could not be given Christian burial and so was laid to rest in a field, without a monument.

Clearly Vatel was an early victim of front-line burnout, or simple, mind-bending stress through overwork. Perhaps he was not well organized. Perhaps he did not delegate properly, but, then, he may not have had a very good staff. Some said that if such a distinguished man could kill himself for a turbot, he'd established cooking among the noble arts. French chef Paul Bocuse echoed this sentiment when he accepted the Legion d'Honneur wearing his chef's uniform of *toque blanche*, the tall white hat, and apron.

Others, ignoring the fact that Vatel was more an administrator than a cook, said that he clearly didn't have the proper character for a chef, as he didn't know how to make the best of a bad job and rise above difficulties. The French greatly prize and admire what they call *Système D*. The "D" is for the verb *debrouiller*, to muddle through, sort things out, make the best of a bad job, and so on.

Nowadays, anyone approaching breakdown is more likely to be sent on vacation than allowed to continue, and clearly there is sometimes a case for this.

In 1998, Bernard Louiseau was one of France's most celebrated chefs and restaurant owner. His culinary group (he owned several businesses) was listed on the stock exchange, making him the only chef in the world to become a public company. On February 26, 2003, Loiseau, 52, committed suicide by shooting himself in the head with a hunting rifle in the bedroom of his house in Saulieu, Côte d'Or, Burgundy. Long before, he'd said that if he lost a star in the Gaultmillau Guide (the rival to the better-known Michelin guide) he'd kill himself. He didn't lose a star, but he dropped from 19 to 17 in the Gaultmillau rating system of 20 possible points. This 20-point system takes into consideration flavor, texture, presentation, and smallness of food portions. A guide spokesperson said that the two points were deducted because the critic received five *haricots verts* (green beans) on his plate, instead of the customary *three*. The spokesperson avered that Loiseau had other problems. The chef's widow, Dominique, revealed that he had recently been very tired, and that he hadn't taken a holiday in years.

There was a general outcry from the restaurant industry against the tyranny of the restaurant guides. Paul Bocuse even went so far as to say that critics killed Loiseau. One glimpses the intense paranoia that occurs at the more rarefied levels of the industry. It might be observed that there are thousands of restaurants that don't feature in any restaurant guide, but do very well, thank you.

Napoleon had a love–hate relationship with food. After the successful battle of Marengo, June 14, 1800, against the Austrians in Northern Italy, his chef Dunand's foragers could only find some onions, potatoes, a scrawny chicken, four tomatoes, three eggs, a few crayfish, some garlic, and a frying pan. (Although the French army on campaign took some supplies, and cattle and pigs on the hoof, they often *foraged,* i.e., lived off the land they conquered. This strategy eventually helped to destroy them in Russia, when they were forced to retreat over country they'd denuded during the advance.)

Dunand was without his normal cooking utensils. No butter was found, but they did find some olive oil. Dunand cut up the chicken with a saber and fried it in oil with garlic and some water made more palatable with brandy from Napoleon's hip flask. A soldier offered some "emergency ration" bread. Eggs were fried in the same liquid and served on the side. Fried crayfish were put on top. Napoleon was delighted, and ordered that this dish should be served after every battle. (One assumes he meant every *victorious* battle.)

Back in Paris, he requested the dish one day. Dunand obliged, but thought crayfish and chicken, though acceptable after a busy day on the battlefield, an absurd culinary combination. He served the dish without the fish, adding mushrooms, and imaginatively substituting white wine for water. Napoleon, a superstitious Corsican, complained bitterly that this would bring bad luck, and crayfish had to be found in a hurry.

On the rare occasions that one encounters Chicken Marengo today, the crayfish are usually omitted and the signature is merely fried eggs on the side of chicken pieces fried in garlic. It should not be thought that Napoleon was much of a *foodie.* He used to gobble his meals, often disdaining cutlery and eating with his fingers. Wine didn't interest him much. He liked Chambertin, but usually watered, and carried a flask of brandy in the field. Often he ate his food so quickly that he would have violent indigestion and sometimes even vomited—hence, presumably, the traditional pictures of Napoleon with one hand nursing a sore stomach.

The British Duke of Wellington, Napoleon's archenemy, was no more interested in food. His Spanish assistant during the Peninsular War said that he never wanted to hear these words again: "Cold meat and red wine." That was Wellington's invariable reply when, after a day's march, he was asked what he'd like for dinner.

KITCHEN STAFF

A polite letter to a grand hotel or restaurant will usually secure a tour of the kitchens. There you may see a full brigade of chefs of various ranks. Some say that the Paris restaurant Maxim's invented the system, but it probably evolved naturally.

You'll meet the apprentices and cooks of varying rank from the various *parties* (departments). The fish chef, the sauce chef, the butcher, the baker, the *hors d'oeuvre, the garde manger* (in charge of the larder), the *communard* (in charge of feeding the brigade), and the *chef tournant*, who is skilled enough to take over any job in the kitchen at a moment's notice. The *chef adjoint* is the second-in-command, and the *chef de cuisine* is the commanding officer.

In a grand hotel or restaurant, the *chef de cuisine* is someone who hires, fires, and spends up to $100,000 a day on food. Yes, this means he's in line for kickbacks. It's an accepted perk of the profession. A legal precedent was set years ago in Boston when a judge ruled that while kickbacks were OK, if they were in the form of cash they should be declared and taxed, just like tips!

You'll be amazed what a genial and easy-going bunch the cooks in these establishments usually are. Most of these highly paid pros despise temperament and talk a lot of teamwork and dedication. Like theater professionals, they never lose sight of their goal—to fill the restaurant's seats. Their responsibilities, and the occasional intensity of effort required, preclude prima donna fits. You'll see no baseball hats worn backward and no precious designer stubble.

Contrary to what TV would have us believe, many top chefs could easily pass as accountants or doctors.

Kitchens generate a lot of waste and dirt. Cleanliness is imposed by law, and a health inspector can close a restaurant instantly. A bang up-to-date modern kitchen will be built like a gigantic shower room, with slightly sloping floors and a drain in the middle, so that the whole place can be literally hosed down. A useful piece of equipment is the "steam wand" a device that enables hot steam to be brought to bear on greasy surfaces.

A typical kitchen crew for a restaurant that seats up to 150 people would consist of a chef (probably the highest paid person in the place) and two helpers. One of these may enjoy the title of salad maker, the other will be the dishwasher. Both will be required to carry out various duties in the course of their shift. The dishwasher will be required to run occasional errands, and, in places too small to employ a busperson, clean up mishaps in the dining room. The salad maker may have to do anything from cutting strawberries to opening clams. It's a good idea to instill a daily routine so that everything gets done automatically, but this shouldn't be done in such a way as to suggest that, outside the regular tasks, nothing else needs to be done. Though most employees will smilingly oblige the boss, you can't always be there. The cry of "It's not my job!" is the last thing the chef or manager wants to hear in any of the mild emergencies that inevitably occur in the course of a day.

In some places the power of the chef is such that many odd jobs are sloughed off onto the waiters and waitresses, from making up their own salads to whipping the cream.

The kitchen crew arrives early in the day in order to set up (or prep), not just for the day, but for the evening dinner shift as well. Sometimes they'll have to prepare food for a special that won't actually be featured for a couple of days. At around 5 P.M., they are relieved by the night crew, whose chef may be less skilled, and thus worse paid, and who only has to dish up that which has been prepared earlier by the day chef. Of course, where, as is hoped, both lunch *and* dinner become very busy affairs, this routine may have to be varied. But patterns of business soon assert themselves. Except in busy travel and tourist areas, there's usually a calm patch in the afternoon when the restaurant can recuperate and various tasks can be accomplished.

Sometimes a state of mutual hatred exists between the two crews. Most commonly, the bone of contention is simply that the job that should have been done has not been done. Once more, it's the job of the owner or manager to mediate and make sure that the show goes on.

DECIDING ON THE MENU

The menu is something the owner and chef work out between them. It will conform to the standard repertoire of cooking with individual touches. These may be provided by local produce and tastes or some special skill of the chef.

When you're inspired to experiment, you can feature a dish as a special. Then, if it's a success, you can make it a regular item.

Ease of production must be borne in mind at all times. If the chef turns out a particular dish that is a bit fussy and time-consuming but is always a sell-out, then there's obviously a case for featuring it. But you don't make work. There's enough to do just attending to the basics.

You should constantly review the menu. Some owners do this very consciously by doing a breakdown of what's ordered every day. If you sell 40 chicken potpies, but only 3 barbecued porks, then you might consider dropping the less popular item.

Also, you should be aware of what gets eaten heartily and what gets left on the plate. Hopefully, the servers will tell you this, but some may not notice. A conscientious owner or manager will draw up a list of what dishes have been sold every day, and consider any changes that suggest themselves. Sometimes the size of portions needs to be changed. The wonderful science of portion control is all about how much you give for the money. Given the current preoccupation with obesity, the operative word here is *less*.

The menu is a good sales tool. There's something engaging about a menu that looks as if it was composed that very day in the light of what was the best food available. With a computer, this is easy to achieve. Make appropriate changes, print, and make copies. Customers often ask for menus to take home, so it's a good idea to have a supply available, with the restaurant's telephone number and general info included.

Menu Changes

It's important that the waiters and waitresses learn instantly those items that have run out. If word of mouth doesn't work, then you should have a black board outside the kitchen to list the items no longer available. Otherwise, busy servers might find themselves making wasted trips and apologizing to customers. They hate this, as it lessens their psychological control over the scene—and not infrequently takes the edge off their tip, too.

Food Quality

Restaurant haters complain that restaurant food is rarely as good as home cooking. This is generally true. Cooking a meal for two or three people, under no great pressure, with a knowledge of how people like their food and with a natural wish to please, is entirely a different task from cooking for hundreds of customers. The chance of finding a used bandage, fingernail, or cigarette butt in your chicken potpie is clearly quite small at home. In a restaurant where many people have had their hands in the preparation of a hundred pies, with regular interruption, obviously the scope for horror is greater. And, inevitably, some of those pies will contain tastier meat than others.

One might expect that a commercial chef with nothing else to do but prepare food, unlike many a working parent with children, would turn out *better* food. In some restaurants, usually the more expensive ones, this is sometimes the case. Expensive restaurants hire more staff in order to increase quality. In the average restaurant, the chef hardly has time to sit down during the entire shift.

Customers sometimes complain about limited menus (hamburger, cheeseburger, baconburger, chopped sirloin, steak, flounder stuffed with crab, eggs of any style, etc.). However, it's irritating to go to a restaurant for lunch only to find that it doesn't feature a standard item like steak, french fries, and salad, but are crowded with chi-chi items. An ideal menu should be like a popular symphony concert program, offering the possibility of a familiar and tuneful overture, a war-horse symphony, or concerto by one of the great composers, something from the less-played repertoire, and perhaps a lightweight, jolly finale. In other words, something for everyone.

Customers learn what to avoid. *Fried* often means deep-fried in a thick, tasteless batter that hides the protein within. *Pan-fried,* by the way, is not a redundant expression—it means fried in a pan as opposed to deep-fried. Duck is often a disaster—to get it right just takes too much time and attention. Pastry dishes, rather a challenge for the domestic cook, are often phony, ready-made tasteless pie crusts inserted on top of separately prepared mini-stews. *Baked on the premises* in many cases ought to read "Faked on the premises." "Flounder stuffed with crabmeat" is another phony description of a deep-frozen favorite that finds a home on many a mediocre menu. Few buy twice. A common and depressing customer's motto is, "I only order the things the restaurant is least likely to get wrong."

Even the most hard-bitten restaurant hater, however, cannot deny that some things are done better in restaurants and would be hard to cook at home. Steak and prime rib, for instance, require more heat than is comfortably generated in a small apartment or house—hence the popularity of the backyard barbecue. Also, the quality of meat supplied to restaurants is generally superior to that obtained in supermarkets or even the ordinary butcher's shop.

The quality of food depends on two factors: the skill with which it's prepared, and the basic quality of the foodstuffs used. To this might be added the perception of novelty factor. Food cooked by someone you don't know has the advantage of a different and original touch. Though mom's sure touch will always be the best, a change will often refresh the palate and perhaps make mom's food taste even better when next sampled. It need hardly be added, though that "hunger is the best sauce." The most demanding gourmet will not disdain the yacht-club-bar hamburger after a cold morning's sailing.

Many chefs lean heavily on cream, a clever move because most American homes don't use it a lot, especially since people have become aware of fat and cholesterol. When real whipped cream (as opposed to the commonly used aerosol stuff, which would be put to better use for shaving) is added to strawberries or good chocolate cake, a glimpse of heaven may be vouchsafed. Heavy cream can be added to soup with good effect, too.

The simple addition of a pinch of curry powder, paprika, dill, bay leaves, or some other herb or condiment, can transform a dish from the banal to the superb. Soup with a pinch of curry becomes *madriléne,* and so on.

So far as mechanical devices go, after the fierce and instantly applied fire of the restaurant stove, the blender is probably the most useful tool. It can be used, for instance, to whip up really tasty desserts quickly.

Food Sources

When "great" restaurants are written up and gushed over by the media—an event usually caused by the restaurant's public relations firm, not the excitement of the editorial staff—sooner or later there will be a reference to the heroic owner or chef getting up at 4 A.M. in order to go to the food markets to select the very best items for the esteemed customers. This scenario has its origins in France, where there really are food markets that open very early, often full of housewives, restaurateurs, and excellent food. They are well worth a visit when in France, if you can stand the sight of pigs' heads on sticks or blinded rabbits at the crack of dawn.

In terms of validity, it's about on a par with the common whine of the sincere and dedicated please-use-me-as-your-ego doormat restaurateur: "I treat my customers like guests in my own home!" Except that they get a bill.

It's true that there are markets that open at unearthly hours in major U.S. cities, and that it's often a case of first come, first served. They are all worth a visit. Considerable savings can be made, but that 4 A.M. reveille—often undertaken by a willing spouse while the exhausted owner who closed the restaurant the previous evening snores on—can be a serious strain on individuals, not to mention marriages. The necessity to attend the food markets has long passed. Food wholesalers, sometimes called *purveyors,* have longstanding business arrangements with producers who provide them with all kinds of food, from swordfish to radishes, of best—and lesser—quality.

Consequently, if you are in the hands of a good supplier, there really shouldn't be a problem in this area, and you needn't lose any sleep. This doesn't mean you should lose sight of quality control. Most wholesalers are ordinary business people, and they want to keep their customers. But the world is full of wise guys, and if some purveyors (or their delivery staff) see you as a sucker, they won't give you an even break. All incoming goods should be checked carefully against the invoice. If you fail to do it once, you may become a *mark*. In many restaurants the highly polished scales in the basement are regularly used to check quantities. One paranoid owner, briefing his manager before taking off on vacation, was heard to say, "Oh, yeah, the lobsters. They come in on Tuesdays. Reject a couple, whether there's anything wrong with them or not. Send them back. Keep the bastards on their toes!" This won't usually be necessary. Purveyors value their clients.

This only affects the gourmet end of the market, but some foods are also genuinely in short supply, and not only white truffles. Only 2 percent of steers qualifies as *prime*. Each prime steer provides about 30 pounds of beef. One steakhouse owner, when questioned about expansion, complained, "I don't know if I can get enough heavy prime to do more." Some foods are, of course, seasonal. With modern shipping and growing techniques, however, almost everything is always available.

In passing, you should insist that your suppliers deliver the goods at reasonable times, preferably before the commencement of business. Diners in silk and satin, lips poised to consume a *Bonne-Bouche* or to deliver a *bon mot,* don't want their restaurant experience spoiled by the sight and sounds of food being delivered.

Phoney Foods

"All that glitters is not gold" runs the proverb. Looking for better profits, food suppliers have come up with some ingenious methods and substances.

Most foods have to meet a legal definition set down by the FDA. This is what brings about such wondrous items as a product called *pork & beans*. When the can is opened, a square 1/2-inch of pork fat can be seen floating on the beans, which may themselves be of mixed ancestry. This makes it, legally, pork and beans! One might also quibble at the can marked *spaghetti and meatballs,* which contains but *one* meatball, and that heavily laced with filler. Where is Ralph Nader when we really need him?

Fresh fish is defined as that which emerged from the waters no more than five days ago. Clearly, this definition doesn't cover those solid chunks that emerge from the deep freeze. But there's nothing to stop you from calling your salmon special the "Catch of the Day."

Veterans of Economics 101 will recall that, whenever a product becomes prohibitively expensive or in short and uncertain supply, substitutes will emerge—hence, plastic for rubber, and polyester for cotton and silk. The food industry has its share of alternatives, too. Atlantic pollack is treated, shaped, and flavored to resemble crabmeat, lobster, and even scallops. When you see a "Lobster Crab Sandwich" for $8.50 on the menu, the one thing you can be sure of is that you aren't getting crab or lobster. And "stuffed with crabmeat" is usually a joke. Often it's a case of the substance being a mere shadow of the description.

Though purists may quite rightly object to this, the small print of the law allows considerable leeway of definition, and it would require both the wisdom of Solomon and millions of dollars in lawyer's fees to make small points. It is a fact of life that the definitions of certain foods are much looser than would be permitted in, say, aircraft safety regulations.

Often the genuine article, real ham, or real crabmeat, is prohibitively expensive for your price range. Sometimes you have to settle for acceptable rather than the best. A good chef will still manage to produce appetizing food. Indeed, one of the definitions of a *good chef* in France is one who makes the very best of available ingredients.

However, the currently popular substitutes for expensive shellfish are much cheaper, of good quality, and certainly the happiest compromise by far in this league. Few can afford Beluga caviar, but salmon caviar is delicious. Bill Buckley once observed that if peanut butter cost the same as caviar, sales wouldn't be affected. Everyone will have their favorites, good and bad. The truth is that many manufactured foods are so good and attractive in price that even a chef with the purest motives will be a fool not to use them. Canned consommé or beef broth can be mixed with other ingredients to great effect, and those little beef or chicken stock cubes can work wonders, too. Although *real* mayonnaise is a delight to the connoisseur, it's a pain in the neck to make and is actually a bit exotic for the average American taste. Most Americans far prefer bottled mayo.

It's possible that many old folks may recall with amusement the disgust with which many postwar youngsters greeted fresh eggs, after having known only the powdered variety.

There are many yarns told about the things used in certain foods. Kangaroo meat was found in hamburger meat in New York several years ago, and the tall story industry seems to date from that time, though it's most likely cyclic. Very few meats are an effective substitute for beef, and most of the stories are urban myths. A favorite myth is the one about the discovery of a skinned corpse in the street that later turned out to be that of a chimpanzee. Investigation revealed that it had died in a local zoo and had fallen out of the truck that was delivering it to a hamburger factory, in keeping with a longstanding arrangement for the disposal of dead animals. Horsemeat, quite commonly eaten in Belgium and France (and definitely not "worth a detour," as they say in the *Michelin Good Food* Guide), is too sweet to pass muster.

Although most of these stories are nonsense, anyone who sees frankfurters being made will think twice before eating another.

Canned ham is meat from a pig, but it is often made up of scraps that have been pounded, shaped, colored, and flavored to give it a farmyard look. This is called *formed* meat. The process is also applied to turkey and chicken. *Formed* must appear on labels in stores, but it's invariably in the tiniest letters imaginable.

Some restaurateurs, notably the quick-turnover kind, are quite unscrupulous about the food they use. What they describe as veal is really pork, and what they call calf's liver is steer liver. In some states, this is actually permitted by law.

When you immerse yourself in trade magazines, you will be amazed at the ingenious devices and foods that exist to enable you to quickly serve food that gives the impression of having been cooked with tender, loving care over a long period of time. They vary from the acceptable to the ghastly.

The proof of the pudding is in the eating. But the truth is that the American consumer often happily accepts food even the English would disdain, let alone the French. Speed is, of course, the enemy of good eating, but it's here to stay, and it won't go away. Restaurateurs must come to terms with it.

Readers may be irritated by the regular references to France and the French, as though they were the supreme arbiters of all things gastronomic. It's simply an easy frame of reference. Undeniably, the restaurant industry has its roots in France, though gastronomy almost certainly originates in Italy. Things have changed. Spain has become a gastronomic destination. One well-known writer recently observed that one could get better food in Noosa Heads, Australia, than in Paris. But France provides the traditions against which newcomers are judged.

FOOD AND TASTE

"Tell me what you eat and I will tell you what you are," and, "He who invents a new dish will have rendered humanity a greater service than the scientist who discovers a planet," are the words of the French gourmet Brillat-Savarin from his entertaining book *The Physiology of Taste*. In the real world of the restaurant, imaginative cooking can be a waste of time. Generally, many American customers like their food cooked in nationally standard ways. Visual pleasure—great cartwheels of tomato and onion and liberal garnishing with dawn-chopped parsley served on huge and strangely shaped plates—can be as conducive to enjoyment as actual taste. Often a chef will devise an intriguing dish that will get the thumbs down from management because it is simply too different, challenging, or strong in taste. Steak and kidney pudding and even quite mild curry dishes are viewed with great dubiety by some, although in general the dining public is becoming much more adventurous, as is demonstrated by the number of ethnic restaurants.

Moving upscale, many restaurants bite off more than they can chew, requiring their chefs to lay on dishes they barely understand that fail abysmally. A young woman of 25 astonished her gourmet uncle by pulling a face at the mention of roast duck. She'd had it twice, each time in a restaurant (full marks for an adventurous spirit!), and had found it rubbery, greasy, and horrible. She was almost certainly correct, because for some reason, many restaurants have taken to serving roast duck in an abominable way. The bird is roasted and cooled. When the kitchen staff get an order, they extract a cooked bird from the refrigerator, "nuke" it (i.e., heat it in the microwave oven), and serve it. It is invariably a disaster. The fat that should have been removed by the application of salt and fierce heat lingers whitely beneath the soggy skin.

Duck is a dish that requires time, care, and attention, and many restaurants simply aren't up to it. This situation is partly what leads to unadventurous tastes. Customers, often on a budget, learn that if they stray from the straight and narrow path of steaks and hamburgers, the chances of disappointment are high. That is why you can sit in a restaurant with 30 entrées on the menu and observe the patrons eating a limited variety of hamburgers and pasta dishes.

Why the industry should shoot for novelty when what the majority want is ordinary, traditional food, cooked at its best, is a mystery. It may be part of that merchandising philosophy that insists on change for the sake of change, which is seen, often pointlessly, in every area of consumerism. Surely the sensible attitude for a restaurateur is, "If you can't do it right, don't do it."

A current obsession in the world of food is with salt and monosodium glutamate, usually referred to as MSG. A small minority are allergic to MSG and suffer when they, perhaps inadvertently, ingest it. This happens because an allergic person's autonomic nervous system causes the heart to speed up, and blood pressure to fall. After a medical study showed that some patients with high blood pressure reacted favorably to lowered sodium intake, the media became so shrill in its condemnation of this vital element of life (Roman soldiers were partly paid with salt, hence the expression, "He's worth his salt") that avoidance of it became fashionable. From using far too much, many chefs went to the other extreme of using none at all, and many restaurants, especially Chinese restaurants, are quite strident in their declaration that they use no MSG.

The two substances work differently. Salt doesn't "bring out" the flavor of food. It stimulates the taste buds. Everyone has different levels of sensitivity in this respect, which is why some people like more salt than others. Consequently, no cook can predict the salt requirement of the consumer, so it's probably best to use a minimum because, just as you can cook a steak a bit *more,* but not *less,* you can add salt to a dish, but you can't take it out once the dish has been cooked and served. For people who must reduce their salt intake (you must have some or you'll die, because without salt/sodium your body can't absorb water), MSG is a happy alternative.

MSG is an amino acid that occurs naturally in most protein and provides the intrinsically savory taste of meat, cheese, and some vegetables. Commercially manufactured MSG (Accent is a well-known brand) is a white crystal, made from fermenting vegetable starches. Thus, it is no more unnatural or natural than, say, yogurt, alcohol, or soy sauce. In addition to stimulating the taste buds in the same way salt does, MSG expands the availability of flavor by chemically linking with related substances in the food.

Only a small amount is needed to be effective, and it is virtually tasteless in itself. Large amounts of MSG are used in many cheap manufactured foods to increase perception of flavor where little exists naturally. A similar dosage of salt would render the food inedible.

Many serious chefs will not disdain using a tiny amount of MSG in order to enhance flavor and savoriness. In blind tastings, between 87 percent and 95 percent of the tasters selected dishes containing MSG as being the most flavorful.

Why, then, are so many people vehemently against MSG, often claiming that they can taste it? Some people talk of the "Chinese restaurant syndrome," blaming it for all sorts of ills from asthma to headaches and general upsets. When MSG is used in large amounts, the taste buds become so sensitive that hitherto unnoticed food flavors are revealed. People mistakenly think they're tasting MSG, but really they are tasting its results.

Tests conducted by the Joint Expert Committee on Food Additives, which advises the World Health Organization, have found no link between MSG and these reactions. However, it is conceded that if one were to eat a large bowl of restaurant soup, which is often loaded with MSG to boost the flavor of weak stock, on an empty stomach, one might feel ill. Soup is quickly digested, and if there's anything wrong with it, the results will soon be apparent. Too much salt, or indeed anything else in the soup, might equally make one feel unwell.

When you consider the extensive lineup of available taste improvers—ketchup, steak sauce, pepper sauce, raw onion, and malt vinegar—MSG appears as a happy alternative because its mission is to enhance food rather than to disguise it. Yes, it does contain some sodium, but only about a third as much as salt, and a little MSG goes a long way, so one need only use small amounts of it.

Preservative sulfites can also affect a small percentage of people. Many are allergic to one or other of the hundreds of chemical ingredients occurring naturally in red wine. The Australian wine industry has been researching exactly what it is that makes red wine a no-no for so many people—it's got to be one or more of the histamines—but haven't yet discovered the answer. Some people find they can tolerate red wine made from the pinot noir grape, but not others. Allergy to shellfish is not uncommon. Shellfish allergy can induce mild epileptic attacks.

DANGERS

The most dangerous place in the world is—home. That's where most accidents occur. And within the home, the kitchen is the center of danger—flood, fire, and fumes are possible threats. The same applies to restaurants.

Fire is an ever-present threat, given the great heat required to cook for large numbers. Consequently, all kitchens must be equipped with fire extinguishers. Staff must know where they are, and they must be checked regularly to make sure they're serviceable. Fire-proof blankets are useful items, too. Experienced staff will take kitchen fires in stride—a pan blazes, they throw a blanket, end of fire, on with the job.

Seating capacity in restaurants, rigorously imposed by the Fire Service, is determined by how efficiently the place can be evacuated should fire break out. Of course, the law doesn't condone fire risks and premises are regularly inspected, but a day-to-day awareness of the risks is essential. The fire authorities have more authority in some areas than the police, and will close a restaurant at a moment's notice if they detect a serious fire hazard. Big fire tragedies have passed into American folklore.

When a restaurant is busy the chance of cooking burns, or scalds, increases. Upon receiving such an injury the casualty should put the damaged area under cold water immediately, and hold it there for several minutes. Plunging a burned hand into ice will be even more efficacious. There used to be much dispute as to the best treatment for such accidents, but the discussion is long over. This is the drill.

Naturally, a comprehensive First Aid box is an essential piece of equipment.

COMPUTERS

Most restaurants these days have computers. The cash register is often a sort of computer, and there is usually an all-purpose computer in the office. It might only be a PC or laptop, but either is very useful. Computers' main function is for inventory. By diligently entering every order to the kitchen, and every delivery, it's possible to keep close control. If no order for food is released from the kitchen until it's been registered on the computer, then the chances of servers pocketing the diner's money is greatly reduced.

However, one shouldn't be too reverential. Before computers, many a small restaurateur would carry the whole inventory in his head without difficulty. There is also a danger that service will be so computer-oriented that servers lose touch with reality. It's not uncommon in the dopier kind of restaurant for a customer to have second thoughts and order an extra creamed spinach on the side, only to be told, "Sorry, sir, I can't get into the computer right now." That is absurd—and it happens. Someone must have the authority to bypass the computer.

There are all sorts of programs especially dedicated to the restaurant industry, and the gurus will welcome the challenge of devising one especially for your operation. You can use it to make a client database. Some restaurants will even record at which table a customer sat so that when next they make a reservation, the employee taking the reservation can ask, "Your usual table?" which adds a nice personal touch. Making people feel special is an important part of the restaurateur's business.

The Internet is useful for finding recipes and suppliers, and placing orders. As in retail stores, it's possible to program a computer to automatically place an order when the inventory is reduced to a certain point.

GROCERY LIST

Here is a typical partial list of groceries from the computer of a successful New York restaurant that is moderately priced with a large choice of genuine cooked-on-premises items and an interesting wine list that changes regularly to allow customers to experiment. If you don't recognize each item and its use, you should.

> Artichoke hearts; arugula; anchovies; A1 sauce; Angostura Bitters; bacon; beef broth; beans (black turtle, dark red kidney, navy, etc.); Baker's spray; barley; capers; canned clams; cranberry juice; cherries; chopped beef; chutney; Coco Lopez; cornstarch; condensed milk; Dijon mustard; eggs; flour; garlic; garlic powder; graham crackers; Grenadine; ham; horseradish; jam; ketchup; Kos lettuce; lemon juice; lemons; lentils; Lea & Perrins; maple syrup; Melfry; mayonnaise; muffin mix; olive oil; olives (cocktail olives); cocktail onions; pasta (fettuccini, tortellini, penne, lasagna, linguine, spirals); pineapple juice; Rose's Lime Juice; rice; saltines; split peas; steak; sugar (white, brown and confectioner's); Sweet & Low; tart shells; Tabasco sauce; tomato purée; tomatoes (whole, plum); tomato juice; canned tuna; vanilla extract; vinegar (red wine, white wine, malt and balsamic); walnuts; walnut oil; spices (basil, bay leaf, chili powder, cinnamon, cloves, cumin, curry, Coleman's mustard, nutmeg, oregano, paprika, parsley, pepper (black and white), salt, tarragon, thyme)

CHAPTER 8

THE DINING ROOM

The dining room is the most important part of the restaurant from the customer's point of view. Except in those restaurants designed to allow a view of all the fascinating goings-on in the kitchen, it's just about all they see. The dining room is the stage where they enjoy their restaurant experience. It's also where they buy the goods and spend the money—the point of sale.

SEATING POSITIONS

Many restaurateurs are not gifted with any particular aesthetic sense. However, there is nothing to stop you from sitting in every single chair in the room at least once and taking in the view. This may lead to the use of a discreet screen or the repositioning of a *bus station*—the corner where backup linen and cutlery and condiments are kept, and where dirty dishes are dumped. Badly positioned lights can offend, as can sudden, cold drafts.

MUSIC

It's usual to have some kind of music in the background in these electronic times—though not compulsory. Some "serious" restaurants, where the diners are mainly there to talk business rather than socialize feature no music, or only very quiet and unchallenging tapes. There are repeating eight-hour tapes that will drive your staff insane before their time. "Music soothes the savage breast," and the researcher who discovered that people consume more, and faster against a loud musical background has a lot to answer for to people who hate recorded background music. Traditionally, music drowns the sound of people slurping soup, just as wine "cuts the grease." Why shouldn't your customers enjoy a little aural satisfaction, along with the oral, tactile, dental, and olfactory sensations you're throwing into your bargain package?

If possible, you should try to accommodate those customers who don't want music. There a still a few people left on earth who actually wish to converse. A creaky old hi-fi, or worse, radio not quite correctly tuned, can be irritating. Sometimes customers are unwilling to be party poopers by diminishing the festive air and will decide to dine elsewhere. One of the worst scenarios is where a waiter agrees to turn down the volume, and does so. Three minutes later, another waiter comes along and turns the music back up again. The saddest victim of noise is the person who, for one reason or another (such as being the host and committed to dine in the restaurant), begs the waiter to reduce the volume, gives him an extra tip, and *still* the next waiter who passes the controls will turn it up.

Jukeboxes can be fun for the young, and even for older people who enjoy golden oldies. But they don't generate much revenue and can be a strain for the staff. One bartender used to sabotage the jukebox the moment he got to work. "What is it with this juke?" the maintenance man would grumble as he made his fourth trip of the week.

VENTILATION AND HEATING

It's not a bad idea to open all the doors and windows every day to freshen the air. Visiting a poorly ventilated, basement club-restaurant after 10 straight days of Christmas parties, when all the amateur drinkers have been out to play, will convince you of the wisdom of this. People have a dual attitude toward cooking smells. Sometimes they're appropriate and welcome, sometimes not. In general, kitchen smells should not be allowed to leak to the dining room, to ruin the effect of all that citrus cologne and musky perfume. Sitting next to a busy kitchen can sometimes mean that a customer goes home smelling of it, as though he or she worked an eight-hour shift. In the days of smoking, waiters and bartenders would get home to find that their very underwear stank of tobacco. It used to cling to the hair, too. Few would risk any kind of social encounter until they'd been home for a shower and a change of clothes. Fiercely efficient ventilation is a good investment.

The larger the room and the higher the ceiling, the more problems you'll have. Sometimes the thermostat controls have to be locked up so that only selected personnel can adjust them. Nothing kills a dining room faster than a cold draft, so if you have tables near a door, make sure it's a double door with a heater. An insoluble problem of the industry is the fact that those who are rushing around at work are automatically warmed, while the seated customers are not. But you can't have a room with two temperatures. Sometimes the Montagues are sweating while the Capulets are freezing, and vice versa. One solution is to put the air conditioner on for a while, then turn it off, and so on, so that all of the people are happy some of the time. And a good antiseptic gargle before retiring can help prevent colds.

Perhaps the worst smell a diner can encounter is the lingering evidence of the exterminator's visit, which is not uncommon, especially in old buildings. If such treatment is unavoidable, it should be done at the crack of dawn, and the windows and doors left open as long as possible.

Some restaurateurs like to spray the place with Forest Zephyr and similar products. Fresh flowers will provide a masking and pleasant smell, as they used to at funerals in the days before refrigeration.

The floor should be vacuumed if carpeted, and mopped if a hard surface, at least once a day. A quick once-over between lunch and dinner will do no harm, either. Garbage tends to accumulate in the bar area and should be cleared regularly. Discreetly placed garbage bags should be emptied promptly, too, especially when they contain wet stuff, because they'll soon start to smell and also become harder to handle.

The presence of breathing bodies will cloud and discolor mirrors, windows, and walls. Some restaurants are successful enough to be able to close for up to two months a year. During this period, the restaurant is painted top to bottom. Not every restaurant can afford to close for such a period. Most will be obliged to paint and mend during the small hours of the night between closing and opening.

A dustpan, broom, mop, and bucket should be placed where they can be grabbed swiftly, that spillages and other accidents can be cleaned quickly with minimum disruption of business.

RESTROOMS

By law, restaurants must post the sign "Employees must wash hands." Everyone sneers at those warm air dryers, hygienic though they are. Disposable paper is generally acceptable. The most elegant drying solution is a pile of small cloth towels, used once and dropped in the bag, but that's another laundry expense. You, your manager, or someone should check the restrooms regularly. Strange things happen in these places. Going into a restroom just before closing to find someone stark naked sitting on the toilet snoring happily because they think they made it home is so commonplace as to be unremarkable. Most important is the possibility of a nasty mess that will curb the appetites of innocent customers. The busperson or dishwasher is a likely candidate to clean up, but it's amazing how often the manager or even the owner has to do it.

In very expensive restaurants and nightclubs, the ladies' room attendants frequently become mother-figures, ever ready with a repair kit to take care of the missing button, tear, or spillage. Some well-known women restaurateurs got their start this way—and many a movie star, too. If you build an upscale clientele, it will do no harm to indulge them with a few chic touches, like linen towels and interesting soap, as this costs little and gives a nice impression.

CLEANLINESS

In a restaurant, as in a hospital or indeed any busy household, cleaning up has to be a continuous process. A successful restaurant is a busy one, and there's a continuous flow of dirty dishes and general refuse that must be removed well before it becomes offensive. The best way to keep on top of things is to establish a routine. At 4 P.M. the busperson checks the bar garbage, replacing the garbage bags where necessary. Either on closing or before opening, the floors all get mopped and swept. Mondays somebody does the front window, Tuesdays somebody cleans the bar mirrors, and so on. Apart from being efficient, this method will eliminate the dismal habit some owners have of wandering about the place with a long face that only comes to life with a snarl when they discover something that needs cleaning.

Owners who prefer the philosophy of *oderint dum temerant* ("Let them hate, as long as they fear")—and they are by no means in short supply—will naturally ignore this observation.

MENUS

Menu design is often appalling. Many menus are unclear, cluttered, misleading, and, worst of all, out of date. Murphy's Law insists that the one item that has been discontinued, but not been deleted from the menu, is the one that will be most frequently requested. Thus, the waiters or waitresses are irritatingly "one down" from the word go because they have to explain and disappoint. Blackboard menus are a good idea in saloon-type restaurants, but they should be checked regularly for legibility.

A neat dodge available to restaurants with computers is to make small alterations in the menu every day. You can have special dishes of the day while retaining your permanent menu. By changing the specials and the date, you can give a very encouraging impression of having had a dawn conference at which the offerings of the day were carefully considered. It's good theater. As mentioned, customers often like to take away a menu, and such menus should have the address and telephone number on them.

Menus can be presented in a dozen ways. Ideally, you should strike a happy compromise between practicality and decorativeness. Where the menus can be wiped clean, they should be, and where they have to be replaced from the printers, a reserve should be held and dispersed before the ones available become too dog-eared, soup-stained, and greasy.

VERBAL MENUS

In the spirit of offering theatrical entertainment, many restaurants insist that their waiters or waitresses tell their customers about the daily specials. Many diners find this ridiculous. They get the giggles when some charming would-be actor secures their attention and then addresses them with all the aplomb—replete with meaningful, engaging glances and occasional witty asides—of Gielgud doing Mark Antony's funeral oration. They feel sorry for the shy youngster who gazes at a point in mid-infinity and rattles off the specials by rote, with occasional stammers and blushes at some unfamiliar word.

Many diners forget what was said halfway through the peroration, descend with glee upon a trapped victim, and cross-examine to death, or demand a recapitulation, followed by further explanation. Others couldn't give a damn what they're going to eat anyway—they're there to talk sex or money. Some will be too drunk to care.

The bottom-line question is: How does this affect sales? At first, one may simply have to rely on trial and error.

But isn't it simpler to change the menu every day on the computer, and have a few copies made? Or have regular specials on different days with detachable slips that can be clipped to the standard menus?

Another current fad in some restaurants—one that smacks of the think tank, restaurant consultants, psychologists, and theme merchants, rather than the result of any common sense consideration—is the business of servers identifying themselves with a gay "Hi! I'm Chris, and I'm your server tonight. My colleague Craig will be with you shortly to discuss the verbal menu . . ."

This phony bonhomie creaks horribly when the chicken arrives rare and the steak burned, and the martini sits on the service bar so long, often in painful sight of its would-be consumer, that it's warm and flabby when it arrives. Again, it's for owners to decide in the light of experience, but perhaps, on the whole, a "Thanks, Suzy" on the back of the check should be the limit of the personal touch. The occasional rapport between staff and customers that results in friendship, romance, stardom, adoption, change of will, or a change of job, is a separate adventure, and no generalizations apply.

DUTIES OF SERVERS

Owners will do well *not* to add casually to the workload of their waiters and waitresses. Before commencement of business they have to set up shop. It can take an hour or more. They have to fill the salts and peppers, combine the ketchups and mustards, check the menus, set up the tables, bring up the reserve supply of linen, fill the cutlery containers, make sure the milk, the iced tea, and the cream supply are in place, and soon. If there's no busperson, they have to sweep and mop. Every little bit hurts, and as the workload increases, their positive attitude diminishes. They are, after all, your front-line salesperson. Every time they go to a table, they have your considerable investment in the palm of their hands. There is no need to explore the importance of just how they feel about *you*, by the way. However, their prime object is to make money from tips, and they usually won't cut off their noses to spite their faces, by letting management down.

A common fault among restaurant staff is that they allow the unusual to dominate their thinking. An encounter with a rude customer will cause a waiter to be rude to polite and pleasant customers. An ungenerous tip will cause frowns and grumbles, whereas a generous one will be accepted without comment. (By the way, any bartender or waitress will tell you that the amount of tips earned in a given shift in an established restaurant will average out almost uncannily, as will the weekly total.) Old hands, who are determined to stay sane in what can be a crazy-making business, give as good as they get to rude customers and maintain a pleasant manner to the others.

It is amazing how frequently in the United States, where so much is made of respecting the individual, that restaurant staff are treated with contempt. However, it may be that one should not make too much of the rapport between the staff and customers. No computer has yet decided how important it is, though common sense tells one that a good rapport is probably better than a bad one.

SYSTEMS FOR SERVERS

In the kind of restaurant under discussion, the waiter or waitress usually takes the orders and delivers the food. This is a standard (but hopefully not inflexible) drill. Once the customers are seated, they are given menus (if the host hasn't already done so, or if it isn't already on the table or on the wall) and asked if they'd like a drink. If they would, the server gets it, then gives them a moment to consider the menu. If they want to order immediately, she waits. If she's busy, she tells them she'll be right back, goes on to something else, and returns. Most people these days understand this choreography perfectly well.

The server has a station of several tables, each with a number, which is entered on the check, on the kitchen order dupe, and on the bar dupe where these are required. Bar dupes are a pain in the neck, and a time-wasting ritual, but some owners find them comforting. They are in no sense a security measure, because no busy bartender has the time to compare documentation *and* make two whisky sours, one up one down, a Campari and soda, two piñas, one is a virgin, and could I get a bottle of number 13, that's the funny label, the one with the—oh, we ran out? Are you sure?

You should have ready instant contingency plans for combining tables in order to make a two into a four, or a four into a six, up to whatever your maximum is. Leave, "Gee, where we gonna put 'em?" to the competition. But when someone calls at 8:30 and says, "We're, let's see, 14. Could you fix us up with a table in 10 minutes?" it's unwise to say yes if you really can't cope. In this regard, beware of phony reservations from pranksters or competitors intent upon sabotage.

Waiters and waitresses are often, but by no means always, backed up by a busperson who serves bread and butter, clears finished plates, and so on. The busperson gets a cut of the tips, and sometimes there aren't enough tips or weight of business to justify employing one. This means the servers have more to do and, inevitably, endure occasional delay. Sometimes the assistant manager, hostess, or seating captain helps clear the tables—never a popular chore, especially since this task may wreak havoc with the smart suits or dresses they are required to wear, as distinct from the cheap and cheerful whites that nobody minds getting dirty.

The owner must discuss the requirement for a busperson with the staff, observe, and make a decision in this regard. Many will risk defective service in order to save a small salary. That's their problem.

Every waiter or waitress has a station, but must be prepared to take note of others. Few words are more depressing to a diner than the dismissive, "Sorry, that's not my station. I'm not your waiter," from a passing waiter from whom something has been requested. Nor is the qualifying, "But I'll send him over right away," very comforting, either. The correct response is, "Yes, what can I get you?" tell the appropriate waiter what has been requested—and double-check to see that the goods have arrived.

A popular system that seems to work very well is the one where there are two sorts of servers: floor servers and kitchen runners. The front server is a combination of captain and ordinary waiter. Having taken the customer's order and placed it in the kitchen, he then assumes a supervisory capacity. The person he supervises is the runner, whose responsibility it is to pick up and serve the food.

The front server has a nice executive feeling—a lance corporal, rather than a private—and some go off on paranoid ego trips. One well-known New York waiter with a shaved head addresses his affluent, but not necessarily highly educated, customers with grandiose, pompous opening speeches such as, "Hi! Lobsters are the special to-night. They're tremendous, and I mean that both literally and figuratively." At this point his victim's jaw drops, the women pull down their skirts, and the men straighten their ties. He claims to be the only Choate-educated waiter in the world ("a dubious claim," sniffed an Old St. Paulian) and, by reference to his pocket calculator and the reservations book, he reckons to be able to gauge his total tips to the nearest dollar on any given evening before the first customer walks in. A simple greeting and a smile are quite sufficient, though of course some customers like a more theatrical approach.

The runner is saved the horror of having to talk to people, a special blessing if he doesn't speak English, though it's a bore for customers who ask for a spoon and get in return a brilliant smile—but no spoon.

In order to ensure that all customers get what they ordered (customers often forget, so it's a good idea to have the edge on them), a system is employed whereby each diner is accorded a number at the table, which is put on the order slip. 1. Chicken 2. veal, and so on. If there's one woman in the party, she's number one. If there are more, then number one is always the person nearest the door, or whatever. The system breaks down frequently, but it's fun straightening things out. Little contretemps in restaurants are often more welcome than owners realize. They're part of the adventure and sometimes help to break the ice.

On the whole, this system works well. A thing to note is that the more people you have on the floor, the less in tips each person takes home. Some owners couldn't give a damn; servers, they say, are a dime a dozen. If they don't like working there, tough. But continuity is a good thing, and rapid turnover of help may be a turnoff for regular customers, especially if you're doing a lot of neighborhood business.

HELPFUL HINTS FOR WAITERS

Get your tables set up in good time, allowing time to put on your fresh shirt and tie, where applicable, and maybe relax with a cup of coffee before the place gets busy.

Good waiters are at ease with people in general. Occasionally, a square peg finds its way into a round hole, and the result can be very bad for business. People who encounter attitude—indifference, demonstrated boredom, ignorance, unwillingness to oblige, an unsmiling face, or plain rudeness, may walk out and never return. Waiters who are tired simply shouldn't be working— often not easy to observe, but it should be.

The secret of efficient service is anticipation. Don't bring out the food or drinks until you know there's space on the table to put them. Don't order the champagne or white wine, then look around for an ice bucket. First find the ice bucket, then get the wine. When people order escargots, locate the requisite dining implements and put them on the table before you serve the snails. Even when people are happily munching, drinking and talking, look the table over once in a while, and see, for instance if there's anything that can be removed to leave more space.

KEEPING DINERS HAPPY

A friendly greeting is the best possible start to a dining experience. People don't require heart, soul, and eternal devotion, just a smile and a cheerful greeting.

If it's busy and you're backing people up at the bar waiting for tables, try not to give false encouragement as to when people will be seated. After yet another round of cocktails at the bar, people's appetites may diminish and they may become bad-tempered. Learn from airline pilots. If there's a delay of 10 minutes, they'll say half an hour. Thus, everyone's pleased when they get off sooner.

Sad though it may be, it's a fact of life that a maitre d' who's tipped in order to find a table in a hurry will give the tipper immediate priority. People may notice this and complain that they've been waiting longer. The lie is, "Sorry . . . they had a reservation."

Complete breakdown in service is always a real possibility. The fundamental reason for this is that everyone wants to dine at more or less the same time— eight o'clock dinner, for instance. Experienced diners know that arriving earlier is usually a good move. Saturday night is, of course, the most likely time for things to go wrong. If a customer complains about a food item, there should be no charge, and an unconscionable wait for service should result either in the bill being waived or a bottle of wine offered on the house.

However, such breakdowns visually indicate either a too-ambitious menu or a weak link somewhere among the staff, and it's probably in the kitchen.

PAYMENT

Bills, checks, or tabs are collected by the waiters and waitresses or the manager. They should include the total for food and drinks, as well as anything consumed at the bar but not paid for there. It's unusual for bartenders to allow this to happen. Most are paranoid about collecting their dues on the spot, before the diners depart to their tables, in order to secure a tip. In fact, most customers who make this request do so because they want to put the whole bill on a credit card and are quite happy to give the bartender a tip, even though they don't pay the bar bill.

To this total, the local tax, if any, should be added, and then it's not a bad idea to write the grand total in large black figures so that it can easily be discerned. Mistakes in addition, which frequently occur, are usually made when transferring from the single column to the tens. When diners are observed departing in an unusually expeditious and purposeful manner, they will almost invariably have been undercharged. Experienced servers develop a feel for the amount, however, and will usually double-check when, after two sirloins, two apple pies á la mode, two martinis, and a bottle of Pommard, the bill somehow only comes to $24.50. In a majority of cases, the money is handed to the bartender, who rings it up on the register.

When servers make mistakes, the boss will usually write off the loss with a smile and a light admonishment. But if such mistakes become too frequent, other solutions must be found.

CREDIT CARDS

There is little doubt that restaurants that refuse to accommodate credit cards may lose business. It is significant, however, that many do not accept plastic money and still do well. A thought that leaps to the cynical mind is that credit card transactions are recorded with a third party, and this may not always suit some operators. Naturally, a service charge is made by the credit card company, and some restaurateurs resent this. However, it is important to consider that some customers are spending company money for business entertainment, and it's highly convenient for them to be able to hand in their credit card bill to the accounts office as a ready-made list of all they spent in a particular month. Tourists also are likely to use them for the convenience, and a growing number of people use credit cards in lieu of carrying more cash. So prevalent is the use of plastic that even fast-food restaurants are beginning to accept credit cards.

If, as is likely, you decide to use this service, you'll be equipped with a machine that enables you to check the validity of cards. There are several designs, but they all follow the same principle. You run the magnetic band of the card through the machine, then enter the amount of the transaction. A prompt on the screen will tell you when to proceed. In the end, you'll be accorded an approval code. If you have this, you are bound to collect your money, even if—and many restaurateurs never quite grasp this—you accidentally retain the wrong copy of the credit card slip.

Some cards require a phone call. They are a pain in the neck, because it sometimes takes ages to get through.

As with so many things in the restaurant, it really helps if you can, *without interruptions*, show new employees exactly how to operate this very simple equipment. The choice is simple: Show them properly once, or waste time in the future half-showing them again between interruptions, invariably at the busiest times of the day.

PERSONAL HOUSE ACCOUNTS

Some regular customers like to be able to sign their bills and pay monthly, and this is to be encouraged as it helps to build customer loyalty. Once in a while you'll get beat. But the steak you sell for $20 didn't cost you $20 so, unless you are prone to pain from opportunity loss, you haven't really been ripped off that badly. The trick is not to let the bills get out of hand.

There is a breed of professional restaurant scrounger who specializes in running up small bills around the town. At first they pay promptly, building confidence. Then, suddenly, they're not there anymore. *C'est la vie.* In these times, you're bound to get a visit from one of those deadbeats who eat their fill and then calmly tell you they haven't any money. It isn't worth bringing in the police. Let them depart in peace. But don't let them in again. Poor souls, one day they'll pull their cunning stunt in the wrong place, and find themselves being taken quietly backstage and liquidated. Some owners wittily write off these visitors under promotion.

It's very nice if you can get company accounts, with certain executives authorized to sign. It means you've got yourself some regular corporate business, and that should produce a warm glow. Incidentally, there's nothing to stop you from visiting companies and promoting yourself—an often neglected means of increasing business.

As part of their *restaurant chic* or *restaurant presence*—variations on the theme of restaurant theater—some regular customers don't even want to sign their bills while they are entertaining at the table. They'll trust you, or your staff, to total it, add a tip, and put their name on it. In the dining room, their guests, if they notice, will be impressed ("Does he own the joint?"). Kindly rich parents will sometimes send young daughters and their swains to a restaurant, having first called to authorize them to put everything on their account.

When a customer wants to ensure that he or she gets the bill, he or she will tell the waiter discreetly, "Make sure I get the tab." But if the bill is brought to the table, there may be a silly squabble, which was precisely what the diner wished to avoid. A better method is for the host to give the manager a credit card and then, under the pretext, perhaps, of popping to the restroom, sign the slip backstage.

TIPPING

A line in *Casablanca* that often elicits a chuckle from some knowing member of the audience occurs shortly after Claude Raines has closed the joint. "Keep everyone on salary," says good-hearted Rick, with a Bogartian, solicitous please hurt-me-more frown. Since, in the United States, a waiter or waitress's paycheck is sometimes precisely zero, after tax computed on salary and tips has been withheld, this would be an empty gesture for the tippable staff—though a bonanza for the others. Also, in places like Casablanca and the South of France, it's not uncommon for waiters to be paid nothing. Their tips are their sole income.

In one sense, tipping is none of the owner's business, but you should be aware of the usual systems adopted. Tipping at tables works out to about 8 percent nationwide for all types of eating and drinking places, but 17 percent in licensed á la carte restaurants

To Pool or Not to Pool

Sometimes tips are pooled and divided equally, after deductions for the buspersons, service bartender, and perhaps the captain or hostess. Occasionally, this leads to suspicions and grumbles, because some waiters or waitresses are better than others. One who receives an exorbitant tip may not put it all in the pool, or *tronc,* as it's called in England. Once a business is established, however, the degree of talent and efficiency will tend to be fairly uniform.

In some restaurants, the staff will keep their own individual tips. This is fine, except that inevitably some stations are more popular than others, and the waiter in the back may fume as tables in the window are turned time and time again while he does a crossword puzzle. Of course, stations should be rotated. But then you have the seniority factor. The waitress who's been with you for three years may automatically get the front station every day, due, perhaps, to a period of turnover when a procession of newcomers meant that they took the easier stations and didn't stay long enough to graduate. This can lead to unrest among the troops. On balance, the pooling system would seem to be the best.

Tipping Other than the Wait Staff

Sometimes the captain or hostess will get tipped. In old-fashioned Maxim's-type operations where a captain in a tuxedo supervises a station, he expects to be tipped, and the customers are usually well trained. You will notice on the slips for some credit cards that there's actually a whole line marked "Captain" in the gratuities area of the column. Occasionally, customers will tip a captain or hostess to get them a table promptly. It's nice if this is done discreetly, because this can lead to bad feeling among the customers and is often forbidden by owners.

Bartenders are tipped an average of 20 percent to 30 percent, but with a usual absolute minimum these days of a dollar. There is a greater variation than at the tables, and in general bar checks aren't as big as table checks. However, since the bartender gets a decent wage as well as tips, there's not much room for complaint and, indeed, complaints are rare. The *decent wage* is usually the union scale, whether the restaurant has a union contract or not. In most states, this is now around $80 a shift, as opposed to the federally guaranteed minimum wage per hour, which is usually what the other staff get. Many think the bartender's job is the best in the house, except that waiters can run from bores, while bar staff are trapped!

Pros and Cons of Tipping

Many consider tipping demeaning and prefer the service charge system whereby 15 to 18 percent is automatically added to a check. This is normal on the continent, where it was introduced because tips tended to be small or nonexistent.

A few owners exploit the service charge system and do not give their employees an even break. Most people who have jobs that attract gratuities prefer to take their chances. It averages out better.

When European customers arrive in American restaurants, some waiters or waitresses will add on a 15 percent service charge, knowing it won't be resented. Otherwise, there's a chance people might glance at the sales tax and conveniently mistake it for a service charge.

A current unpleasant trend in some restaurants is to levy a service charge, but leave the tip/gratuity line open on the credit card slip. Thus, a customer may pay a service charge, and also add a tip. It's a deliberate rip-off. No customer who discovers such a ruse will return to the guilty restaurant—unless to create an angry fuss.

One irate customer examining his credit card slips discovered that he'd added a tip to a bill that already included a service charge. Imagine his mirth when he realized they'd forgotten to charge him for the vintage champagne!

From a customer's point of view, the tipping system is a godsend. Some jobs just wouldn't be worth doing if there were no tips involved. What luggage porter is going to struggle across a crowded foyer to grab heavy bags if there's no reward involved? If you're a regular customer and tip well, you'll amass brownie points entitling you to all sorts of extras, possibly including warm smiles when you call for extra butter. Business people are far and away the best tippers.

In Russia, where tipping is forbidden, the service in restaurants is usually as rotten as the food—as many tourists have reported. Strangely enough, in Japan, where tipping also is forbidden, things seem to go smoothly.

Restaurant employees easily lose sight of the way in which everything averages out, and they rarely rejoice when they get an exceptionally generous tip. It's said that *tip* derives from the phrase "to ensure promptness."

The worst aspect of tipping is the mean attitude it provokes. It's unpleasant to see young servers' lips curl as they curse some customer for leaving an ungenerous tip. It rarely seems to cross their minds to reflect that the absence of generosity may be a comment on the quality of service. Even if this point is grasped, there may be a whine on the lines of, "I know the fish was cold. This damn chef never gets things out together. It wasn't my fault!"

The owner is responsible for declaring employees' tips for IRS purposes. In fact, the IRS (not ungenerously, though they can hardly employ an agent to shadow servers as they go about their duties) allows each employee to declare a daily amount, and this is agreed among the help. The accountant will normally take care of all this for you. While the IRS is generally benign in its attitude toward restaurants, when it descends, its attentions tend to be ferocious. Often, it is in hot pursuit of organized crime money launderers.

In Italy, customers can be stopped within a statutory distance of the restaurant they've just visited and required to show their restaurant bill to the official tax inspector, whose job it is to make sure that restaurateurs are declaring all their takings. Quite who gets prosecuted if the person has lost the receipt or thrown it away is unclear. It smacks of bad law, but it is a scene tailor-made for a *Pink Panther* movie.

STEALING

Due to the accessibility of cash and goods, stealing, sadly, is common in the restaurant business. Many owners are obsessed by it. They will solemnly inspect all employees' bags on leaving, and sometimes will not allow bags to be brought in at all. They will require their employees to undergo screening, including lie detector tests, before they're hired. The security firms they hire—presumably retired thieves who've turned state's evidence, poachers turned gamekeepers—will send spies, called inspectors, to restaurants to observe and report.

Their reports may go something like this: "The bartender greeted us with a smile. His appearance was neat and his fingernails were clean. He placed a clean bevnap in front of each customer. Two Beefeater martinis were ordered. They were correctly prepared, chilled, and served with the requested garnishes, an olive in one, a twist in the other. The drinks were immediately rung up on the cash register and the check placed in front of us."

Well, whatever turns you on. You probably pay the security firm more than the bartender steals, but there you are.

An amusing story emerged from the 1970s at the wildly successful and always busy New York restaurant, Maxwell's Plum. A security firm was employed to survey the bar, and a solemn meeting was held to discuss the findings. The investigator droned on " . . . and this transaction was correctly rung up on the number three cash register." The meeting continued until one of the assistant managers suddenly woke up and said, "Number three cash register? Surely there are only two registers on this bar?"

The resourceful bartenders had actually brought in their own private cash register. Everything that went into it was theirs.

In Europe, theft paranoia is surreal. In some places in Italy and France, if you sit at a bar and order a cup of coffee, the bartender will solemnly go to the cashier and hand her a slip saying "one coffee." The cashier will then authorize the serving of a cup of coffee. The customer will put up his money, which will be solemnly handed to the cashier.

In the United States there are many restaurants where bartenders handle no money at all. Drinks served at the bar are put on the diner's bill by a supervising bar manager. Owners rejoice because they know that this is a safe area, from which they are not being ripped off. But an untipped bartender is a sorry fellow or lass. No latest jokes, no character, no football, no baseball, no politics, no nothing. The turnover of personnel is constant, and the restaurant never establishes any character. Sadly, but realistically, such is the gross over-population of the earth that this sometimes doesn't matter. Some heavily advertised locations don't need repeat business and a regular crowd. People just come.

Some owners, upon noting that the bartender is stealing, will calmly assess just how much is being stolen. If the bartender is doing a good job and boosting business, provided his regular take doesn't exceed an acceptable amount, he's allowed to continue. Many owners appoint spies among both their employees *and* their customers. Their cover is soon blown, though. Far from liquidating them, the other employees will simply warn acceptable newcomers whom to watch out for, in much the same way as the British often leave terrorist leaders alone and under supervision, on the grounds that if they're arrested, it will take months to identify their replacements.

A hilarious aspect of restaurant work is that sometimes a new employee being shown the ropes will also be initiated into the little wrinkles that help to swell the take. Occasionally, a new employee is embarrassed to discover that the staff are stealing *far too much,* and knows that one dreary day everyone will be fired.

Hotels are notoriously paranoid about stealing. Each bottle of liquor delivered is stamped, sometimes invisibly, to ensure that only the house booze is being sold. The point is that bartenders have been known to bring in their own bottles in order to show an acceptable percentage profit while actually pocketing most of the bar proceeds. At the crack of dawn, assistant managers will take the bar inventory down to a tenth of a bottle. Often as not, they have nothing better to do. Maybe some restaurants can afford it, but the average restaurateur probably cannot.

Some larger restaurants are completely computerized. This makes excellent sense once everyone has mastered the system. This replaces the *dupe system,* whereby, having taken an order, the waitress makes out a duplicate kitchen order slip and enters the number of the check, so that later the check and the kitchen dupe can be compared by the owner or manager. With the computer, nothing is sent out unless and until it's entered on the computer. But again, you may have to pay an extra wage for someone to monitor all this. *Quis custodet ipsos custodiens?* Who will monitor the monitors?

Some restaurants give the server a bank to make change. Then, at the close of business, the server has to pay up for everything he or she has entered on the computer.

By the way, the computer systems don't come cheap. Most restaurants wait until they're going strong before investing.

Servers can steal in time-honored ways. They'll use the same check over and over, if a common order in the restaurant is two hamburgers and two beers. But what about the dupe they have to put into the kitchen to get the food out and the dupe they have to give the bartender to get the beers? They wait until no one is looking, grab them, and destroy them—or cut the chef in on their ill-gotten gains.

In busy places, servers will give *verbal checks,* simply stating the amount and making change from their pockets. But supposing the boss is watching? Then they go to the restroom and make the change there. If they've got the money for a check in their pockets, they may put it on the next credit card they get hold of and keep the cash. But what about when the customer finds she's paid two bills instead of one? Either the server will shrug it off ("That's weeks ago. How can I remember?") or won't be working there anymore anyway. Some employees automatically pad their checks with small amounts. Two dollars per check on a busy day can mount up nicely. Just as liars need to develop good memories, restaurant thieves need to be on their toes, and they'll tell you it's exhausting having to remember what moves they've made.

Bartenders have their wrinkles, too, but the owner can always compare the liquor takings with the amount issued, so it doesn't pay them to be too greedy.

Generally, the happier the restaurant, and the better managed it is, the less stealing there will be. There's no point in being paranoid about it, although a majority of restaurateurs are. If all your employees are in cahoots, they'll cover their tracks carefully and you'll go crazy trying to find suspected leads.

A weather eye on the profits is your best protection in this respect. Half an hour spent on your books in a morning will save an awful lot of suspicion and anxiety. In a reasonably happy restaurant, a frown and a tut-tut from the boss to an employee will often curb greediness. "Joe, I must say, the PC doesn't reflect the increase in bar trade we've noticed lately. I wonder why that is?" Or, to translate this into restaurantese, "Mary, the new help. What are they doing? Either they straighten out or I'm going to have to fire the whole lot of them."

Customers are quite capable of stealing, too. It's mainly souvenirs such as attractive showplates, but the box containing the tips is a favorite target, as are tips allowed to sit too long in plain sight on vacated tables.

Ah, the warm, smiling, carefree joy of the restaurant business! One's faith in human nature and love of mankind are bolstered at every turn! If you have ever felt that Mine Host's Falstaffian laugh sometimes has a rather hollow ring, when you become a Mine Host yourself, you'll soon realize why.

CHAPTER 9

HYGIENE, HEALTH, AND SAFETY

The inevitable dangers that exist in any public place where people are gathered, and particularly where they are eating and drinking, are too great to allow safety measures to be left to the goodwill and wisdom of owners and customers. That's why the law requires attention to hygiene, health, and safety. It appoints inspectors to check premises at random. If standards are not met, owners will be warned and required to correct their omissions. If violations are not corrected, then premises are closed. However, authorities are generally helpful in these matters and willing to advise businesses on their requirements. With certain notable exceptions that are unavoidable where the deadly hand of bureaucracy lurks, these requirements are based on common sense standards, and you should have little trouble complying with them.

HYGIENE ISSUES

A century has passed since Doctor Lister started insisting that hospital doctors should wash their hands after examining one patient and before examining another. The law now requires the following sign to be hung in restaurant bathrooms: *Employees must wash their hands before leaving this room.* Absence of this notice constitutes a violation, though it's unlikely that a restaurant would actually be closed for this reason.

There is no requirement for the sign to be printed in any language other than English. Many restaurant employees do not read English. The thought of kitchen staff emerging from a lavatory and going straight back to work cutting vegetables and dipping veal slices into flour isn't pleasant. Thus, all employees should be frequently reminded to wash hands.

Food Contaminants

There is a greater reason than aesthetics to insist on clean hands at all times. Salmonella, the most common form of food poisoning and one that can kill the elderly and infirm, is often transmitted by urine. Diarrhea and dysentery often come from feces.

However, the good news is that the *least* likely source of food poisoning is a dirty person. The classic case of "Typhoid Mary," an itinerant dishwasher who spread typhoid wherever she worked, is long gone.

Far more dangerous are bad food storage disciplines. Raw meat and cooked meat must not collide. A butcher or chef who has handled raw meat must not handle any other food item until he's washed his hands thoroughly in serious soap and water. The quick rinse under the faucet doesn't do it.

Food stored in a refrigerator must be placed in a way that will not allow accidental drippings from one item to another.

What saves society from regular epidemics of food poisoning is the cooking process. Germs insinuated into food by dirty workers or natural deterioration are destroyed by heat.

Other germs may be present in food from other sources. Chicken has been targeted as the main source of salmonella in the United States. That's why it should be thoroughly cooked, though it's not unusual in dubious restaurants to see a little ooze of blood as one cuts into a chicken breast! Such a sight is likely to extinguish the heartiest appetite, so make sure your chicken—and all other appropriate items—are properly cooked, or you'll lose customers and even risk lawsuits. Apart from the fact that pork tastes better when well cooked (though the French sometimes eat pork chops medium rare!), there is the danger of trichinosis, a common disease carried by pigs that can be fatal to humans. The dietary laws of some religions preclude the consumption of pork, and originally the reason for this may have been practical rather than religious.

The most dangerous food is that which, having been cooked, is then reheated. At certain temperatures germs spring to life with a vengeance, particularly in meat and quite horrifically in sausage. The simple way to avoid this danger is to make sure that food is served either thoroughly cooked and piping hot, or cold. Of course, this leaves your poor old *salade de canard tiède* (warm salad of medium rare duck breasts and vegetables) out in the cold, but some gourmets are happy to take a chance.

Sadly, fish is a well-known source of poisoning, and fish allergies are common. Although it's not likely to be a danger to Westerners, there is some curio value in mentioning the highly dangerous puffer fish, so called because when threatened, it gulps water and doubles its mass, making it harder to swallow. The trade-off is a 50 percent reduction in speed of withdrawal. Other names for this fish, of which there are more than a hundred species worldwide, ranging in size from a few inches to two feet, are blow fish, swell fish, globe fish and, in Japan, where it's considered a great delicacy, *fugu*. Many parts of this fish, including the liver, skin, and ovaries, contain a strong paralyzing poison, 1,000 times more deadly than cyanide, called tetrodotoxin. There is no known antidote for this poison. The immediate symptoms of ingestion are a slight numbness of the lips and tongue. Diarrhea, vomiting, collapse, and paralysis follow. Eventually, the central nervous system is destroyed, and the patient dies between 20 minutes and eight hours later, often remaining mentally lucid to the end. In Japan, only specially trained and licensed chefs are allowed to prepare *fugu*. There have been many casualties over the years. Some call this dish the gourmet's Russian Roulette. Read that sushi menu carefully.

At the risk of sounding gruesome, it should be mentioned that ordinary (i.e., ghastly but non–life-threatening fish poisoning) will often produce the same immediate symptoms, as well as fierce facial flushing, which will sometimes reduce the sympathy factor as beholders assume the poor victim is simply drunk.

Fortunately, there is usually no mistaking fish that has deteriorated, but accidents do happen, and even the strong smell of rotting fish might get lost in the jumble of aromas that pervades the kitchen at busy times. Interestingly, fish inspectors at central markets are often allergic to the histamines that occur in deteriorating fish. Their noses are thus super-sensitive. One threatening whiff will define the quality of a batch of fish.

A properly trained Western cook simply follows the maxim, "When in doubt, throw it out." But anyone unfamiliar with the fundamentals of hygiene should make an effort to acquire them.

Cleanliness

The price of cleanliness is eternal vigilance. Bored assistant managers will usually find time to run inquisitive fingers along picture rails and examine the glasses containing the bar garnishes. Indeed, some of them manage to fill their whole shift doing little else!

Cleaning routines must be established. Cleaning materials must be readily available so that jobs don't get put off and then forgotten. Some things get cleaned every day, others once a week. A list pinned to the employees' notice board will help. All employees must get into the habit of cleaning up as they go along.

Consumer watchdogs fiercely monitor the chemicals used to promote the growth, or enhance the appearance, of fruit and vegetables. Most people, even strawberry lovers, are happier if these items are washed in running water before being used. Some gourmets require each leaf of the lettuce in their salad to be dried so as not to dilute the salad dressing. The little worms that sometimes cause such alarm and fuss in salads and fruit dishes are sometimes the least harmful things in the dish—and a good source of protein, too!

If you poison people, they may sue you. A famous example of this some years ago was Yul Brynner's successful case against Trader Vic's in New York. He complained that he and his family had become ill after eating spareribs. No doubt the company was insured.

Any kind of dirt is a potential source of infection. Even basically clean people can have accidents or overlook things. That's why the authorities inspect premises from time to time. A fresh eye will often see what the accustomed eye ignores.

Few things are more depressing to the diner than an encrusted fork, a clouded knife, or a glass with a smear of someone else's lipstick on it. However, even in the best-run establishments, accidents can happen. Though a conscientious bartender will check glasses automatically during work, the light in bar areas is often subdued. So it sometimes happens that a glass is sent from a gloomy bar area to a window table, where the lipstick smear is revealed in all its glory.

This is an area where official hygiene requirements and reality collide. Many regulations require a rinse water temperature that is acceptable in the dishwashing machine, but that would cause serious injury to those foolish enough to put their hands in it. Thus, the bartender, who usually washes many used glasses in the bar sinks, has to compromise. He or she will normally send glasses that have been used for creamy drinks such as Brandy Alexanders or Piña Coladas to the kitchen, in order not to grease up the bar sink. But kiss-proof lipstick will often survive boiling water. Sometimes the electric revolving brushes in the bar sink will remove it, but the best way is to wipe it off with a damp paper napkin before washing.

Some regulations specify which types of detergents must be used for washing up. But detergents sometimes leave a thin film, which, though invisible on inefficiently rinsed china, is visible on glass. So the extra expenditure for spot-free dishwasher detergent is well justified.

Vermin and Exterminators

Vermin play an important role in spreading infection. In the Middle Ages, huge swathes of populations fell victim to the bubonic plague, which was efficiently spread by mice and rats.

In most cities and states, restaurateurs are required by law to employ an exterminator at regular intervals and to post a report in a prominent place for the health inspector to examine. Exterminators know where to spray and they have all the proper equipment. They are well worth the $50 or so they generally charge for a visit because they go all over the premises, usually in less than an hour.

Exterminators often work very late at night, thus sparing customers the smell of insecticide. Their most disagreeable, though efficient, weapon is the glue mousetrap. Sometimes the first person to enter the restaurant in the morning will be faced with the prospect of administering the *coup de grâce* to a live mouse enveloped in glue.

By the way, some professional exterminators collect dead mice and other offending creatures. They take them to premises they've been hired to clean up, and pull them out of their pockets at appropriate moments with a sigh saying, "Yeah, that's one o' the critters . . . !"

Health Inspections

Health inspectors are just regular people. From time to time, some of them lose their jobs because they accept bribes. Some owners would rather resort to the bribe than attend to their perfectly simple responsibilities. Such is the cynicism of our times that owners persist in believing that corruption is more rampant than it really is. One owner said, "It's always tough when two of them come together. The other day I had a guy and a young girl, a trainee. I cornered the guy by himself in the basement. I had two $50 bills in my pocket. I pulled one out and said, 'I'd like to take care of you. Christmas is coming.' 'No, no,' he said, 'I can't take that. I'm a supervisor!' So then I found the girl in the ladies room where she was just making a note of the fact that somebody had removed my 'Must wash hands' sign. 'Why don't you buy yourself a little something?' I said, offering her the money. 'No, no, that's OK,' she said. 'Don't worry, you'll pass!' And I did. It must be the new generation of health inspectors!"

If you don't pass, you may be called in for a hearing. If things aren't put right, you'll be closed.

Restaurants that are closed down are often run by inexperienced people with questionable standards of hygiene. They are often in old properties that have been infested for a century or more and suffer from erratic plumbing.

In some cities, retired health inspectors make a living by carrying out unofficial inspections of premises. For a small fee, they will go over your premises with great zeal—probably more than when they were acting in an official capacity! This will help keep you out of trouble.

Warning: Rivals and disgruntled ex-employees will sometimes exact revenge by anonymously complaining to the Health Department about some fictitious breach of hygiene regulations. The department must act on such complaints for legal reasons, even if they strongly suspect that they're frivolous or malicious. This may mean regular visits from inspectors who will take up the time of an owner or manager for an hour or more, depending on the size of the establishment. It doesn't happen often, but it happens.

Garbage and Sanitation

Restaurants generate vast amounts of garbage. Take a stroll down any busy city avenue around 11 P.M. and you'll see the minions dragging out great black plastic bags. Big restaurants and hotels often use huge metal containers that are specially designed to be loaded onto a truck.

Such is the quantity of restaurant garbage to be collected that the regular sanitation department cannot cope with it. This is where the private sanitation companies come in and, again, if you stroll along city streets late at night, you'll see the garbage trucks with private company names on the side.

Don't fuss about finding a suitable company. About three minutes after you sign the lease on your premises, a representative from the company that, by long-established custom, covers your area will arrive on your doorstep. The fees are about the same wherever you go. Once you've agreed to give the company your business (and you'll have to give it to someone!), you'll find you're protected from being bothered by a visiting sales rep from other companies. A discreet sticker in your front window will indicate to other sanitation folk that everything is taken care of. Private sanitation companies are renowned for their efficiency.

Typical Violations

The New York City Department of Health regularly releases lists of food establishments cited for violating the health code. In addition, it lists restaurants that were allowed to reopen after correcting earlier violations and those closed for having failed to do so. Here is a selection of violations.

Mouse droppings
Dead roaches and old food under coffee station
Flies and roaches in the kitchen
Old food on walls and floor
Wall tiles missing in bathroom
Material stored improperly
Debris under preparation table
Old food on potato slicer
Glass cracked in kitchen cabinet door
Food stored improperly
Rinse water too cool
Gas burner improperly placed under dishwashing sink
Kitchen door not secure against rodents
Holes in basement and kitchen walls
No protection certificate
No hairnets for food handlers
Some food too warm
Ice cream scoops not rinsed in running water
Old food on can opener
Grease on shelves
Seams in cutting board
Leaky pipes under sink
Boxes on floor
Improper detergent
Most recent inspection report not available
No guards on fluorescent lights over preparation area
No ventilation in bathroom
Dust on refrigerator fan guard
Ceiling tiles missing
Dishwashing equipment inadequate
Basement door not secure against rodents
Material under sewer line

Flies, grease, and dust on kitchen floor
Grease on work stove and filters
Food and grease on stove and behind equipment
No extermination report posted
Standing water on basement floor
Carbon dioxide tanks improperly secured
No guards on lights
Uncovered garbage
No backflow prevention in basement hose
Seams in table
No soap or towels in employees' bathroom
Faucet leaks in dishwashing sink
Foods kept at improper temperatures
Food uncovered in refrigerator
Live or dead mice in kitchen and storage areas

It's hard to quarrel with any of these being classified as violations. The "Grade 1" violations, which can get you into trouble, are immediately health threatening. When the inspectors find a place in an appalling state, they will naturally tend to throw the book at the owner. Then you will see violations such as "No chemical test kit." By law, restaurants must have, but not necessarily use, a little gadget that changes color when immersed in wash water, indicating the level of chlorine, detergent, and other chemicals. It is a farcical example of bureaucracy hitting reality, and nobody takes it very seriously unless they're looking for trouble. Another persnickety violation sometimes cited is material stored on unfinished wood.

Personal Hygiene

Restaurant workers are required by law to be clean, and the restaurant owner is required to provide them with the necessary supplies of soap, towels, and, for the kitchen staff, clean work clothes. Long hair is supposed to be pinned back in the dining room, and actually covered in the kitchen, though this requirement is often ignored.

Sometimes owners will have to be brutally rude in order to correct carelessness. Employees who come to work with sweaty, greasy hair, perhaps straight from their gym, just have to be straightened out. They may cry, but they will be wiser. Sometimes you have to be cruel to be kind. A manager at Maxim's in New York caused great consternation by insisting on a military-style parade at which shoes and fingernails were checked. As a result, at least *one* area of the restaurant was efficiently run, though what effect this had on business is not known.

Bad breath is rarely noticed—people don't get *that* close in restaurants—

but body odor will certainly offend diners. Some owners actually have a little book of rules which employees must read and sign. However, on the whole, personal hygiene isn't a problem in the restaurant business. But in a society bombarded for decades by advertisements for soap, toothpaste, and deodorants, when someone offends in this area, it really glares.

Getting someone to take care of his or her body odor is a problem for our well-scrubbed times. One method is to make deodorants available free to employees and make a great fuss of it so that, hopefully, everyone gets the message. But they might not. Most of us would rather attack a machine-gun post than inform someone that he or she smells, but sometimes it's the only way, other than the last sad recourse, which is to fire the offending person on some pretext—and this happens.

HEALTH OF RESTAURANT PERSONNEL

The health of restaurant workers is important. From a business standpoint, a healthy employee is a happier, more productive, and more dependable employee. From a personal standpoint, you will be a happier person if your employees are more to you than cogs in the wheels of industry.

Alcohol Abuse

Alcohol is often available in abundance. You will be doing your help no favors by allowing employees unlimited access to it. Many restaurateurs restrict their employees to a drink with their meal and perhaps another on completing their shift. But it is quite usual for alcohol to be forbidden completely. In larger establishments, there's little choice because the chance of generosity being abused is too high. Some employers wisely spell out the rules when they hire someone new. Drinking too much on the job is a very good way to get fired.

Alcoholism is common in the industry, particularly among bartenders. The mysteries of this problem have not yet been fully explained, but it's obvious that access to the stuff is likely to accelerate the process. Some bartenders are strict teetotalers, often as a result of revulsion at the sight of what alcohol does to some people, sometimes because they are rehabilitated alcoholics, and sometimes because a clear head enables them to steal more efficiently from customers and the house! Others like a drink in order to put themselves on the same level as their merry customers. This is a dubious reason, especially when the bartender is required to make change for the dining room as well as the bar. The owner-manager who takes regular little sips of wine throughout the day in order to maintain a gentle buzz is a well-known figure in the trade.

The revered chef or cook can usually do no wrong and often is allowed—even encouraged—to drink, sometimes with disastrous results. Chefs are the least supervised of all employees. One often has the impression that some owners live in fear of their chefs. Owners and managers often apply their executive zeal to every area of the restaurant except the kitchen. It's hot in there, perhaps they don't know much about cooking, and, anyway, it's more satisfying to check the cutlery or tell the bartender to get more sipsticks. Part of the chef's privilege stems from the fact that the chef is the hardest employee to replace in a restaurant. All other jobs can be filled quickly. But if you lose the chef who's gotten used to the restaurant and to you, there's a danger of having to endure a procession of incompetent agency temps who are often drunk when the arrive, let alone when they finish.

Owners will have to make their own rules on this subject and decide just how tolerant they're prepared to be. Sometimes you must turn a blind eye for the sake of a comparatively quiet life.

It will do no harm to repeat that bartenders can be held responsible for the actions of their drunken clients after they leave the premises. Restaurants must be insured against this risk. Some wicked cynics have opined that this is a splendid example of the law business and the insurance business getting together to feather their own nests.

Overwork

The job of waiting tables and tending bar is extremely demanding, mentally and physically. This perplexes some newcomers to the job. After all, the work isn't usually heavy, unless there are steps to be negotiated with heavy trays. And it isn't furiously busy for eight solid hours.

But the constant switching of attention from one person to another and from one task to another is mentally taxing. This is transformed into physical fatigue by a means the medical profession would like to understand but does not. The cumulative effect of unnatural hours also can be a strain. People who don't get to bed until three or four in the morning show and feel all the signs of jet lag, a depressed state of fatigue brought on by disruption of the *circadian rhythm,* commonly known as the body clock.

It's generally agreed that four shifts a week is plenty in restaurant work. A few owners insist on a four-shift week because they don't like their employees to become bad-tempered and snappy toward the end of their working week. It's common for owners to *order* their help to take a vacation as they approach burnout. Others, however, especially in French restaurants, insist on a six-day week, and they close on Sunday simply because this eliminates the brain-teasing task of organizing a work schedule!

Unfortunately, it's tough to tell an employee with a mortgage and three kids under 18 that the limit is four shifts a week. Employees may feel they need the wages and tips from a fifth or sixth day to make ends meet, no matter what this is doing to their health. Some restaurants enjoy a phenomenal initial success, and when everyone is making so much money, they will want to work every shift they can against the day when business levels off!

The evidence of overwork is easily discerned in some restaurant employees: that hangdog expression, that dreadful shuffle! Most people's memories of restaurant work are of sheer exhaustion. Long after the amusing little incidents have been forgotten, the ache will be recalled.

Again, this is an area where owners must make their own decisions. Some restaurants are very successful and keep everybody smiling by employing part-time students who are delighted to work only two or three shifts a week. With a good crew, there's always a fill-in available at short notice, but as an owner-manager, you must make sure you're covered, and if things get too disorganized, you may have to impose a stricter schedule. Employees usually respond to this situation in a positive and responsible manner. They are happy to have flexible hours so that they can pursue other interests. They won't want to add to your workload and stress by making you feel insecure.

Health Hazards

Occupational health hazards include hemorrhoids, varicose veins, sore feet, cuts, burns, and tension headaches. There is sometimes a lot of stress involved, and this is increased when employees are unhappy. Owners may not be in the business of promoting health and happiness, but they will do well to take such steps as they can to keep their employees as happy as is feasible, given the constraints of the working situation. It is not unknown for restaurant workers to move on to jobs that actually *pay less* to get out of an unhappy place or to escape uncongenial hours!

Restaurant workers should be encouraged to wear suitable shoes. How some waitresses get through six or eight hours on a stone floor in silly little slip-on pumps is perplexing. Thick soles and laces are highly recommended.

SAFETY

The most important aspect of safety in a restaurant is the risk of fire. Fire alarms, extinguishers, and other equipment such as asbestos blankets, are usually required by law. Emergency exits must be clearly marked, and the maximum occupancy must not be exceeded. Restaurant fires are not remote possibilities. They happen all the time. Fat is spilled, flames spread a little too far from the boiler, kitchen help are inattentive or drunk—the gamut of possibilities is endless.

From time to time, the story of the disaster at Boston's Coconut Grove in the 1940s is recycled in the press. It is a cautionary tale. Hundreds died in this restaurant fire.

Burns and cuts are an occupational hazard, too, so a first-aid kit is essential. Owners should watch for dangerous habits, such as improper use of cutting implements, slamming glasses into the ice instead of using the scoop, and so on.

Cleaners should be trained to make a great ceremony of mopping floors so that everyone knows it's been done. Too many people get hurt because the dry surface they crossed five minutes before is wet and slippery when they return, though there's no visible evidence of the work having been done. Ideally, a "Wet Floor" sign should be displayed. Spillage should be dried immediately.

Hundreds of people die every year from choking. The most common situation is one in which a person, who's often had a bit too much to drink, gets bored chewing a piece of steak and tries to swallow it as an alternative to inelegantly spitting it into a napkin. Not everyone has attended West Point and been taught that there should never be more in your mouth than can be disposed of with two chews and a swallow. Indeed, watching people eat in restaurants can be a nauseating sight, and there may be a germ of truth in that old joke about the purpose of music in restaurants being to drown out the sound of people slurping their soup. Some people make the food scene in the movie *Tom Jones* look rather tame!

The health department will happily supply posters describing the *Heimlich maneuver.* If one of your customers is choking and desires help, you may try administering the Heimlich maneuver. You should only try this with a conscious adult, and not with a child or pregnant woman. Stand behind the choking victim, make a fist with one hand, and place it thumb-side two finger-widths above the victim's navel. Place your other hand over the outside of the fist, and then administer quick inward and upward thrusts until the object obstructing breathing has been expelled. You might wish to consider paying for a first-aid course for some of your floor staff.

CHAPTER 10

PUBLIC RELATIONS

"Good wine needs no bush," runs the proverb, dating from the time when a vineyard would announce that its most recent vintage was for sale by displaying a bush on the roof. It's true that some of the very best restaurants rely solely upon word of mouth for their business, but they're often small, expensive, and appeal to such an élite group that they only need a small pool of customers in order to prosper. Once a restaurant achieves this level of distinction, it will not need to advertise or employ a PR firm. If a restaurant becomes an icon, or the sort of place that the media will be happy to mention *gratis* as "news," then all a restaurant has to do is maintain its standards and it will flourish. A few restaurants have no standards yet prosper. Every industry has its accidental and undeserved successes and there is nothing to be learned from them.

EXAGGERATED CLAIMS

It could be argued that the restaurant industry has brought its love-hate relationship with the public upon itself. Restaurants try to attract customers by exhorting them to believe that they'll get more for their money than just a meal. Worse, they promise things they can't hope to deliver consistently.

Claims are casually made in advertising that can't possibly be substantiated more than half the time, at best. Airlines try to sell their potential customers dreams and experiences, but what airline would dare run an advertisement that said, "Our planes *never* crash"? Again, one looks to the world of theater and movies for similar absurdity: "The perfect play" or "If you only see one movie this year."

One restaurant describes itself as "conducive to good conversation." Another runs a radio ad, delivered in a sepulchral voice better suited to lines like "unfortunately, there is no known cure for this disease," which informs the customer that its menu is so constructed as "not to allow you to make a mistake." As though such an event were the end of the world. The plenitude of feeble egos in the industry is such that the cry, "I *never* make a mistake!" is a common one.

One restaurant just bluntly promises in its advertising "Int'l celebrities." Could a customer who stayed all night and didn't see so much as a third cousin twice removed of Paris Hilton claim a refund? Jack Nicholson and Donald Trump can't be everywhere, every chef gets it wrong once in a while, reservation mistakes are made, and sometimes customers are going to have to accept the idea of dining with the unsmart set.

A very good line used by many restaurateurs is: "Sure, Jennifer Lopez and Clint Eastwood are in here all the time. But they don't like a fuss. If people started gaping, they'd leave, and they wouldn't come back. So we just give them that quiet table in the corner there, and treat them like regular folks."

Some restaurants plug the image of exclusivity, often to their eventual chagrin, as the public heartily agrees with them and doesn't dare darken their doors.

THE NEED TO ADVERTISE

Many restaurateurs will wish to advertise. It is significant that at a certain point of success, many stop advertising, and the sudden reappearance of blurbs for a restaurant that hasn't advertised in years may indicate a dropping off in business or an expansion of space that needs to be filled.

Viscount Leverhulme, founder of the mighty Unilever soap empire, once said, "I know half my advertising is wasted. Trouble is, I don't know which half!"

That was long before the age of market research, but even in the nineteenth century, surely, it must have been possible to draw some correlation between advertising and increased or unaffected sales. Today, no one needs to linger in doubt for long. It's perfectly simple. If you run an ad in a local paper or magazine and business increases, then your expenditure is worthwhile. If business doesn't improve, then you discontinue the ads. It's usually worth a try.

There are some strange anomalies, and it's interesting to observe which advertisements continue to run, on TV, radio, or in the press, and which are swiftly discontinued. A plug in a gossip column will usually generate business, whereas a straightforward ad may fall flat on its very expensive face. Unless you are in a busy location, with lots of casual passing trade, you are pretty well bound to advertise unless you intend to rely solely on word of mouth—and that's risky. If there's heavy local competition, if you must bring in customers from other neighborhoods, or if you're in the suburbs or country, it's very hard to see how you can let people know where you are and what you're offering unless you advertise. It isn't always an option. Sometimes it's a necessity.

Placing an Ad

Advertisements should clearly state location, phone number, business hours, credit card facilities, type of food, and sample prices. One of the most elegant advertising formats, though rarely used, is simply to display a sample check for two people with all the relevant information on it, placed on a background photo of the restaurant's dining room.

When you call the advertising departments of the illustrious organs of the press, there'll be no shortage of help. Selling advertising space is murderously competitive, and when *you* go to *them*, they love you. Never forget that advertising is the single most important source of revenue for the whole of the media industry. They need you. You might also consider local radio advertising, which isn't cheap but is believed by many to be extremely effective. The proof of the pudding is in the eating.

Arranging a mob murder outside your entrance might be a little difficult to engineer. But if you have an interesting location, or stereotypical décor (old Irish bar, bodega, art deco), you might be chosen as a movie set (à la New York's P.J. Clarke's in the movie *The Lost Weekend*) and this can make a restaurant a tremendous success. If the restaurant is closed while the shooting takes place, then a considerable fee can be charged. By tradition, the staff are compensated as though they'd worked a full shift and receive the equivalent of a day's pay with tips where applicable.

Using a Public Relations Firm

Publicity is a subbranch of advertising where you hire a company (very possibly consisting of one person, a dog, and an occasional bit of help from family and friends, but that's okay) to devise ways of bringing you and your restaurant to the public's notice.

One way is to persuade celebrities to attend your restaurant. You'll be amazed at how rich people will simply leap at the chance of a free dinner. If you decide to graciously allow your PR firm's nominees to come and sample the goods, be careful that the surliness of your staff, who may sense that a tip is in doubt, doesn't turn their experience into a bore. You might even promise to tip the staff yourself, should the movie star and her date turn out to be *stiffs* (i.e., fail to tip). Sometimes you just have to bite the bullet. No figures exist to prove or disprove the value of this kind of promotion, but the feeling is that it's very hit or miss.

PR people will also get you mentioned in gossip columns. Once in a while, they'll even get you on TV—very important and a tremendous boost for the old ego. Nothing sells quite as successfully as TV. It's an integral part of the consumer society—a fact sometimes overlooked as people agonize over whether or not it's really a good thing.

To find the PR person of your dreams, you should ask around and check the telephone books. If you see a nice article in the paper, you could ring up and ask who handled it. One contact leads to another. PR people can be retained quite cheaply at a monthly rate. For about $2,000 a month in New York, there are several firms that will take care of your affairs imaginatively and efficiently. Obviously, as one moves away from New York, prices come down.

Celebrity Power

If you can genuinely become the haunt of a celebrity or two, and if they are not deterred by publicity such as mentions in the columns, you can earn a useful cachet. Some restaurants kept a photographer on duty at all times to snap any celebs who should wander in. But at one cheap-and-cheerful blue jeans and hamburgers type of place, this policy backfired, as the very casualness that the celebs were seeking was eliminated by the presence of the photographer—and the gawkers that followed.

A few celebs like a restaurant where they are not stared at. Sometimes celebrities will ask not to be photographed. This is a strange psychology since media exposure is the oxygen of their success. Possibly, the star wants to demonstrate that he is a regular guy, unpretentious and private. Possibly, the star has been photographed all week and just wants to eat a meal in peace.

You pay your money and you take your choice. It's unfortunate that the most common cachet a restaurant builds is as a hangout for "characters"—artists, musicians, actors, and writers. These people may be interesting, but they're also notoriously and frequently broke. Be assured, the business community is the restaurateur's best friend.

In business terms, it makes sense to have people say, "Luigi's Tavern, that's the place where all the big names in fiber optics hang out." There are not known doctors' or airline pilots' hangouts (except, of course, near hospitals and airports), though many restaurateurs, when asked who frequents them, will look the world straight in the eye and say, "Pre-meds, pilots, stockbrokers, and beautiful young models, mostly."

A lot of people are so partied and blurbed-out these days that they're impervious to most of the devices favored by PR agencies (Oh no, not another hot-air balloon party!), and if you find you're paying out and seeing nothing for your money, you'll have to think again.

Special Deals

Especially in suburbia, the mom, pop, and kids market should never be ignored. Saturdays and Sundays are long days, and schools get out early during the week.

Gimmicks such as free drinks, happy hours, and "With this voucher one person eats free" sometimes work well, but they should be approached with caution. Any right-minded person should be suspicious of anything "free"" in this world, anyway.

However, special prices for "pre-theater" dinners, which will help you fill the restaurant in the early evening when diners are sometimes sparse, are a good idea. The customers feel they're getting good value, and you're looking at customers instead of empty chairs. Also, you may coax customers to trade up to more expensive evenings.

Your most important PR person is *you*. By taking an interest in neighborhood affairs or joining the local Chamber of Commerce, you can often do yourself some good, and others, too. You need to be a bit steely sometimes, as there will be no shortage of people coming around, asking you to donate to all sorts of worthy causes, and some of them will be of dubious validity. Your ever-ready restaurateur's smile will be taken by some as a sign of weakness. If you feel your customers will enjoy the attention of panhandlers, and you're content to let them work the crowd you attract, then let them in, by all means!

THE FOOD CRITICS

Lord Byron, whose appetites for other areas of life unfortunately left little time for gourmandise, observed:

> A man must serve his time in every trade
> save censure—critics are ready-made.

Almost every branch of consumerism now has its professional commentators and its critics. The restaurant industry is no exception. There are several newspaper and magazine reporters who've turned the assignment of restaurant critic into a highly paid profession. To be fair, some critics really know their stuff. They've actually been in the trenches and know when to forgive and make allowances. The best food critics don't file their report until they—or their appointed agents—have been to a restaurant three times.

A good write-up from a major critic can *make* a restaurant. It's hard to prove, but there are enough people with time and money on their hands that curiosity alone will bring people in. The pattern most commonly observed is one where business booms for up to six or eight months after a rave review, at which point your fashionableness abruptly wanes. It is at this point that maximum effort needs to be made. The business is vulnerable to whim. Several restaurants are reviewed every week, and competition is constant.

Reviews and Their Consequences

Many restaurateurs are expert at the game of "in and out." They raise money quickly, move in, and get the doors open in record time. They have enough contacts to get some good reviews, and then, at the height of fame, they sell. There's a luck element here, and it isn't nearly as easy to do as it is to write about it. A group of three men, all old hands at the restaurant game, opened a yuppie paradise, a sort of brasserie, in the mid-1990s on New York's Upper West Side. The restaurant was an instant success, largely as the result of a quite accidental visit and subsequent glowing report from a major critic. They almost immediately opened a similar operation at what proved to be a disastrous location. Imagine their sighs of relief when a large corporation offered to buy them out on the strength of the first successful operation. They could afford to absorb the less glittering performance of the second. After less than 18 months of work, the partners were each $300,000 richer, and they stayed on to operate the business.

Restaurateurs froth at the mouth with rage when they're ill-served by critics. One state restaurant association moved to pass a bill whereby restaurant critics would be licensed. This bill was spurred by a restaurateur who claimed a 20 percent loss of business due to an inaccurate report. Another restaurateur, who had lost two of his four stars to a well-known critic, sympathized. He opined that a bad review could break a new restaurant. A critic replied, "Restaurateurs and chefs should be licensed. Beyond meeting health department regulations, all any idiot has to do to open a restaurant is spend some money."

Again, the emphasis is on food, when, in reality, there are scores of reasons for going to restaurants, none of which are connected with sustenance and nourishment. Business people go to restaurants to talk business; lovers, or would-be lovers, to talk about love, old pals to reminisce; lonelies to enjoy the presence of others; jazz lovers to listen to jazz; and countless others to observe some human ritual, such as graduation, marriage, birth, death, retirement, or success. A sales rep about to clinch a deal, a swain about to propose, or a writer discussing a novel won't care whether they're eating pâte de foie gras or donkey liver, as long as it's edible. They'll be much more impressed by prompt service and a table where they can think, as opposed to one where any conversation is drowned out by the neigh-bores. But food is the only tangible material given, so it's the inevitable focus.

The restaurateur who has a cosy corner location, ample parking, a loud jukebox in one room, laser-beam-curtain silence in another, Chateaubriand at $20, famous habitués, attractive, smiling, multilingual servers, quirk-accommodating kitchen staff, and an intensely moving view has nothing to fear from critics. Others may pay them some mind.

A young (intensely talented) chef in one restaurant—where the "lobster cocktail" was a whole lobster at $40 a piece—perused an order which had come down the tube from the dining room one night and, after a moment's reflection, called the maitre d'. "Say, Joe," he said, "Check out Table five, will ya? This looks to me like a food critic's order. I'm gonna be real careful with this one!"

One restaurant chain procured a picture of a food critic, posted it on the notice board, and instructed its employees that on no account was he to be served. Some critics send friends, for that reason.

In order to understand just what the critical eye is looking for, what's noticed and what isn't, restaurateurs will do well to read critics' write-ups carefully. Surprisingly, few of them ever refer to the "rick factor" or the great convenience of the location. They seem to prefer showing off their knowledge of what *carpaccio* should really be like, and whether *trompe l'oeil* decor is really appropriate to the *je ne sais quoi*. You may sniff the unmistakable odor of humbug, but these people are very influential.

Although they comment on service ("the kitchen was very slow") and ambiance ("a romantic, dark-cornered room"), they concentrate inevitably on food. Often, they apply gourmet standards that are irrelevant to the operation. When they really get going, they say things like: "The raw beef was cut thin as Brussels lace. A tracery of light and fruity olive oil gleamed on the surface. There were a few flakes of parmesan, and then down came a blizzard of white truffle on top of the *carpaccio con tartufi*. It was, explained the man at the inappropriately named Ristorante L'Assassasino in Milan, only simple *cucina del paese*, but it was the closest I wish to come to paradise on this earth."

Bribes

Is it possible to bribe food critics? Of course it is. But it has to be subtle, done through friends, and it isn't cheap.

The bribery of chefs and food and beverage managers is so common that such payments have even been held up in law as legitimate business expenses. Whether your friendly IRS would take a similar view of payments to critics is open to conjecture.

DEALING WITH THE PUBLIC

A tragic byproduct of the restaurant industry, or indeed any people business, is the sheer hatred of humanity engendered in some people who must deal with the public. You see dead eyes set in the glum faces of otherwise attractive servers, and you endure their gratuitous rudeness. From their expressions, you might deduce that their only child has just been ripped from their breast, when in fact all that's happened is that the people at Table 7 have politely asked if they could move to Table 8.

To be blunt, a major reason for all of this is the low caliber of many restaurant employees and the poor management qualities of some owners. Most people shudder at the prospect of having anything to do with the public. Small children want to be engine drivers, pilots, doctors, nurses, soldiers, actresses, writers, and teachers—not hostesses, bartenders, or maitre d's. Inevitably stress and threat, real or imagined, will reveal personality defects and character weaknesses.

An awful lot of workers in the restaurant business should never be allowed to have anything to do with people. Some feel that this is the age of the repressed, inward-looking loner, happier with electronic stimulus of one kind or another than with the ordinary give and take between people. The dwindling interest in marriage, and the divorce figures, may substantiate this to an extent. Whatever the sociological reasons for it may be, the fact remains that the industry contains an unusual number of misfits. Nevertheless, everybody has to get through the day.

MANAGEMENT QUALITIES

Management qualities involve several factors:

Leadership
Relationships with people
Stability and stress tolerance
Planning and organization
Spoken communication
Written communication
Motivation
Flexibility
Decisiveness
Problem analysis
Initiative
Originality

You may have fun deciding to what degree some of your favorite restaurant people have mastered these talents. Don't be surprised by low scores. The following statements demonstrate these management skills:

Leadership: "Let's all pull together, enjoy the job and make money . . ."

Relationships with people: "You don't seem too happy. Is there something you want to get off your chest?"

Stability and stress tolerance: "We're a person short and there are lots of reservations. But we can do it!" "Monday and Thursday were disasters. But the week's average will be okay if we get a busy weekend."

Planning and organization: "We won't need three waiters on Tuesdays. Two will be fine."

Spoken communication: "Terrible weather, isn't it? How about a nice fireside table?"

Written communication: "Dear Mr. Smith: I'm so glad you enjoyed your lunch here. I take pleasure in sending you our new spring menu for your perusal. With so many of your colleagues interested in fishing, I'm sure you'll be amused to hear that world champion Sigi Galoomi has become a regular customer . . . "

Motivation: What the military call "the will to win." First cousin of self-confidence. "The more thoughtful and efficient we are the easier the work will be."

Flexibility: "If it rains, don't bother putting out the umbrellas on the patio." "If people keep asking for Fuzzy Navels, then make them."

Decisiveness: "That new waitress is terrible. We'll have to let her go."

Problem analysis: "Why do I get these regular complaints from the front station? What's wrong? How can I speed up service?"

Initiative and originality: "There isn't a brunch place for miles. Let's do it. And let's give them a really exciting omelet!"

EMPLOYEE QUALITIES

The talent most required of restaurant employees is simply *speed*, not an ability to relate to fellow members of the human race, though this quality will often be welcomed. If you can carry six salads along your arm, or make three piña coladas in 20 seconds flat, the fact that you communicate in small words and grunts won't matter much. Admittedly, good looks can sometimes help, and, indeed, many restaurants have little else to offer apart from their good-looking floor staff.

That much-vaunted quality, leadership, is difficult to apply to employees who, on the whole, would rather be doing something else, thank you, but happen to need a job. In the days when navies were crewed by men who had been rounded up by press gangs, it was the threat of being flogged or keelhauled that made the navy work, not the winning charm of the officers. Now that threat is countered by the stronger threat of a ruinous lawsuit, so employees have to find other means of incentive.

PEOPLE STRESS (OR COMBAT FATIGUE)

The restaurant business is very much a people business, and thus has a heavy built-in stress factor. Although you simply cannot run a business like a platoon or a scout troop, the happier the crew and the customer-employee relationships, the less stress will be generated. A wise restaurateur seeks opportunities to reduce stress as assiduously as areas of greater profit.

A small number of precious people actually enjoy the chi-chi aspect of restaurant theater. "Alphonse knows my favorite table, Luigi knows exactly how I like my linguini," and all that guff. They live for pipsqueak fuss about nothing. Some restaurateurs are better equipped to deal with these monsters than others.

The tragedy is that 9 out of 10 restaurant customers—who may or may not sometimes fall into a special psychological group—are harmless, undemanding, and nice. They may not always be wildly exciting, but they are rarely obnoxious. Yet the nice often pay the price for the nasty at the hands of incompetent restaurant personnel.

Some might wisely observe that, even if only 1 in 10 people is unpleasant, if you deal with a hundred people a day, that's plenty! But it does seem that a lot of tension and stress is generated unnecessarily. It's an unfortunate aspect of American life that rudeness commands an absurd amount of respect. Behavior that would be laughed out of court in most European countries reduces many Americans to terror, and worse, the rude take it out on the undeserving.

Everyone in the business has to live with all this. The public is to the restaurateur what the land is to the farmer or the sea to the fisherman. There's no choice but to dig and trawl. Basically, the majority of your customers are more interested in themselves and their conversations and appetites than they are in the detail of your restaurant. If their restaurant experience is satisfactory in this regard, they'll retain a nice memory of the place, whether the food was good or not.

GREETING

If you employ a maitre d', host, or hostess—and remember that this might well be *your* spot, at least initially—you should remember that the worst thing that can happen to an entering customer is to be ignored.

We live in the age of the plastic smile. It doesn't have to warm your eyes; it just has to signal your general agreeableness. "Hi, folks, how are you doing?" is as good a greeting as any, unless you immediately sense (as a good restaurateur should) that "Good evening, sir," will go down better.

It doesn't matter much. A smile and a greeting are what you should deliver. Everyone should keep an eye on the door, and all your employees should be trained to take a general and overall interest in what's going on in the joint, not just in their own corner. The waitress nearest the door and the bartender can greet customers if the host is seating people in the rear of the restaurant.

This isn't only good manners. It's good marketing. The greeting should never be, "Sorry, I don't have a table right now," unless it would be patently dishonest to pretend otherwise. Rather it should be, "I should have something breaking in 10 minutes."

You should instill in your employees the conviction that they must convey an atmosphere of welcome. Customers will not respond well on slow nights to the intimation that they're the party poopers, the ones who interrupted an exciting game of Name the Show Stopper by their untimely entry and willingness to spend money.

The bottom line is bad training. When things go wrong it's usually the owner's fault.

RESERVATIONS

It gives a nice professional air when your telephone is answered politely and smartly, and reservations are taken accurately and cheerfully. "We shall look forward to seeing you!" should be the watchword. "Serious" restaurants, with few tables and high prices, can lose money by keeping tables for someone important, who fails to show, while turning away casual drop-ins.

It's nice to be able to check your book and gauge how busy you're going to be. It makes you feel like you're running a grown-up business.

If, because of its informality and speed of turnover, there's no great point in making reservations at your restaurant, this fact must be admitted in a positive manner. Many restaurants don't take reservations except for large parties. This information shouldn't be given in a negative way ("Sorry, we don't take reservations except for large parties.") but positively: "No need for reservations if you're only two—unless you want a special table." This usually indicates that the turnover is steady and nobody should have to wait more than 5 or 10 minutes. A surly, "We don't take reservations" is a negative attitude often heard, it turns away would-be paying customers. It's just as easy to say, "We don't take reservations, but how many are you? Two? For eight o'clock? There might be a five-minute wait, but don't worry."

For large parties of six or more, it makes sense to take reservations, because this may entail moving together several small tables.

The old restaurant con trick of backing people up at the bar so they can spend a little more money while awaiting their tables works fine when you really *can* seat the people in a reasonable amount of time and get those names ticked off the list in your pocket. Only time and practice will enable you to gauge turnover speed. It isn't always easy, particularly as yet another cross the restaurateur has to bear is that the whole world wants to lunch at 12.30 and dine at 8 P.M..

Those unfortunates who, after drinking far too many cocktails than they really like at the bar, finally realize that they aren't going to get a table before their appetites have disappeared and their conversation dried up anyway, will never return to your restaurant. Not only that, but they'll bad mouth it all over town.

Strangely enough, some will be intrigued by the hard-to-get ploy. They actually feel triumphant at being allowed, at last, to spend their money at your table. But this doesn't work with everybody. And even if they do collapse with relief onto a table, the memory of the long wait, and the lurking certainty that someone who arrived after them got a table *before* them, will linger. As already discussed, this does happen when a maitre d' has been bribed.

Again, time and practice will enable you to read the situation accurately and ensure maximum satisfaction to yourself and your customers. If you ever sense dissatisfaction in customers a polite and concerned inquiry will usually help. "Is everything fine and dandy?" will work better than "Is there a problem?"

DRESS CODES

If you are bold enough to stipulate a dress code, which usually means jacket and tie for the men, or no blue jeans, then you immediately kiss the bulk of casual diners good-bye before you have even said hello. Although the desire to strike a blow for old-fashioned standards may be laudable, it isn't very practical in an age when everyone seems to be competing to be "more laid-back than thou."

Some restaurants have a little brass plate that proclaims rather pathetically, "Proper Attire Required." This gives the host a small edge. If unsuitable people appear, the host can sometimes turn them away on the grounds that they're not properly dressed. Some restaurants keep a supply of ties and jackets to accommodate those would-be customers who aren't wearing either.

But what do you do when the movie star of the month and her glamorous crowd in their white Reeboks, designer jeans, and designer stubble suddenly appear at your door, creating waves of excitement? What you usually do is make an exception, which can be dangerous. "Oh, sure, you can go to Rick's in blue jeans—if you happen to be a star!" your neighborhood customers may grumble.

One of the many stock restaurant situations, repeated time after time, features an earnest hostess obeying orders to the letter and refusing to admit Mick Jagger or Dustin Hoffman or some other worthy because he's not properly dressed. The owner, lurking in the back, will react with horror. A moment of glory is about to escape! She runs down the block beseechingly, "Come back, all is forgiven!" But the celeb is bound for one of his usual haunts where he knows he won't be turned away.

Another scenario features the owner arriving and seeing a customer improperly dressed. "Go tell that man he has to have a tie," he orders his host bravely, not having the courage to do it himself. The host tries to make his point and is told to bleep off. Suddenly, it's all *his* fault, and the boss still hasn't found the courage to approach the customer directly.

If your restaurant proclaims itself in every way as exclusive and expensive, then you may be able to insist on a dress code, and, indeed, if your service and decor are up to it, your clients may enjoy the theatricality of dressing up. But in an age when many men sit at restaurant tables with their hats on, drinking beer straight from the bottle, you are on dangerous ground trying to educate them. Most cruise lines, once famous for requiring diners to dress for dinner, have abandoned the custom. For the majority, even a clip-on bow-tie is too much to ask. Billy Graham caused sighs of relief when he told the world that it was okay to be rich. But America got the message long ago that it was okay to be a slob. The chewing gum industry is an $800 million industry that employs a lot of people. Somebody out there has got to chew that gum, dammit. And if some of it (usually the green variety) shows up under your table-tops, you just have to be grateful they put it where no one would sit on it.

DRESSING THE ROOM

This means putting attractive people where they will be seen to advantage by other customers as they arrive. You put the well-dressed, good-looking yuppies at a nice table near the door and the grumpy old pair who snarl at each other and complain the whole time in the back. Sometimes they resent it. You then have to explain that the star table is reserved. They'll then watch it like a hawk and very possibly query whether the people who eventually get the table really had a reservation.

Some celebs are wise to this one and will strenuously insist on being in the back. There are two or three restaurants in New York, however, where the reverse is the case, and the same old faces sit at the same old tables in mutual admiration day after day. The maitre d' who awards the power table can always be sure of a good tip. When restaurants are featured in movies, people will call from all over the world months ahead of time to reserve the table where, for example, Candy Frabazoni and Hank Strutt finally plighted their troth in the

Oscar-winning movie *A Vulnerable Girl*. The table that Gene Hackman had to observe while standing in the cold in *The French Connection* was similarly sought after.

Visitors from outer space after the nuclear holocaust will open time capsules and marvel at the beauty of the human race as displayed in current glossy magazines. In your early days as a new restaurant, you may be so glad to have a customer that you make a fuss of people who are *banned* from every other restaurant in the neighborhood on account of their loudness, their falling-down drunkenness, their coughing, their spluttering and spitting, or whatever. So don't be *too* generous with your bonhomie. It may come back to haunt you.

But one day, when things are going a little better, you'll see a girl whisper in her escort's ear, while studiously not looking in the direction of the table where dear old Joe is swishing his dental plate in a glass of water. They'll leave, with vague assurances of "Catch you another time." You may judge this to be the time when dear old Joe, and perhaps a few other worthies, should be "eighty-sixed"—they may no longer be served. A greedy restaurateur who is happy to serve anybody is to be despised.

The law is a little woolly on this subject, but roughly, no restaurant is obliged to serve anyone if they have good reason not to. And if a person clearly shows signs of having drunk too much alcohol, then a restaurant can be penalized for serving them—if they later cause an accident, for instance.

AVOIDING NASTY SITUATIONS

Customers are right 90 percent of the time. You might as well indulge their whims—you may have promised to in your advertising. But unpleasantness of one kind or another does sometimes occur. Sometimes it's more practical to just look the other way and ride out the storm, rather than escalate the incident by asserting your authority. It isn't satisfying, and you may despise yourself a bit, but you can congratulate yourself on having happily resolved ominous events if (1) other customers haven't been disturbed, (2) there has been no violence, and (3) you've suffered no serious loss of revenue.

Apart from the people who just aren't very pleasant to look at or listen to, you may be unlucky enough to attract a group of mean nasties intent on causing trouble. They'll insult your staff, make noise, swear at the tops of their voices, and even throw things around. It must be stressed that this doesn't happen very often, but it happens.

One much-despised owner spied troublemakers in his restaurant whose behavior had once required calling the police. Instead of asking them to leave, he merely warned the staff to make sure they got the money. They didn't get the money, and one of the staff was assaulted. Before the police arrived, the troublemakers had run away, full of fun.

Experience has shown that the best thing to do is to wait for nasties to leave, then hope your headache soon subsides and your entire staff doesn't walk out. Your aim must be at all times to minimize the risk of physical violence. Going over to the table and asking a bunch of guys to behave themselves may be just the trigger they've been hoping for. There's no point in being brave and putting your fists up to a man with a gun or a knife. Sometimes you may have a happy arrangement with your local police station, and the pressing of a button will bring help. But this should be a last resort. If a precinct starts getting too much aggro from a restaurant, it might take a close interest in it, which will not be to the place's benefit. Some restaurants employ armed doormen—often moonlighting cops. This is an excellent idea, and if you're trying to build a club, it gives members a nice sense of security. Sometimes you can combine host and bouncer in one person, where a tall, strong man also has a congenial manner. Nowadays, quite harmless-looking people are often martial arts experts, and if this talent exists among your staff, it's a useful bonus. But a strenuous effort to avoid trouble is your best bet.

ROBBERY

If you take the view that robbery only happens to other people, then you need read no further. Some restaurants are robbed regularly. In the classic instance at Mortimer's, where all the customers were made to lie on the floor at gunpoint by crooks in tuxedos while the cash register was emptied, the late Glenn Birnbaum laconically remarked afterwards, "Thank God the Aga Khan had just left!"

The standard drill when approached with a gun or other weapon is to hand over the cash calmly and immediately. You then pray the criminal won't kill you anyway, either for fun or to prevent you from identifying him or her later in the event of arrest.

Criminals mark places and stake them out. They observe routines. At 11 A.M. every day the guy with the glasses comes out of the restaurant with a canvas bag in his hand and goes to the bank. What can be in that bag, the criminal wonders?

Knowing this, casually hired employees will sometimes stage a phony mugging and hand the bag with the money to a pal. "It was horrible, he had this big gun. I just gave him the money." "You did the right thing, son." Similarly, many a delivery person has been known to pocket the money for the four deluxe dinners to go and disappear into the night. This will be relieved rather heart-sinkingly when an irate customer rings up and says "I ordered four jumbo deluxe pizzas half an hour ago. Where the . . ."

Whenever two or three people come in purposefully, and one stays at the door while another strides briskly to the back, the third one is probably the one who will announce the stick-up. Some of these incidents make hilarious telling after the event—when everyone survives, that is. Sometimes situations grow and grow, with no one aware of what's happening, then suddenly violence erupts. Your best defense is awareness, which is at its lowest when you're very busy. That's when trouble strikes.

SECURITY

On closing, all money should be deposited in a hidden safe. The cash register should be left open, so that if there's a break-in, they may get some money but they won't break your register. Some of the new computerized registers cost more than $3,000. You may be insured, but it'll take a day to replace your register, and your premium may go up. The less money there is in the register during working hours, the less there is to steal. In supermarkets, you'll sometimes see the supervisor going to the registers and taking away the large amounts of cash that will have accumulated. Some restaurants have the same discipline.

The two most vulnerable times of day are opening and closing, when there are few people present and the staff is preoccupied with setting up or closing down. Late at night, when only the bartender and a manager are present, it's a sound precaution to lock the door and only admit known faces—neighborhood regulars looking for a nightcap, or the porter coming in to clean.

CHAPTER 11

EMPLOYEES

A standard moan among restaurateurs is "It's hard to find good people." It's true that the restaurant industry has special problems that dissuade many from working in it. There's steady attrition because many restaurant workers are students, or in the process of putting together some project, and at a certain point, they'll quit. Many people get to a stage where they can no longer take the contact with a demanding public, a demanding owner, and co-workers who really defy belief in their horrific attitude to life and their comrades but who are adored by the boss. Add to this the unsociable hours and the physically tiring nature of the work, and you can still see what people are grumbling about. The best solution to the general stress is plenty of time off.

In New York and Los Angeles, it's easy to recruit people from among the struggling would-be show-biz types. In other cities, you are looking for students and part-timers with a few reliable pros. In the country you'll have to cast your net wide, not only for customers but for employees, too.

Very few restaurateurs exercise any imagination in this area. Many seem to have an unhappy knack for hiring the wrong people all the time, so that they're faced with a running disaster with harder work for the other employees.

Hiring the chef, as has been discussed, is a crucial business and a separate exercise. They almost invariably call their own shots and carve out their own empires. Kitchen staff can usually be recruited satisfactorily from agencies. You apply trial and error until you get reasonable people. Cloakroom attendants are usually either part-timers or work for the person to whom you've leased your cloakroom concession.

It's the rank and file of servers and bartenders who present the most problems. There is always a certain turnover among them, and you constantly have to be on the lookout for suitable replacements. They are often poorly motivated, which is a shame because they really are important in the running of a restaurant—they talk to your customers; they're your PR people and sales reps all in one.

If you can arrange it, it's a good idea to have a limit of four shifts a week for your floor staff. That way they won't get too tired, fed up, and snappy. As has been discussed elsewhere, this may not always yield a satisfactory wage for a parent with responsibilities, but it's often a godsend for younger, single people. They don't feel enslaved, and they have time to do their own thing.

FINDING HELP

Agencies are the single worst source of restaurant employees. There are happy exceptions, but they're few and far between. Sometimes restaurant personnel walk into jobs that are like paradise. But most often, agencies supply people for the seedy places way off the beaten track, with quirky suspicious owners and regular cantankerous customers. Such places often deliberately mitigate against the employee's chances of earning decent tips and are *happy* to accept a constant turnover of personnel. Life being what it is, that often doesn't prevent such restaurants from being highly successful places of business.

The single best method of recruitment is word of mouth through friends. Just as a waiter and waitress start their job hunt by ringing everyone they ever knew in the business, so must the restaurateur.

Newspaper advertising is okay from a restaurateur's point of view, but it is a notorious nightmare from the employee's point of view. Experienced people simply don't read the Help Wanted columns. Why not? Because when you put on your best bib and tucker and trundle halfway across the country for your interview, you find there are 30 people ahead of you, and more coming in. The interviewer will take an intelligent interest in the first two or three people she sees, then the faces blur.

Sometimes the interviewer is really looking for sexual opportunity, not employees. The restaurant industry isn't the only one in which the job often has been allocated even before the sham interviews start. Why the farce continues is anybody's guess. Sometimes there are internal political reasons for making it look as though a fair effort has been made to recruit external talent. One well-known and well-hated owner of a famous New York restaurant has a running ad in the newspaper and interviews every Monday. What he's looking for is anybody's guess, but it isn't employees. He never hires.

You get a positive *attitude* from people who've just finished a training course, but often they haven't yet acquired the confidence and zip necessary for a busy, successful restaurant. If they learn fast, and you have the patience to train them, this can work out very well indeed.

Since personal manner and looks are so very important in the business, a good way of finding a job is simply to make the rounds. Every restaurateur becomes accustomed to people walking in and asking for jobs. Some are embarrassed, and it doesn't work for them. Some jobseekers are pretty ridiculous, slouching in, chewing gum, not even bothering to take off their sunglasses or remove their earphones, and not able to cite references and experience. Perhaps they believe the main talent is to be cool.

If someone with reasonable vibes comes in, you should simply note their name and telephone number. Before long you'll have a large pool of potential employees. When you call one up, he or she may have found a job, in which case you have to call the next one on the list. Unless you're convinced that they're competent, perhaps from having had a word with a former employer, you ask them to come in and *trail*—that is, observe the method of service you use and see how they adjust to it. After an hour of having them around, you should have a good idea of how they'll shape up. If you have an old, established crew, it will be important that the trailer fit in, so you might seek confirmation from your senior server or bartender. Some owners pay their trailers, some don't. They never get any tips, but they should at least get a bite to eat.

One well-organized restaurateur has a little booklet printed in which the rules of employment are spelled out very simply—not in an intimidating military style. When someone nice comes in looking for a job, he gives them the booklet and asks them to take it home and read it. If they feel they'll be happy, and there is a position open, they can talk a bit more on the phone, then trail, and so on. It may sound a bit elaborate, but it eliminates the embarrassment of having to correct people's dress or whatever.

There's no shortage of ancient wisdom to help you lead your staff to glory and get the best out of them. Start as you mean to go on, man should be led as though you led him not, and so on. You should at least try to be fair in your dealing, although it won't always be possible. Remember, no man can serve two masters, but many of us have to try. And also, masters who make themselves like honey are eaten by the flies.

THE EMPLOYEES' POINT OF VIEW

Here's what a happy server had to say:

> I really like this job. The boss knows his stuff and is always cheerful. His wife comes in with the kids sometimes. She doesn't give a damn; in fact, sometimes she wants to gossip when we have work to do! If we need to change the schedule, it's okay as long as we give plenty of notice and make sure our shift is covered. The only thing he hates is when people are late because that gives him one more thing to worry about. He does have his private quirks. Why shouldn't he? It's his movie. But he always makes his point with a smile, so nobody ever gets upset. There's every reason to be prompt, because then you can sit down and have a bite to eat at leisure. You can also have a snack when you go off, if you like, and a drink or two, although he has fired one or two people for overdoing it. He's no patsy! The law doesn't require him to let us have that, but he doesn't mind. We don't have union membership, but we're paid union rates and he gives two weeks paid vacation after a year, even to part-timers like me—I only work four shifts. Boy, it's enough. That place gets so damn busy! But Al, the chef, is a real nice guy. I think he writes plays or something, and he's always talking about

writing a cookbook, although we never seem to see much progress. If you make a mistake, as often as not he'll pick up on it and put it straight. If there's something funny about an order, he'll just ask you politely what it's all about. The bartenders are great. They make the drinks promptly for the floor and get the change right. Also, they get our credit card tips right. We don't mind giving them 5 percent of our tips at the end of the shift. The menu's simple, and there's always plenty of cutlery and linen, so there's no need to get tense about trivia. The money averages out very well.

But an unhappy server said:

What is it with this restaurant business? Why does every customer and employee turn into an idiot the minute they walk through the door? What kind of homes could they possibly have come from to talk the way they do? It's gotta be the last bastion of slavery, the way people talk to you. I've hit three chefs, a maitre d', and a customer in my time. Every one of them deserved it. I wish I'd hit them harder. One was in the hospital for two weeks. The customer sent his beef back three times, saying he wanted it cut in a certain way that I couldn't explain to the Chinese chef. Apparently, he was a valued customer. Of course, I blew the job, but who cares? And the money isn't that good unless you're at an expensive place, and then there's so much regimentation it's a pain in the neck. I just don't know who I hate most: the customers, the chefs, or the owners. Some chefs are animals, the way they scream and shout and cause trouble deliberately. You don't meet a lot of nice ones. But owners are the real weirdoes. They are like curios from a psychiatrist's museum, most of them. And even when they're successful, most of them seem to be miserable. Some of their wives are pretty good numbers, too. There was one who used to walk in with a face like stone, look around the place for a moment, then walk up to her husband, who was terrified of her, and say, "There's a fork missing on Table 3." She would announce it like it was the end of the world. He was such a jerk he put up with it. If I could just get off the booze and get some money together, I wouldn't mind opening my own place.

A happy bartender said:

I love the job. The money's great and the crazy hours suit me fine because I'm a night person. The job is my social life, too. I often meet people who are customers on my own time. We go to ballgames and stuff. And yes, I meet a lot of girls. Bartenders are like priests and doctors. Women find us fascinating. Of course, the main thing with me is I'm a people person. The chef's a great guy and gives me anything I want. I give the busboy a few bucks and he does all the donkey-work, brings up the beer and ice, and cleans up, too.

An unhappy bartender said:

Alcoholics disgust me. I like a drink, but when you find yourself pouring whole bottles of hard liquor into people, and they still appear to be sober, it's scary. The regulars are the worst. They won't stop talking. They're lonely, and it's easy to understand why. Who the heck could put up with them if they didn't have to? Sometimes I give them a couple of drops of [an over-the-counter medicine]. They start throwing up in 10 minutes and go home. The tips are good, but you always feel you earned them. Sometimes with an alcoholic you can give him the same check twice and he won't notice. A lot of bar-tenders try to screw up the waiters so that the boss and the man-agers will concentrate on them and stay away from the bar. I don't do that myself. I need their tips! The element of violence always lurks. I've been attacked, had drinks thrown at me and stuff. Fortu-nately, the people were too drunk to be dangerous, but you might not always be lucky. It's no good saying you shouldn't serve them. How do you know how many drinks they had before they get to your place? They'll often fool you, come in nice and proper, and order a drink very politely. Then, wham, the noise starts, they start bothering the other customers, whatever. You have to throw them out. Then you never know when they might come back with three friends and a shotgun. Owners very rarely back you up in these situa-tions. They often create them. I once saw the owner's wife break step and run the length of a bar to drag in some guy. "Dinner for one?" she cooed. Anyone could see he was a bum except her, of course. I thought about letting him have his fun, then leaving it to her to get him out on the principle of, "You let him in. You get him out." But I thought better of it and whispered confidentially that the drinks were $6 each, and there was this great bar just round the corner where . . . Sometimes you have to do everybody's thinking for them, and it's exhausting. By the time I finish my five-shift week, I'm exhausted, physically and mentally. It takes me one full day to recover. The next day I'm okay, but not exactly full of energy. Then, just as I feel recuperated, it's time to go back to work. I've got to get out of this.

DRUGS

As blissful as you want your working conditions to be, you should be alert to employees who seem just a little bit too happy, especially bartenders. They may be on drugs. Worse, they may be selling drugs on your premises, and that's big trouble. If you're suspicious, you should fire them.

Some employers require recruits to undergo a drugs test. This is demeaning to many and will hardly promote a positive attitude. Far better if the owner is able to exercise worldly judgment and have confidence in his or her choices.

MANAGERS

If good help generally is hard to find, good managers are *really* hard to find. If they know enough to be good managers, there's only a short space of time between achieving that happy status and owning their own restaurant. It can be a dreadful job, involving everything from bussing tables to answering the phone, with a taxed salary but no tips, and only the dubious privileges of not having to wear a uniform and being able to eat from the menu to cheer it up. Some managers work out a few kickbacks here and there, but it isn't common in a medium-sized restaurant.

You can get the best out of managers by explaining their duties and not making them the culprit for everything that goes wrong. The major complaint among managers is the long hours often required of them. A generous salary may not soothe if the employee realizes that the hourly rate is $3. Specified shift hours are the best solution.

They often irritate other staff members by embarking on a power trip, especially if they have the right to hire and fire. This is usually a bad thing, but it's your movie, and it may suit your purposes sometimes.

The area of personnel is the one in which your ideals can be put to best use.

Although some miserable restaurants make fortunes, happy restaurants are much more likely to prosper. Besides, since you have to spend so much time at work, why not make it as congenial as possible? The author makes no apology for the occasionally harrowing descriptions of just what goes on in the wonderful world of restaurants. None of them are even faintly exaggerated. Forewarned is forearmed. If you can keep your head when all about you are losing theirs, the restaurant business will make you rich and give you a rewarding and occasionally amusing career.

How can you be a successful restaurateur and still stay sane and happy? The answer seems to be the ability to detach. Take those weekends off, and insist on those vacations. As one very successful restaurateur used to say to his staff, "When I leave, I don't want to be called for any reason whatsoever, unless it's a matter of life and death."

Let's face it, there's a little bit of Rick in all of us!

CHAPTER 12

MAKING YOUR DECISION

There is a certain hollowness about deciding whether one is wise in becoming a restaurateur. Very few people do the ideal thing with their lives. The world is full of square pegs in round holes. Some are shunted into careers in which they have no particular interest because they have no particular interest in anything, but are still faced with the necessity of earning a living. Doctors' sons and daughters don't exactly *drift* into medicine. They simply never entertain the idea of doing anything else with their lives, and the same is true of many military people. Many restaurateurs are also born to the business. Although sometimes efficient, they rarely have enough personality to do more than a mundane job; however, the mundane can be just as profitable as the brilliant.

THE "UP" SIDE

These are the attractions of the restaurant business: The abilities and talents it requires are not very esoteric. You don't have to charm people into laying down their lives for you with hypnotic words. You just have to say, "How're you? You're lookin' good," to your regular customers. If you're a soldier and made lance corporal, you have enough management talent to succeed. Even if you've failed at everything else you ever did in your life, you still have an even chance of making it. Apart from local health department requirements, no other qualifications are needed to be a restaurateur. If you call yourself a restaurateur, then that's what you are!

It's a freer free-for-all than most businesses. The business is in a constant state of expansion, but there's been a shakeout at the lower end of the market due to crazy real estate spirals. Profits can be enormous. There's always the chance of being bought out at a considerable profit.

People who are well adjusted with a reasonably optimistic view of life and possessed of education, intelligence, humor, and a healthy skepticism can do very well in the business and stay sane. They are the sort of people who would do well at whatever they attempted, but, clearly, running your own show is preferable even to a long, safe career with IBM.

It's hard to disdain the perks of owning a restaurant. There are obvious advantages that the criminal element exploits, such as the ease with which accounts can be adjusted. There is also the simple bonus of being able to eat, drink, and entertain on the firm, to say nothing of the deductible expenses for cars and so on.

But beyond the ordinary, practical day-to-day considerations of a restaurateur's life, there's a deeper satisfaction in creating a success.

It's small wonder that so many people from the creative side of life, perhaps having been disappointed in their first careers, find total satisfaction in the restaurant business. That's because their greatest source of energy, their creative urge, is used all the time in different situations. Not only do they have to plan menus and decor, but they have to reach compromises on the personality level, too, like a diplomat.

The respect of your employees and customers can be very heartwarming. The sight of familiar faces who've become regulars at your establishment is a daily confirmation that you are doing something right. This, of course, is one of the major satisfactions of all service industries.

If you get it right, you've succeeded in inventing your own world, and there can be no greater satisfaction than that.

THE "DOWN" SIDE

This is a convenient point at which to begin the list of disadvantages of being a restaurateur. The luxury of being able to carve out your own leisure time may be elusive and hollow. When the cat's away, the mice will play. Unless you are a good manager with the good fortune to have recruited a first-class staff, then you must accept that the business will only run efficiently when you are there in person. Even when you go to the back for a bite to eat yourself, the service on the station out of sight from you will slack off, and customers will start looking around to find the waiter who has become immersed in a game of Show Business Trivia.

The tetchy, pale sight of the restaurateur who has taken the weekend off and decided just to look into the joint on the way home is a cliché of the trade. All worst possible fears are almost invariably confirmed. The lights are set too high or too low. On the front station, a couple with the helpless look of shipwrecked sailors are looking around, holding their menus in a way that suggests they're ready to order—and have been for some time. The music will be blaring heavy metal, not soft rock. Suzie will have her hair down, and Ira will be wearing blue jeans, in contradiction of house rules. There'll be smoke in the kitchen, and some of it will be percolating into the dining room. There'll be an unusual number of empty beer bottles in the kitchen garbage. Juliette will be polishing off a lobster and a glass of Chardonnay at the back table, heavily involved in a rehash of some movie or other. Where's Pete? He went home early "because there wasn't much business." If the reading on the cash register is a disappointing one, then it will be clear that the nagging fears that have blighted the owner's skiing, sailing, or sunbathing were totally justified. One more step on the road to ulcerdom, bankruptcy, severe depression, divorce, or massive coronary.

Until and unless the near-perfect manager and staff are found, the restaurateur will have to spend far more than eight hours a day on the job. A bitter cliché of the business is that people who are capable of doing a job unsupervised will be in business for themselves anyway, not working for others. This, though clearly an exaggeration, is the general belief. But a leader who cannot success-fully delegate whether in business, sport, or battle is less likely to succeed.

True, being in charge isn't nearly as tiring as being in a subservient role, but it still requires a lot of hours of concentration. This concentration is of a curiously harrowing kind, because a restaurateur's day is one of constant in-terruption. Very few people seem to have the self-discipline to finish one thing at a time or to resist phone calls. It's hard to discipline yourself to finish the funny story you're telling a regular customer if you see that the daily special is being served without tomatoes and with the wrong fork. Customers in restau-rants often get headaches from all the interruptions while they're trying to talk to the boss or the bartender.

An apt metaphor may be borrowed from the technical world. As was re-vealed after a bizarre air accident in Hawaii, aircraft "age" more through the number of take-offs and landings they make than by the miles they fly. Thus, an aircraft used for island hopping and comparatively young in terms of miles flown may be comparatively old in terms of take-offs and landings when com-pared, say, with a plane used mainly on the London–New York run. Planes there-fore become prone to metal fatigue at an earlier stage than might normally be expected.

Some restaurateurs, however, appear to thrive on the constant switching of attention. They're only happy when problem after problem is brought to their attention to be solved brilliantly with a Solomon-like pronouncement that produces gasps of admiration to their faces, but much groaning and rolling of eyes when their backs are turned.

All restaurant staff are oppressed by the strange antisocial hours. True, for people who are trying to do something else with their lives, this can sometimes be a tremendous advantage, especially if they're fortunate enough to be able to work part-time. But, especially for a married person who enjoys family life, the long absences from home can be a strain, often barely compensated by the cash rewards of a flourishing business. The routine of returning exhausted (stinking of kitchen smoke), with no appetite for dinner at home and falling asleep in front of the TV news, isn't very good for some people, though there are undoubtedly some who hardly notice. Really late hours, such as those worked by some cocktail and supper club servers, do induce a form of jet lag, and lead to depression.

The availability of alcohol, and the subliminal effect of seeing so many people drinking it, can be a trap for those whose drinking habits, if any, are not already formed. Alcoholism is common in the business and often ruins it. Dealing with the public can be a strain. There's a curious tradition, expounded by Hollywood, that it's all right to be rude to restaurant personnel. Every yuppie worth the name knows how to put down that "snotty" maitre d', despite the fact that most maitre d's these days are more likely to err on the side of overfamiliarity than arrogance. When the hero knocks over the fruit bowl and the apples and oranges roll, to the consternation of the comically distressed waiter, it's considered funny. Some people take a delight in ordering finicky things that cause a disproportionate amount of stress backstage. Maybe their companions are impressed by the masterly approach. You can't kick out everyone you don't like, least of all in the beginning. When you're turning away business, then you can start to be a little more selective.

Any sensible person can see that you should be able to organize yourself around all this. If that's your reaction, then there's hope for you.

It may well be that the unhappy restaurateur laughing on the outside, crying on the inside, is a cliché easily accepted because he or she is somehow more prominent than the happy kind. If you are wise, you will make the demonstration of that point one of your major goals.

Getting away from the mystical, the major practical reasons for avoiding the restaurant business are the large capital investment required, the chance of losing every penny, and heavy competition in many urban areas. The brave fellow with $200,000 raised from several sources is in competition with multimillion-dollar corporations that will snap up any suitable location that comes on the market and accept a low return on their money for a longer period than the average individual could possibly afford. Against this may be balanced the more aggressive search efforts of the individual. A sharp, probing eye will often see more than that of a large corporation nodding over its interdepartmental memos and endless meetings. But there is never a shortage of people looking for suitable premises, and the brokers are every bit as aggressive in their sales tactics as other real estate operators.

QUESTIONS BEFORE DECIDING TO GO INTO BUSINESS

Every pilot has a checklist. A businessman needs one, too. Here's a suggested list of pertinent questions.

Am I confident of being able to realize a significant profit within a reasonable time—say, a year?

Do I have enough money to cover all financial outgoings for a reasonable period?

Is the location under consideration at least workable? That is, are

there no serious negative factors whatsoever, either now or loom-
ing on the horizon, due to local zoning plans or building?

Have I enough general experience of every aspect of the business to
feel completely confident?

Can I keep a healthy amount of leisure time, in spite of the rigorous
demands of the setting-up phase?

Can I hire and fire people?

Can I get good, or at least acceptable, help?

Do I know enough about people and life to choose winners over losers?

Am I going to be able to get along with the customers?

What does my spouse think about it all?

Is my partner reliable? How well do we know each other?

What's the competition locally?

Is there a real, natural demand for my restaurant?

If not, am I going to have to bring customers in from other areas by
various means?

Supposing everything about the agreed format turns out to be wrong,
am I flexible enough to change quickly?

UP AND RUNNING

While the day you open is exciting, your *real* opening day comes when you
decide to proceed into business. You must really force the pace to open those
doors and get some money coming in. This can be an exhilarating and creative
phase, and, if you're successful, you'll look back on with surprising pleasure.

There is a lot to be said for inviting friends for a *shakedown* evening so that
you can see whether or not things work as planned. Rome wasn't built in a day.
Some restaurants are an instant success, but most take time to develop. You
should neither rejoice when you have a good day nor wail when you have a
bad one. When you begin to spy growth patterns and familiar faces among the
customers, you may permit yourself some self-congratulation.

At the end of every week you should ask yourself three questions:

Did I attract enough customers to meet the average number of
covers I need to operate at a profit?

Did the vast majority of my customers get what they ordered
promptly and to their apparent satisfaction?

Did they pay?

If you can answer yes to these questions — you're in business!

EATING OUT FOR RESTAURATEURS

Some restaurateurs complain that they're so steeped in the business they no longer enjoy going to other restaurants. When they do, their critical faculties are too sharp, and instead of relaxing they find themselves examining every detail of the place.

This is part of the price you pay. But especially when you are thinking of opening your first restaurant, you have so much to learn that you would be extremely foolish to ignore what's happening in the restaurants available for your discreet inspection. The education is free—apart from what you spend in the place, of course. It can also be fun.

Being only human, your first and main focus will be on the food, because that's the easiest thing to criticize. Your main interest here should be the scope of the menu, the flexibility of the kitchen, and interesting dishes—especially high-profit items, of which a good example is the delicious *Moules Marinières* (mussels in wine). Mussels, like squid, are practically a giveaway item in the fish market, but will bring in gourmets by the score if they're done well. Some dishes are a bit fussy to do in a domestic kitchen, but easy to cope with in a restaurant kitchen, where the quantity sold justifies the effort.

If you are taking a properly professional approach, however, you will not wallow in criticism of the food. You should be noting the servers' system, determining why some servers are better than others, and asking yourself what you might do to improve the service or in any way to make the restaurant more attractive.

Once you start looking you may be amazed by what you see. Has the boss noticed the dirty sneakers that waitress is wearing? (Oh, that's his wife.) Are two inch-square pats of butter really enough for two people, with six rolls in the breadbasket?

Things you never thought about before will catch your eye, and ear. The hostess who says "Hi, folks, how ya doin'?" with the cheerfulness of a well-trained parrot every three minutes, the waiter who glances stagily at his watch to note the time he took your order, and the bartender who ignores your second attempt to get his attention will irritate. You should ask yourself whether the restaurant is making maximum use of available space. Has space been carved out for just one more deuce, while the kitchen is like a space capsule?

Naturally, you should also try to see the reasons for the restaurant's success. Location? Is it a landmark? Relentless advertising? Consistent high quality? Good value? Amusing gimmicks? An owner with personality? Appeal to a special area of the market? What's the rent? Does the restaurateur own the building? Is it just a flagship, not intended to make a profit? If there are any apparent disadvantages, how have they been overcome?

You should put yourself in the shoes of an insecure but determined social climber in the Victorian age who's been invited to a smart party and who notices every nuance of pronunciation, phrase, and dress with a cold, Proustian eye.

There is no such thing as a *Good Food Guide to the United States*. England has one, and France has its famous *Michelin* guide. But there are reliable restaurant guides for all the major cities, such as the Zagat Survey and the Mobile Travel Guide. Most states have a restaurant association that will be happy to provide lists.

It's always wise to reconnoiter a restaurant you propose to visit, either by looking it up in the local guide or going to it, looking in on some pretext, and examining the menu. It's not unknown for people to ring up restaurants and say, "How much is dinner for two with a bottle of wine?" Most often the response is the true, but weak and not very constructive, reply, "It depends on what you have." A better reply is, "We have a varied menu—and our coq au vin is world-famous. If you had a couple of martinis, two shrimp cocktails, two coq au vins, two lemon tarts, two coffees, and a bottle of Beaujolais, your bill would be $100, excluding gratuity." Or, perhaps better because quicker, "Our entrees average $12, and our wine list goes from $12 to $50. The average bill for dinner for two here is $90."

What you find yourself noticing consciously is noticed by other customers subconsciously, and will implant a general impression in the mind, resulting in either a positive or a negative impression. "Let's go to Cocky Leekie's," says one diner. "Yes—great idea. I like that place," says the friend. Or, with a frown, "Let's find some place else." "Why?" "Oh, I don't know."

Few people are sufficiently articulate to be able to say *why* they dislike or like anything. They'll often say they didn't enjoy the food when really they mean something quite different. But most people know what they themselves like.

Restaurateurs should always be on the lookout for new ideas, and regular reconnaissance of other restaurants will not be time wasted. Some restaurants are wildly expensive. You should check them out before reserving your table. If you really can't afford it, perhaps you can have a drink at the bar. If our fabled friend the haughty maitre d' asks if he can help, you can always say you're meeting Doctor Weinstein or Henry Kissinger, but you're not sure whose name the reservation is under.

Like writers, few restaurateurs are ever reluctant to steal the ideas of others. Although keeping up with trends is clearly important, one should not be entirely a slave of fashion. Sometimes restaurateurs invent whole new approaches to the industry that find a successful market. As Jimmy Goldsmith, the late successful financier, observed, "If you spot the bandwagon, it's too late. You've got to *be* the bandwagon."

GLOSSARY

WINE TERMS

Acidity. The tang or bite of a wine. The right amount of acidity is necessary to all wines—without enough, a wine is weak and uninteresting; with too much, it is sharp and unpalatable.

Alcohol content. Most table wines have an alcoholic content of between 9 percent and 13 percent. In lower percentages are many Moselles; in the higher, Chateauneuf-du-Pape or Barolo. White wines with higher alcohol content tend to be heavier-bodied; they can lack the delicacy of those with lower proof. Wines with low alcohol levels are meant to be consumed as soon as possible, since they do not age well.

Alsatian. Fragrant, dry, usually white wines from an ancient French province bordering the Rhine, made from the Gewurztraminer or the Riesling grapes. Alsatian wines are usually shipped in green *flutes*—tall, slender bottles like those used in the nearby Moselle Valley of Germany.

Amontillado. The most popular of the Spanish sherries, with an unmistakably nutty bouquet and flavor. The unique flavor is said to mimic that of the wines of Montilla, in the province of Cordoba; hence, the name. An aged fino. Dry.

Aroma. This key term, when combined with bouquet, refers to the *nose,* or the composite of all the fragrances found in a wine. A wine's aroma specifically describes the varietal character of the grape—it is, very simply, its unique grape smell.

Austere. This is a flattering term, and it refers to the crispness and dryness of a white wine. Initially, an austere wine is too sharp for pleasurable consumption; connoisseurs use the phrase to indicate a positive aging potential. It may seem *tight* or *closed* *in,* but in a positive way that shows restraint and subtlety. Especially used in conjunction with Chablis Grand Cru and other leading white Burgundies.

Balance. This is the harmony of the basic elements of a wine—its dryness, acidity, aroma, bouquet, body, and finish. In a good wine, one element must complement the other; none should be overpowering; a sweet wine should have acidity. For instance, a wine with a light, soft bouquet should have a relatively light body; a wine with an intense bouquet should have a more substantial body.

Bardolino. A very light Italian red wine, almost a rosé in color, produced near the town of the same name close by Verona in northeastern Italy. This wine is usually drunk quite young (one to three years old) and has a charming, fruity flavor.

Barolo. Considered one of the great European wines, this powerful, deep-colored Italian red is produced in Piedmonte, the Italian province closest to France. Sometimes heavily sedimented (even after three years in a cask), this wine is stored standing up, in Burgundy bottles.

Beaujolais. An uncomplicated yet fruity, full-bodied red wine produced in Burgundy, north of Lyon. It is usually served cool—at cellar temperature—and drunk very young, sometimes as early as mid-November of the harvest year.

Beaune. Distinctive, graceful Burgundies, both red and white (but more often the former) from the southern half of the Côte d' Or. Beaune is the town that divides the "Côte de Nuit" from the "Côte de Beaune."

Blanc de Blancs. Literally, a white wine made from white grapes. Traditionally used only to identify a distinctively made champagne (usually produced from a blend of white and black grapes or just the black grape, Pinot Noir), the term is now frequently employed by the white grape vintners of some of the secondary wine areas (such as Provence or the Loire Valley) to add prestige to their labels. Refers to a champagne made exclusively from Chardonnay.

Body. The body of the wine is the feel of it on the tongue—its roundness and its texture upon the palate.

Bordeaux. Elegant and aesthetic red and white wines, produced in the Province of Gironde, surrounding the port city of Bordeaux, in southwestern France. Shipped in the traditional straight-sided, high-shouldered bottle. Also, the largest of the great wine areas of France.

Bouquet. The bouquet differs from the aroma in that it refers to the scent of the wine, derived not from the grapes but from the process of aging, cooperage, and fermentation. Usually not used when referring to young wines.

Burgundy. Rich and sensual red and white produced in the ancient Duchy of Burgundy southeast of Paris and always shipped in a distinctive, slope-shouldered bottle. Since Burgundies are often made from a blend of wines from a given area, the shipper's reputation is critical. Reds are always made from Pinot Noir, whites from Chardonnay.

Cabernet Sauvignon. A strong red wine from the grape of the same name, produced in the North coast counties of California. This long-lived, slow-maturing red wine is considered by many wine experts to be America's finest; it is often compared to the red wine of Medoc, in which the Cabernet Sauvignon grape also predominates.

Chablis. A dry white Burgundy, produced near the town of the same name southeast of Paris. Made exclusively from the Chardonnay grape, it has a pale straw color and a distinctive flinty flavor. The name has been widely appropriated in the United States and other wine-producing countries to describe a variety of white wines using some proportion of Chardonnay grapes.

Chambertin. One of the truly great red Burgundies, produced in very limited quantity in the northern portion of the Côte d'Or. This rich, long-lasting (and frequently expensive) wine has a long tradition dating back to 600 A.D. It was a favorite of both Napoleon and Alexandre Dumas.

Champagne. Generally, a sparkling wine. In France, a specific dry, white sparkling wine, made by a special process (using only certain varieties of grape) in a legally limited area east of Paris. The unique shape of its bottle and cork have evolved from the fermenting process, which involves the removal of accumulated sediment from the neck of the overturned bottle.

Chewy. Chewy is used to describe a good, full body for red wines. Once you have a chewy wine in your mouth, it feels good, rich, and full-bodied. A Pinot Noir should be chewy, as should vintage port and Barolo.

Chianti. The best known Italian red wine. Produced in Tuscany, south of Florence. Refreshing and piquant, Chianti is made from a wide variety of grapes and bottled in squat flasks that, until recently, were usually wrapped in straw. Even its better grades, bottled in bordeaux-shaped bottles, are usually drunk young.

Color. A good wine's color should be clear and even throughout, exhibiting no cloudiness whatsoever. A dry white wine should have a greenish-yellow tint, and the sweeter types a golden hue. An oxidized white wine has a brown tinge, a bad sign, and is said to have *maderized*. Inferior corks usually cause this, it won't be a problem with the new plastic "corks." Red wine should be purplish when young, acquiring brownish tones as it ages. Pelure d'oignon, or onion skin, refers to the thin, light-brown band that is visible around the rim of healthy, vintage wines. Beware of any wine that has a muddy appearance.

Côte de Nuits. Red wines from the northern half of the celebrated Burgundian Côte d'Or. The better Côte de Nuits wines are known by their commune or vineyard names (Chambertin, Musigny, Nuits-Saint-Georges, etc.)

Côte du Rhône. The general name of the red wines bottled in burgundy-style bottles that are produced on both banks of the Rhône River between Lyon and Avignon. These wines are deep red and somewhat heady; the best are known by their vineyard names, such as Côte Rôtie, Hermitage, and Chateauneuf-du-Pape.

Dryness. Very simply, this is the absence of the taste of sweetness. Some popular dry wines are Chablis, Muscadet, Verdicchio, and Graves.

Finesse. This word refers to the breeding or style of a wine. It is a very subjective term that attempts to combine the qualities of body, color, and finish. Finesse is that highly elusive element that is found in a superior wine, as opposed to very good or excellent ones.

Finish. The sensation that lingers after the wine is swallowed is the *finish*. If a wine finishes well, there is no unusual aftertaste, no unpleasant bitterness, no excess of acidity. What remains, instead, is a general feeling of warmth in the mouth. A good finish is a difficult characteristic to achieve.

Flowery. A flowery wine has a soft, floral nose that can remind one of violets, roses, or spring mountain flowers. Northern Italian wines often have very definite flowery qualities, as do several outstanding German Moselles.

Foxy. This interesting term has nothing to do with foxes—it refers to the pungent grape flavor of native American grapes. New York State Concord wines—made from the species *vitis labrusca*—are foxy and remind one of jelly or jam.

Fruity. The element of the wine's nose reminiscent of the fresh fruits. This element is found in most young wines, such as those of Beaujolais. New York State wines, especially the foxy types, are very fruity.

Graves. Red and white Bordeaux from the gravelly districts on the left bank of the Garonne south of the city of Bordeaux. The whites are generally better known (the reds usually carry the chateau name); they run dry to medium sweet, pale yellow in color, with a distinctive metallic character.

Legs. The legs of the wine—or the paths the wine forms when it runs from the robe or rim of a glass—tells something about its body. The faster the legs drop and the thicker they are, the more body the wine has. Fairly uniform spacing of the legs also indicates wines of fuller body.

Macon. A solid, bourgeois wine produced north and west of the town of the same name on the River Saone in southern Burgundy. Macon reds are sound and pleasant, but less fruity and not as firm as a good neighboring area Beaujolais. Macon whites are frequently known by their district, most notably, Pouilly Fuissé.

Marsala. The best-known of Italy's fortified wines, produced in the town of the same name on the west coast of Sicily. Sherry-like in texture, and usually served as an aperitif, Marsala is deep brown and vaguely molasses-like in flavor.

Meursault. The dry, nutty white Burgundy produced around the towns of Meursault and Volnay in the Côte de Beaune. Green-gold in color, Meursault is full-bodied, yet tangy; it is among the best white Burgundies.

Montrachet. The classic white Burgundy, Montrachet is probably the most celebrated and expensive dry white wine of France. Produced in the Côte de Beaune, solely from the Chardonnay grape, Montrachet is pale gold, with a hint of green, and has a soft, yet extraordinary bouquet and flavor.

Moulin-a-Vent. The best red wine of the Beaujolais area north of Lyon. Deep colored and sturdy, Moulin-a-Vent improves in the bottle for 8 to 10 years (for longer than the two- to three-year life of a typical Beaujolais).

Muscadet. The charming and delicious light white wine of the lower Loire Valley. Muscadet has a small flavor when compared to white Burgundies, but it is pleasantly dry and fruity.

Musigny. Recognized as one of the best Côte d'Or red Burgundies, Musigny has a haunting delicacy that increases in the drinking. Only slightly lighter than a Chambertin, it is often thought of as being *feminine*.

Nuits-St.-Georges. A fine red Burgundy produced around the town of the same name on the southern end of the Côte de Nuits. Nuits-St.-Georges is a generous, soft, well-balanced red; as a Côte de Nuits red, it has a longer life and deeper color than the reds of the Côte de Beaune to the south.

Orvieto. An Italian light white wine produced near the town of the same name in central Italy, between Florence and Rome. Orvieto's vineyards actually mingle with trees and crops. This typically sweet wine is shipped in a truncated, Chianti-like straw-covered flask.

Pinot Chardonnay. Probably the best white table wine made in the United States today, Pinot Chardonnay is produced primarily in the California North Coast counties. The name is derived from the grape that produces the best white Burgundies and champagnes of France.

Pomerol. One of the most attractive red Bordeaux, from a single township of the same name 25 miles east of Bordeaux. Recognized as the gentlest yet richest of Bordeaux reds, Pomerol matures quickly (typically in 5 years versus the 8 to 10 of a Medoc) and possesses a lustrous red color, a velvety texture, and great depth of flavor.

Pouilly Fuissé. The superior dry white Burgundy produced exclusively from the Chardonnay grape in the area west of Macon in southern burgundy.

Pouilly Fumé. A dry, white upper Loire Valley wine made most frequently from the Sauvignon blanc grape. In its best years, it is smoky, green and spicy, with a metallic fragrance. It should be consumed a year or two after bottling.

Rosé. The French word for pink, the color of these wines. The best rosés are not made from a blend of red and white wines, but rather from black (red wine) grapes whose skins have been removed from the processing shortly after fermentation begins.

Saint-Emilion. The red wines from the most productive of the Bordeaux districts. The chateau-bottled vintages rank with the best wines of the Medoc; in general, St. Emilions are simpler. They are rich, sturdy, warm, and generous, maturing less quickly than the neighboring Pomerol but faster than the wines of the Medoc.

Saint-Julien. The smooth and gentle red Bordeaux of the middle and least productive of the Medoc districts. A St. Julien is said to be fuller than a Margaux, more fragrant than a St. Estephe, and to mature faster than a Pauillac.

Sediment. The better wines, usually those that improve with age, deposit a sediment. In white wines it emerges as crystals at the bottom of the bottle, in red it may take the form of a thick crust or appear as large brown flakes. Sediment is a positive sign—an aged wine with no sediment is suspect. If the wine is served properly in a restaurant, the sediment should remain in the bottle and not get into your glass. You can ensure this by asking the wine steward to decant any bottle of fine wine for you. This means simply pouring the wine off the sediment in the bottle and into a wide-mouth decanter for breathing.

Sherry. The most popular aperitif, Sherry is a gold-to-amber-colored fortified wine, traditionally produced and shipped from the district surrounding the town of Jerez de la Frontera in southeastern Spain.

Soave. Probably the best-known Italian white wine, Soave is produced in northern Italy, east of Verona, in the foothills of the Alps. It is a plain, dry, pale white wine with a distinctly fresh flavor. It is shipped in tall green "Alsatian" bottles and should be drunk before it is three years old.

Tavel. One of the oldest and most famous rosé wines, produced in the Rhône River valley north of Avignon. Orange-pink in color, with a strong flavor and bouquet. Tavel rosés are usually drunk when less than two years old.

Valpolicella. The distinctive northern Italian red, produced northeast of Verona, in the foothills of the Alps. A beautiful cherry red in color, Valpolicella has a sweet bouquet, a young, fruity, light flavor, and smooth body. Typically bottled after 18 months in wood, it improves in the bottle, but should be drunk before it is five years old.

Vanilla. This is the flavor imparted to wine from the substance vanillin, which is present in the oak in which the wine is stored. A young Bordeaux or Burgundy has a milk vanilla flavor derived from the barrel. The younger the barrel, the more apparent the vanilla flavor will be. The influence of this element is most noticeable in the better California Chardonnays.

Verdicchio. One of the most popular Italian white wines, produced in central Italy near the Adriatic part of Ancona. Verdicchio is dry and pale but full flavor; it is shipped in a distinctive, slender vase-like bottle.

Vermouth. A fortified white wine, flavored with herbs, bark, roots, seeds, and spices. Usually served as an aperitif or cocktail ingredient, vermouth comes in either of two varieties: French—pale in color and quite dry; usually aged three to four years before shipping; Italian—dark red and sweet, usually aged two years before shipping. Both French and Italian vermouths are made in both France and Italy.

Volnay. A Côte de Beaune red burgundy produced in the districts of Volnay and Meursault. (Whites from both districts carry the Meursault name.) Volnay is a particularly soft and delicate red, with a round texture and a fragrant aftertaste.

Vouvray. The best-known of the Touraine wines, produced on the north bank of the Loire River, near Tours. One of the longest-lived white wines, Vouvray can be, in turn, depending on weather and vinting, bone-dry and fruity, rich and Rhine-like, or pale and sparkling.

MENU VOCABULARY

Italian

Abbacchio. Baby lamb.

Abbacchi Arrosto. Roast baby lamb.

Abruzzese, all'. Made with red peppers, in the style of Abruzzi.

Adriatico, dell'. Marinated in oil and lemon juice and then grilled over a wood or charcoal fire.

Agnello all Arrabbiata. Literally, "angry lamb," lamb cooked over a high flame.

Agnello in Guazzetto. Lamb stewed in an egg and cheese broth.

Al Dente. Literally, "to the tooth," refers to pasta that is cooked firm.

all'Amatriciana. Prepared with onion, ham, and tomatoes; literally means in the style of the women of Amatrice, a town in the Abruzzi.

Ancbellini. Ravioli stuffed with meat and fried.

Antipasti di Pesce. Appetizers made with fish.

Antipasto. Hors d'oeuvres; appetizer.

Aragosta. Lobster.

Arista. Roast pork loin.

Asparagi alla Fiorentina. Asparagus tossed in butter with Parmesan cheese and topped with fried eggs.

Baccalao. Salt cod.

Bagna Cauda. Hot dip for vegetables flavored with anchovies.

Besciamella. White sauce made with milk, flour, and butter.

Ben Cotto. Well-done, to describe meat.

Biscotti all Anice. Anise-flavored cookies.

Biscuit Tortoni. Dessert made of egg whites, whipped cream, and topped with chopped almonds.

Bistecca. Beef steak.

Bocconcini. Small pieces of veal cooked in white wine sauce, also called *olivette* because the pieces are the size of olives.

Bollito Misto. Mixed boiled meat, served with a tomato or pepper sauce; what goes into the mix depends on the chef and the region of Italy he or she is from; it may include veal, tongue, sausage, calf's head, beef brisket.

Bolognese, alla. With a sauce of meat, milk, and tomatoes.

Braciola. Roast pork meat stuffed with pine nuts, raisins, and almond paste; a Sicilian specialty.

Broccoli al Formaggio. Broccoli with melted cheese sauce.

Broccoli all' Agro. Broccoli served with olive oil and lemon juice.

Brodette. Fish stew.

Brushetta. Garlic bread.

Bucatini. Long noodles.

Cacciatore, al. Prepared in the style of a hunter; with mushrooms, herbs, shallots, tomatoes, wine, etc.

Caffe Cappuccino. Coffee with whipped cream topping and cinnamon flavor.

Calamari. Squid.

Calzone. Pastry crust with ham and cheese filling.

Campagnola. In the country style; usually with onions and tomatoes.

Cannelloni. Meat-stuffed rolls of pasta, baked.

Cannelloni alla Catanese. Baked pasta stuffed with meat with a sauce of tomatoes and pecorino cheese.

Cannoli. Custard-filled pastry in tubular shape with candied fruits and rum flavoring, powdered sugar sprinkled on top.

Cantarelle. Chanterelle mushrooms.

Capelli d'Angelo. Very thin noodle, literally means *angel hair.*

Caponata. Mixture of eggplant, onions, and tomatoes.

Carciofi alia Romana. Artichokes cooked with mint leaves and cloves of garlic.

Carpaccio. Sliced raw steak in a vinaigrette sauce.

Carrettiera, alla. With basil and tomatoes.

Casalinga. Homemade.

Cassata. Ice cream with candied fruits.

Cervella Dorte alia Milanese. Calves' brains seasoned with salt and pepper, dipped in egg and bread crumbs and fried in butter.

Cipolline in Agrodolce. Sweet and sour onions.

Conchiglie. Pasta shells.

Coscia di Agnello Arrosto. Roast leg of lamb.

Cotolette alia Milanese. Veal chops that have been breaded and cooked in butter.

Cotolette alia Valdostana. Veal or pork chop with ham and fontina cheese.

Cotolette di Agnello. Lamb chop.

Cotolette di Vitello. Veal chop.

Cotolettine. Baby lamb chops.

Cotoletta. Sice of veal, turkey, or beef or some vegetables like eggplant.

Cotoletta di Tacchino alla Bolognese. Turkey breasts cooked with ham, Parmesan cheese, and truffles.

Cozze alla Marinara. Mussels cooked in white wine with garlic and parsley.

Crema al Mascarpone. Cream dessert made with a soft, yellowish cheese.

Crespelle alla Fiorentina. spinach-filled pancake.

Crocchette di Pollo. Chicken croquettes.

Crostacei. Shellfish.

Crostini. Rounds of bread, sprinkled with cheese and then toasted or bread fried in garlic oil.

Crostini in brodo. Croutons in broth.

Cuscinetti di Vitello. Veal roast.

Del Giorno. Of the day, equivalent to the French *du jour*.

Della Casa. Of the house; in the style of that particular restaurant.

Dolci Assortiti. Assorted sweets.

Fagiano. Pheasant.

Fagioli in Salsa. Cold bean salad.

Fegatelli di Maiale con la Rete. Pork liver wrapped in caul fat and then broiled.

Fegato alla Veneziana. Thinly sliced liver and onions cooked in olive oil; a very popular dish.

Fettuccine. Ribbon-shaped noodle.

Fettuccine al Burro. Noodles with melted butter.

Fettuccine Alfredo. Immensely popular dish in New York, noodles tossed with butter, cream, and Parmesan cheese; the creation of a Roman chef named Alfredo.

Fettucine al Sugo di Vongole Bianco. Noodles with a white clam sauce.

Fiamma, alla. Served flaming, like the French *flambé*.

Filetto di Sogliola. Filet of sole.

Filetto di Bue. Filet of beef.

Filetto di Sogliola alla Parmigiana. Filet of sole baked with Parmesan cheese.

Finocchio al Burro. Fennel cooked in butter.

Finocchio. Fennel; a green, celery-like vegetable with a slight taste of anise.

Fiorentina, alla. Beefsteak rubbed with crushed peppercorns and broiled over charcoal.

Fonduta. A fondue made with fontina cheese and truffles.

Formaggio Grattugiato. Grated cheese.

Fra Diavolo. With a spicy, tomato-based sauce; in the style of the devil.

Frittata al Formaggio. Omelet with melted cheese.

Frittata alla Paesana. Omelet with bacon, potatoes, and onions.

Frittata Genovese. Omelet with grated cheese, basil, and spinach.

Frittella. Fritter.

Fritto in Padella. Sautéed.

Fritto Misto alla Bolognese. Brains, liver, zucchini, cheese-stuffed puffs, and pasta stuffed with chopped chicken giblets, all fried.

Fritto Misto di Pesce. Assortment of fried fish; Italian version of the fish fry.

Frutta Affogata al Vino Rosso. Fruits poached in red wine.

Frutta Composta. Compote of fruits; may be made from fresh or dried fruits.

Frutta di. Fruit that is in season.

Frutta di Mare. Seafood.

Frutta Fresca. Fresh fruit, one of the favorite Italian desserts when served with cheese.

Funghi Trifolati. Sautéed mushrooms.

Gamberi Fritti. Fried shrimp.

Garganelli. Macaroni made by hand from an egg dough.

Gelato. Ice cream.

Gelato Agli Amaretti. Ice cream with a macaroon mixture.

Genovese, alla. With pine nuts, cheese, basil, garlic, and other herbs.

Giardiniera. A mixture of vegetables, marinated.

Gnocchi alla Romana. Dumplings made with semolina.

Gnocchi di Riso. Rice dumplings.

Gnocchi di Patate. Potatoes, flour, and eggs made into dumplings.

Gnocchi Verdi. Gnocchi made with spinach.

Granita de Caffe. Coffee ice.

Granita di Limone. Lemon ice.

Gratinati. Baked with a golden crust; usually of bread crumbs and cheese.

Grissini. Bread sticks.

Il rotolo di Pasta. Sheets of pasta rolled and stuffed with spinach and then sliced.

Imbottito. Stuffed.

Imbrogliata di Uovo con Pomodoro. Omelet with bacon and tomatoes.

Insalata. Salad.

Insalata alla Lucia. Artichoke hearts with an oil and vinegar dressing; served cold.

Insalata alla Russa. Cooked vegetables cut up and mixed with mayonnaise.

Insalata Siciliana. Tomatoes with basil and garlic and an oil and vinegar dressing.

Involtini. Stuffed rolls of veal.

Lasagna. Pasta in broad sheets; may be either white or green; also refers to the same pasta baked with meat and tomato sauce, mozzarella, ricotta, and Parmesan cheese.

Lasagna Verdi al Forno. Green lasagna baked with a meat sauce.

Lingue in Salsa. Tongue in a sauce of white rolled around slices of prosciutto ham and sautéed in butter and Marsala wine; literally, "jump into the mouth."

Linguine. Narrow noodles.

Lonza di Vitello. Loin of veal.

Lo Scrigno di Venere. Spinach fettucine baked in a pasta bundle.

Luganega. A sausage.

Lumache. Snails.

Maccheroni al Forno. Baked macaroni.

Macedonia di Frutta. Fruit cup; salad of fruit.

Maggiorana. Sweet marjoram.

Maigletto. Suckling pig.

Maionese. Mayonnaise.

Maltagliati. Triangular noodles.

Manicotti. Large, pancake-like noodles that are stuffed and baked with a sauce.

Manzo alla Lombarda. Pot roast cooked in red wine with parsley, carrots, celery, and onions.

Marinara. Sauce made with tomatoes, olives, and garlic, no meat.

Medaglioni di Vitello. Fillet of veal.

Melanzane alla Siciliana. Eggplant halves stuffed with pulp, olives, anchovies, and capers and then baked.

Menta Peperina. Peppermint.

Milanese, alla. Coated with bread crumbs and cooked in butter.

Millefoglie. Flaked pastry, like a napoleon.

Minestra. Term used to describe the first course of an Italian meal; may also mean soup.

Minestra di Funghi. Mushroom soup.

Minestra di Riso e Fagioli. Soup with rice and beans.

Minestrone. A thick vegetable soup; the variety of vegetables that may go into a minestrone is endless and as variable as the regions of Italy.

Meringhe di Castagne. Chestnut meringues.

Monte Bianco. Dessert of chestnuts and whipped cream.

Mozzarella ai Ferri. Grilled mozzarella.

Mozzarella in Carrozza. Two pieces of bread soaked in consommé, dipped in egg, and spread with cheese, then fried, sandwich-like, in olive oil.

Nasello. Whiting.

Naturale. Plain, as is.

Nocciola. Hazelnut.

Noce. Nut.

Olive Nere. Black olives.

Olive Ripiene. Green olives stuffed with pimento.

Olivette di Vitello. Boneless veal cut into small pieces and cooked in wine.

Oreganato. Baked with oregano; appears on menus most often as a way of preparing clams.

Osso Buco. Veal shank stewed in tomatoes and wine.

Ostriche. Oysters.

Pagello. Red snapper.

Paglia e Fieno. Literally, straw and hay; two kinds of noodles, one green, the other white; in a cream sauce with prosciutto and peas.

Pan di Spagna. Light cake covered with cream or jam and soaked in liqueur.

Pane. Bread.

Panettone. Yeast cake filled with candied fruit; especially popular at Christmas time.

Panizza. White beans, rice, tomatoes, onions, and bacon.

Panna Montata. Whipped cream.

Pappardelle. Broad noodles with a crimped edge.

Parmigiana, alla. Prepared with Parmesan cheese.

Parmigiano. Parmesan cheese.

Pasta. The first course in a classic Italian meal; dough made into a variety of shapes that may be eaten alone, in a broth, or with a sauce.

Pasta all' Uovo. Pasta made with eggs.

Pasta e Fagioli. Soup of beans and pasta; the beans will probably be of the great northern variety in New York restaurants.

Pasta Verde. Spinach noodles; lasagna is often made with spinach added.

Pastina. Noodles used primarily for soup.

Penne. Short, tubular pasta.

Peperonata. Stewed green peppers, tomatoes, and onions.

Peperoni alla Calabrese. Peppers fried in oil with tomato.

Peperoni alla Piemontese. Peppers stuffed with a mixture of tomatoes, garlic, anchovies, egg, and bread crumbs.

Peperoni Ripieni con Ricotta. Green peppers stuffed with ricotta cheese.

Perciatelli. Elongated macaroni.

Pesce al Cartoccio. Fish baked in oiled paper or parchment.

Pesto. Paste or sauce made from fresh basil, garlic, cheese, and olive oil ground in a mortar or, more likely, in a blender.

Petto di Pollo. Breast of chicken.

Piccante. Highly seasoned.

Piccata al Limone. Veal sautéed in butter and lemon juice.

Pignoli. Pine nuts.

Pizzaiola. Sauce of tomato, garlic, and marjoram; a popular method of preparing veal and beef.

Pizza Rustica. Cheese pie with ham, sausage, and hardboiled eggs.

Polenta. Cornmeal simmered in water; some like to equate it to cornmeal mush.

Polenta al Burro e Formaggio. Polenta mixed with butter and cheese.

Pollo alla Griglia. Broiled chicken.

Pollo alla Romana. Chicken sautéed with peppers and tomatoes.

Pollo al Diavolo. Spicy chicken; literally, *devilishly hot.*

Pollo Disossato. Chicken that has been boned.

Pollo in Vino Bianco. Chicken in white wine.

Pollo Novello. Spring chicken.

Pollo Spezzato alia Sabinese. Chicken cooked in a sauce of olives, capers, and anchovies.

Polpette. Meat balls.

Polpettone con Ripieni. Meatloaf with a stuffing.

Polpi alla Luciana. Octopus cooked in a sauce made with oil and hot red peppers.

Pomodori Ripieni. Tomatoes stuffed with rice.

Pomodori Ripieni alla Romana. Tomatoes stuffed with rice and mozzarella cheese.

Poverella, alla. Method of preparing pasta with eggs and bacon, literally, "the way the poor woman makes it."

Prosciutto. Smoked ham, sliced wafer thin.

Prosciutto e Melone. Smoked ham, sliced very thin with melon; a popular appetizer.

Pure di Patate. Mashed potatoes with Parmesan cheese added.

Radicchio. Red lettuce.

Ragno. Sea-bass.

Ragu. May mean a sauce or a meat stew with garlic, tomatoes, and herbs.

Ragu di Fegatini. Sauce of chicken livers.

Ravioli. Envelopes of pasta that are stuffed with either meat or cheese and eaten in soup or with a sauce.

Rigatoni al Forno con Ragu. Rigatoni baked with a meat sauce.

Risotto. Rice dish prepared by sautéeing raw rice and onion and then cooking the rice by gradually adding broth; to be true risotto, the rice must not be boiled.

Risotto alla Milanese. Risotto with saffron, Parmesan cheese, and ham added.

Rognoni. Kidneys.

Rugola. Field lettuce.

Salmone Affumicato. Smoked salmon.

Salsa alla Milanese. Sauce of ham and veal cooked in butter with fennel and wine.

Salsa di Burro alla Gorgonzola. Sauce with gorgonzola cheese and melted sweet butter.

Salsa di Funghi. Mushroom sauce.

Salsa di Pignoli. Cream sauce, with pine nuts.

Salsa di Vongole. Clam sauce; served on pasta.

Salsa Verde. Green sauce served with fish or boiled meats.

Salsiccia. Spicy pork sausage.

Saltimbocca. Slices of veal seasoned with sage.

Scalloppine. Thin slices of meat, most usually of veal.

Scalloppine alla Bolognese. Veal cooked with prosciutto and potatoes.

Scalloppine alla Fiorentina. Thinly sliced veal on spinach with a white sauce.

Scalloppine al Sedano. Veal cooked in butter with prosciutto and celery.

Scaloppine di Vitello. Thin slices of veal.

Scampi. Shrimp.

Scampi fra Diavolo. Shrimp in a spicy tomato sauce.

Scarola. Escarole; a popular side dish when cooked in a chicken broth.

Sedano alla Milanese. Celery prepared with white sauce and grated cheese.

Sfogliatelle. Flaky pastry in the shape of a small fan.

Sorbetto. Sherbet.

Spaghetti al Burro. Spaghetti with butter.

Spaghetti alla Carbonara. Spaghetti tossed with oil, eggs, bacon, and cheese; literally, "in the style of the charcoal gatherer."

Spaghetti al Pomodoro. Spaghetti with tomato sauce.

Spaghetti con Aglio e Olio. Spaghetti with garlic and oil.

Spaghetti con Carne. Spaghetti with meat.

Spaghettini. Very thin spaghetti.

Spiedini. Pieces of meat or anything else on a skewer.

Spiedini alla Romana. Mozzarella and bread dipped in batter, put on a skewer, and deep-fried.

Spiedino di Mare. Fish roasted on a skewer.

Spumone. Dessert of ice cream and candied fruits with whipped cream and nuts.

Stracciatella. Bouillon of eggs and Parmesan cheese; the Italian version of egg-drop soup; literally, "little rags," because of the shape the eggs take when dropped in the soup.

Stracotto al Barolo. Beef cooked in a sauce of red wine and tomatoes.

Stufato. Beef stewed with white wine and vegetables.

Sugo di Broccoli e Acciughe. Anchovy and broccoli sauce.

Suprema di Pollo. Chicken breast.

Tagliatelle. What the people of Bologna call *fettucine*.

Tagliolini. Thin noodles, most often used in soup.

Tonnato. In a sauce made from tuna; veal prepared this way is a popular dish in New York's Italian restaurants.

Torta con Formaggio. Cheesecake.

Trenette. Fine pasta, the thickness of a match; cut in long pieces.

Trippa alla Bolognese. Tripe fried in olive oil, bacon, onion, and garlic with egg yolks added.

Uccelletti. Small birds.

Veneziana, alia. Cooked with onions and white wine.

Verdure. Vegetables.

Vitello all' Uccelletto. Veal cut into small, thin slices, cooked in white wine and flavored with sage.

Vongole al Forno. Baked clams.

Zabaglione. Dessert made with egg yolks, Marsala wine, and sugar beaten to a froth; may also appear as *sbaglione* or *zabaione*.

Zeppole. A type of fritter.

Zeppole alia Napoletana. Fritters with a brandy flavor.

Ziti. Large, tubular pasta.

Zuppa de Pesce. The Italian version of bouillabaisse; a fish soup with ingredients that vary from chef to chef and season to season.

Zuppa Inglese. Sponge cake soaked in rum with candied fruits and either whipped cream or custard.

Zuppa Pavese. Broth with toast and poached eggs topped with grated cheese.

French

Abatis de Volaille. Chicken giblets.

Agneau de Lait Persillé. Baby lamb grilled and served with parsley.

Aioli. Garlic-flavored paste that is the consistency of mayonnaise.

Allumettes. Potatoes cut to the thickness of matchsticks.

Amandine. Prepared with almonds; often used for fish fillets.

Andouille. Large sausage made with tripe and pig intestines.

Anglaise, à l'. Cooked in either water or stock.

Artichauts, à la Vinaigrette. Artichokes in a dressing of oil and vinegar.

Aspèrges Mornay. Asparagus with a thick cheese sauce.

Aspèrges Mousseline. Asparagus with a sauce of egg yolks, lemon juice, and whipped cream.

Aubergines à la Nicoise. Eggplants with garlic and tomatoes.

Baba au Rbum. Cake that has been soaked in rum after it's been baked.

Baguette. Long loaf of French bread.

Ballottine. Boned meat, fish, or fowl that is rolled into a bundle-like shape and served sliced.

Bananes a Crème Chantilly. Bananas with whipped cream.

Bar-le Duc. Currant preserves.

Béarnaise, Sauce. A thick sauce made with shallots, tarragon, thyme, bay leaf, vinegar white wine, and egg yolks; most often served with grilled or sautéed meat or grilled fish.

Béchamel, Sauce. Milk blended with a rowx—a mix of butter and flour.

Belon. A French variety of oyster.

Beurre à la Maitre d'Hotel. Butter melted with parsley, salt, pepper, and lemon juice, served with meat or fish or vegetables.

Bigarade, sauce. Made from the pan drippings of duck, orange juice, lemon juice, and a touch of curaçao; used on duckling.

Billi'bi. Cream of mussel soup (sometimes spelled billy-by).

Blanquette d'Agneau à l'Ancienne. Lamb stew with cream, onions, and potatoes.

Blanquette de Veau. Veal stewed in a cream sauce.

Boeuf à la Mode. Braised beef in red wine.

Boeuf Bourguignon. Braised beef prepared in the style of Burgundy; with small glazed onions, mushrooms and red wine.

Boeuf Miroton. Beef stewed with an onion-based sauce.

Boeuf Rôti. Roast beef.

Bonne Femme, à la. Cooked with bacon, onions, potatoes, and a thick brown gravy.

Bordelaise, Sauce. Brown sauce made with wine and bone marrow.

Bouillabaisse. A well-known dish from Provence; made with fish cooked in either water or wine with garlic, parsley, pepper, oil, and tomatoes added; the ingredients will vary with the restaurant; one French poet was so inspired by the bouillabaisse he ate that he wrote a poem about it.

Bourgeoise, à la. Prepared with carrot and onions.

Brioche. A roll made of yeast dough in a circular or loaf shape.

Brioche de Foie Gras. Brioche dough stuffed with goose liver paté.

Brochette. A skewer; anything cooked on a skewer may be called a *brochette*.

Bûche. Swiss roll; sponge cake rolled around a jelly or cream filling.

Bûche de Noel. A special Christmas cake made to look like a yule log.

Café Glacé. Cold coffee with whipped topping.

Canapé. A toasted slice of bread; also applied to these slices when topped with a variety of spreads; used as an appetizer.

Canard a l'Orange. Duck in an orange sauce.

Câpres, Sauce aux. Caper sauce; frequently used on lamb.

Carbonnade à la Flamande. Beef cooked with beer.

Carré d'Agneau aux Herbes. Loin of lamb with a variety of herbs.

Cassoulet. A stew made with white beans and pork; may also include lamb, goose, or duck.

Cassoulet Toulousain. Navy bean stew with lamb, pork sausage, or poultry.

Cêpes Farcies. Stuffed mushrooms.

Champignons Farcis. Stuffed mushrooms.

Chanterelles. A type of mushroom that is extremely popular in France; may also appear on menus as *girolle.*

Chateaubriand. Thick slice of steak, classically grilled and served with a garnish of potatoes cut in strips and with a bearnaise sauce.

Chaudfroid. Cream sauce containing aspic.

Choucroute Garnie. Sauerkraut baked with ham, bacon, and sausages.

Confit d'oie. Goose that is preserved in its own fat.

Consommé. Meat stock that has been enriched, concentrated, and clarified.

Coq au vin. Chicken prepared in a wine sauce with mushrooms, garlic, small onions, and diced pork added.

Coquilles St. Jacques à la Parisienne. Scallops and mushrooms in white wine sauce.

Côte de Boeuf Grillé. Grilled beef rib.

Coulibiac de Saumon en Croute. Salmon, rice, and mushrooms baked in a rectangular pastry shell.

Coupe de Fruits Frais. Fruit cup made with fresh fruit.

Court Bouillon. The liquid in which meat, fish, and some vegetables are cooked; may contain a variety of spices and vegetables and will vary from dish to dish.

Crème Caramel. Custard with a burnt sugar flavor.

Crème Chantilly. Whipped cream.

Créole, à la. Prepared with rice.

Crêpes de Homard. Pancakes stuffed with lobster chunks.

Crêpes Suzette. Thin pancakes made with a batter flavored with curacao and the juice of mandarin oranges, usually served flaming.

Croissant. Crescent-shaped roll made with puff pastry or yeast dough; most often served at breakfast.

Croque Madame. Grilled chicken and cheese sandwich.

Croque Monsieur. A ham and cheese sandwich, fried.

Croustade. A dish made with a flaky puff pastry shell or from bread that has been hollowed out.

Crudités. Raw vegetables served as an appetizer.

Cuisses de Grenouilles. Frogs' legs.

Daube. Chunks of meat stewed with vegetables.

Délices. Strictly speaking, this refers to a particular pastry, but on American menus it can mean anything that is reputed to be especially tasty.

Diable, sauce. Spicy sauce of white wine, vinegar, shallots, pepper, and other ingredients.

Dijonnaise, sauce. Egg yolks, Dijon mustard, salt, and pepper beaten with oil and lemon juice to the consistency of mayonnaise.

Duglere, à la. With a cream sauce made with wine and tomatoes and served with fish.

Duxelles. Mushrooms chopped and browned in butter and oil, mixed with onions, shallots, and a bit of wine and parsley.

En Bordure. Served with a border, commonly of duchesse potatoes.

En Croute. Baked in a pastry crust.

Endive à la Normande. Endives simmered in cream.

Entrecôte. Literally, "between the ribs"; the steak cut from between two ribs of beef, usually grilled or fried.

Entrecôte Marchand de Vin. Steak cooked with red wine and shallots.

Epinards au Beurre Noisette. Spinach in browned butter.

Escalopes. Boneless slices of meat or fish, usually fried in butter.

Escargots à la Bourguignonne. Snails baked in their shells and served with garlic butter.

Escargots de Bourgogne. Snails of Burgundy; famous for their succulence.

Feuilletté de Fruits de Mer Puff. pastry filled with a variety of seafood.

Feuilletté de Homard. Puff pastry with a lobster filling.

Feuilletté de Ris de Veau. Puff pastry with a sweet bread filling.

Filet de Boeuf en Croute. Fillet of beef in a pastry crust; beef Wellington.

Filet Mignon. Small, choice cut of beef prepared by grilling or sautéeing.

Financière, à la. Made with a garnish of sweetbreads, mushrooms, and olives.

Flamande, à la. With cabbage, carrots, turnips, bacon, potatoes, and sausage.

Flambé. Describes a dish that has been ignited after it has been doused in a liqueur.

Florentine, à la. Foods cooked in this style—usually eggs or fish—are put on spinach, covered with mornay sauce, and sprinkled with cheese.

Foies de Volaille en Brochette. Chicken livers, mushrooms, and bacon grilled on a skewer.

Foie Gras. The livers of especially fattened geese and ducks; the "foie gras" of Toulouse and Strasbourg are the most highly prized and may weigh up to four pounds each.

Fondue Bourguignonne. Beef cut into small pieces and cooked at the table in boiling oil; a variety of sauces accompany the meat.

Forestiere, à la. With mushrooms, bacon, and diced potatoes.

Fraises aux Liqueurs. Strawberries, sugared and sprinkled with a variety of liqueurs.

Fraises Chantilly. Strawberries with whipped cream.

Fricassé. Meat braised with spices and vegetables and served with a thick sauce; most commonly used to prepare veal and poultry.

Fromage Rapé. Grated cheese.

Fruits de Mer. Seafood.

Galantine. Boned turkey, duck, or chicken stuffed into a sausage, shaped and cooked in wine-flavored bouillon, and chilled; usually served in aspic. According to Julia Child, "A galantine is not built in a day."

Garbure. Thick peasant soup made with cabbage.

Gâteau de Crèpes à la Florentine. Layered crepes filled with spinach and topped with a cheese sauce.

Gâteau de Crèpes à la Normande. Layered crepes with apple slices.

Gigot d'Agneau. Leg of lamb.

Glaces Tous Parfums. Ice cream in all flavors.

Gratin, au. Prepared with a crumb topping of toasted breadcrumbs; usually includes grated cheese, most often Parmesan.

Gratin Dauphinois. Scalloped potatoes with browned top.

Grenobloise. With capers, brown butter, and lemon.

Grenouilles à la Provençale. Frogs' legs in garlic and butter.

Haricots. Beans.

Haricots Verts à la Maitre d'Hotel. Green beans tossed with butter, parsley, and lemon juice.

Haricots Verts Sautés au Beurre. Fresh green beans sautéed in butter.

Hollandaise, Sauce. Hot sauce made with egg yolks and butter; served with vegetables and fish.

Homard à l'Américaine. Lobster sautéed in oil with onions and tomatoes.

Homard Newburg. Chunks of lobster cooked in a sauce of brandy and fish stock.

Homard Sauté. Chunks of lobster sautéed in butter with herbs added.

Hors d'Oeuvres. Appetizers, hot or cold.

Jambon Bayonnaise. Smoked ham from near Bayonne, a French town in the Pyrenees.

Jambon Fumé. Smoked ham.

Jardinière, à la. Garnished with fresh vegetables, served with roast, stewed, or braised meat and poultry; the vegetables may be boiled or glazed and are placed around the meat.

Julienne. Meat or vegetables cut into thin strips.

Laittue Braisée. Braised lettuce, usually Boston lettuce.

Langoustine. Crawfish, small lobster.

Lyonnaise. Prepared with onions; onions grow abundantly in the Lyonnaise region of France.

Macedoine. Fruit or vegetables, diced and then mixed.

Madère, Sauce. A sauce made with Madeira wine.

Madrilène. Clear soup with tomato; served chilled.

Maquereaux au Vin Blanc. Mackerel in a white wine sauce.

Marchands de Vin, Sauce. A brown sauce of butter and red wine.

Marguery. Prepared with a sauce of white wine and stock made from mussels; most often used for fillets of sole.

Marrons Glacés. Candied chestnuts.

Medaillon. Food cut into a round or oval shape.

Meringue Glacée. Egg whites and sugar beaten and baked, served with ice cream.

Meunière. Method of preparing fish; it's first seasoned, floured and fried in butter, then served with lemon juice, parsley, and melted butter.

Miropoix. Diced vegetables cooked in butter.

Mornay, Sauce. A cream sauce with cheese added.

Moules à la Marinière. Mussels cooked in broth and served with a mixture of broth and melted butter.

Mousse. A light and airy dish that is made with cream and eggs; may be of fish, chicken, etc., or fruits and chocolate; served either hot or cold.

Nantua, sauce. A shrimp sauce.

Nicoise, à la. Prepared with tomatoes, zucchini, garlic, sometimes potatoes, green beans, olives, capers and anchovies; may also mean with tomatoes and garlic.

Noisettes de Chevreuil. A cut of venison, round or oval shape.

Normande, Sauce. With oyster juice; used with fillet of sole.

Oeuf. Egg.

Oeufs à la Russe. Hard-boiled eggs with a mayonnaise sauce of chives, onion, and a bit of tabasco.

Oeufs Argenteuils. Scrambled eggs with asparagus.

Oeufs Benedictine. Classically, eggs over salt cod with a cream sauce; in a New York restaurant this refers to an egg and ham on an English muffin with hollandaise sauce and possibly even a slice of truffle.

Oeufs en Gélée. Eggs in aspic.

Oiseaux sans Têtes. Rolled sliced meat with a stuffing.

Omelette aux Fines Herbes. An omelet made with parsley, tarragon, and chives.

Omelette Bonne Femme. An omelet with onions and bacon.

Omelette Provençale. An omelet with garlic, tomatoes, onions, and olives.

Paillard de Boeuf. A boned shell steak that is pounded very thin.

Papillote, en. Cooked in a sheet of oiled paper or parchment.

Pâte. Dough, pastry.

Pâté. Originally, the term was applied only to a meat or fish dish enclosed in a pastry and baked; now it describes any dish of ground meat or fish baked in a mold that has been lined with strips of bacon.

Pâté Maison. A pâté unique to a particular restaurant.

Paupiettes de Sole. Slices of sole, rolled and stuffed.

Paysanne. Peasant style; with vegetables and bacon.

Persillade. Chopped parsley, usually mixed with garlic.

Petite Marmite. Clear soup made with meat, poultry, marrow bones, stock pot vegetables, and cabbage; usually served with toast and sprinkled with grated cheese.

Piperade. Omelet with peppers, tomatoes, garlic ham, and onions.

Plat de Fromages. Choice of cheese.

Point, au. Medium done; refers to beef.

Pois à la Francaise. Peas cooked with lettuce leaves and onions.

Poitrine de Veau. Breast of veal.

Pommes de Terre Duchesse. Potatoes put through a sieve and mixed with butter; salt and pepper; may be served as is or put through a pastry bag to make a border.

Pommes de Terre à l'Huile. Potato salad with vinaigrette sauce.

Potage Clair. Clear soup.

Pot-au'Feu. French version of the boiled dinner.

Poule au Pot. Chicken stewed with vegetables.

Poulet Chasseur. Chicken prepared with sautéed mushrooms, shallots, and white wine and tomatoes; literally, "hunter's chicken."

Poulet en Cocotte. Chicken roasted in a casserole.

Poulet Rôti à l'Estragon. Roast chicken with tarragon.

Printanière, à la. Garnished with a variety of vegetables.

Profiterole. Eclair-like pastry; may be filled with ice cream or any puree or with a custard, jam, or other sweet filling.

Provençale, à la. With tomatoes, garlic, olives, and eggplant.

Purée de Pommes de Terre à l'ail. Mashed potatoes flavored with garlic.

Quenelles. Dumplings made with either fish or meat.

Queue de Homard. Lobster tail.

Quiche Lorraine. A tart made with eggs, cream, cheese, and bacon.

Rable de Lapin. Saddle of rabbit.

Raclette. Hot, melted cheese; served with baked potatoes and gherkins, a dish of Swiss origin.

Ragout. A dish made from meat, poultry, or fish that has been cut up and browned; may or may not include vegetables; a navarin is a popular ragout of lamb.

Risotte. Rice baked in chicken stock.

Rissolo. Meat-filled turnover that can be either fried or baked.

Robert, sauce. Sauce of onion, white wine and mustard; served with grilled pork dishes.

Rognons de Veau. Veal kidneys.

Rossini. Garnished with truffles and foie gras.

Sabayon. The Italian Zabaglione; a frothy dessert made of beaten eggs, sugar, and wine.

Salade de Cresson. Watercress salad.

Salade Nicoise. Potatoes and string beans with an oil and vinegar dressing; trimmed with olives, capers, anchovies and tomatoes.

Sang, au. With a sauce made from the blood of the meat used

Saucisson. Large sausage; sliced for serving.

Sauté. Cooked over a high heat in butter, oil, or other fat.

Savarin. Molded yeast cake soaked in liqueur-flavored syrup; may be served hot.

Sorbet. Sherbet; made from fruit or liqueurs.

Soubise, sauce. Cream sauce with onion, puree added.

Soufflé. Dish made with pureed ingredients, thickened with egg yolks and stiffly beaten egg whites; the varieties are limitless and may be made with vegetables, fish, meat, fruit, nuts or liqueurs; served as an appetizer, a main dish or a dessert.

Soup au Pistou. Vegetable soup with garlic, basil, and cheese; a specialty of the Riviera.

Steak au Poivre. Steak made with crushed peppercorns.

Suprèmes de Volatile à Blanc. Chicken breasts poached in butter with a wine and cream sauce.

Tacon. Young salmon.

Terrine. Meat, fish, or fowl chopped finely, baked in a dish called terrine, and served cold; often called pâté in the United States.

Tournedos. Small slice of beef, round and thick, from the heart of the fillet of beef; sautéed or grilled

Tournedos Rossini. Tornedos sautéed in butter and arranged on toast; a slice of foie gras and truffles tops the meat, and there's a sauce over all.

Tripes à la Mode de Caen. Tripe made with calf's feet, vegetables, and cider.

Truffle. Truffle, a fungus that grows underground.

Turbot Poché Hollandaise. Poached turbot served with a sauce of egg yolks and butter.

Varié. Assorted.

Verte, sauce. Green mayonnaise, colored with spinach, watercress, tarragon, or other green herbs.

Vichyssoisse. A cream soup of leeks, potatoes, and chicken broth, served cold.

Vinaigrette. Mixture of oil and vinegar, seasoned with salt and pepper, and at times herbs; a vinaigrette sauce is often served with asparagus, cauliflower, or boiled fish or as a green salad dressing.

Vincent, sauce. Green herbs pureed and added to mayonnaise with hard-boiled egg yolks.

Volaille. Fowl, poultry.

Vol-au-Vent. Pastry shell filled with a variety of mixtures, bound together with a brown or white sauce.

Mexican

Aceituna. Olive.

Acitron. A dried citron or candied biznaga cactus.

Agrio. Used to describe something with a sour taste.

Antojito. Appetizer, called tapa in Spain; on some menus, refers to the main course, literally, "little whims."

Arroz con Pollo. A dish eaten throughout Latin America made mainly of rice, yellowed and flavored with saffron, chunks of chicken, peppers, onions, tomatoes, and other spices. Other ingredients may be used depending on the locale's offerings.

Barbacoa. Barbecued meat.

Birria. Seasoned meat, steamed or barbecued.

Bistec Mexicano. Filet mignon charbroiled, served with salsa ranchera.

Bola. Ball, bolita—a little ball.

Botana. Appetizer served with drinks.

Budin. Pudding.

Bufiuelo. Fritter.

Burrito. A flour tortilla rolled and filled with beans, beef, and cheese, or a combination of those.

Cabrito. Kid.

Cacahuazintle. White corn with large kernels.

Cafe. Coffee.

Cajeta. Dessert, generally of fruit and milk.

Camarones al Ajillo. Shrimp in garlic and butter sauce.

Camarones Empanados. Shrimp coated in a light egg batter and deep-fried, served with coriander, jalapeno peppers, and sour cream dressing.

Camarones Malaguenos. Shrimp in wine butter and almond sauce.

Carne Asada con Tortillas. Steak slices wrapped in flour tortillas with beans, onions, and cheese, and topped with guacamole.

Carnitas. Small pieces of cooked pork; on some menus cooked and marinated beef chunks.

Ceviche. A fish dish served as an appetizer and eaten throughout Mexico and the rest of Latin America. Its main ingredients are fish marinated in lime juice, onions, and tomatoes and also oregano, olive oil, and coriander.

Chayote. Vegetable pear.

Cheese Crisp. Large flour tortilla topped with melted cheese, refried beans, onions, and ortega peppers.

Chilaquiles de Liza. Fried tortilla strips covered with shredded chicken, sour cream, and cheese.

Chile con Queso. (Mexican fondue). Blend of melted cheeses made with green chilies and often served with a basket of crisp corn chips.

Chiles Rellenos. Chilies or bell peppers stuffed with cheese or meat, coated with a light batter and fried.

Chiles Rellenos en Escabeche. Pickled pablano chilies stuffed with a filling made of pinto or California pink beans, chorizos, onions, spices, and cheese.

Chili Bean Soup. Spicy pinto bean soup, often made with ground beef and served with onions and grated cheese. Also called chile con carne.

Chimichanga. Burritos filled with chicken, cheese, beans, and onions served with sour cream and guacamole.

Chocolate. The much tastier Mexican version of hot chocolate. The original chocoholic was probably the Aztec ruler Montezuma II. He demonstrated his obsession by drinking 50 cups a day and providing 2,000 cups each day for his staff.

Empanada. Butter pastry tart filled with cherries, fried and sprinkled with powdered sugar.

Enchilada. Tortilla filled with either meat or cheese and coated in a chili sauce.

Enchiladas del Mar. Enchiladas made with shrimp, crabmeat, fresh coriander, and salsa ranchera, topped with cheese and sour cream.

Enchiladas Suizas. Enchiladas made with chicken and tomatillo sauce and topped with melted cheese and sour cream.

Envinada or Envidado. With wine added.

Failsan. Pheasant.

Flan. A caramel custard dessert.

Flauta. Large corn tortilla filled with chicken marinated in salsa ranchera, deep-fried and topped with sour cream.

Frijoles a la Charra. Pinto bean soup made with bacon, fresh coriander, and a splash of beer.

Gallina. Hen.

Garnacha. Round antojito of tortilla dough.

Gazpacho. A raw vegetable soup, served cold; a specialty of Spain, but also served in Mexico.

Guacamole. Dip made with ripe avocado, onions, and spices, served with corn chips.

Guayaba con Queso de Crema. Guava shells with sweet white cheese.

Haba. Large bean.

Habanero. Extremely piquant chili.

Hueves Revueltos a la Mexicana. Scrambled eggs made with serrano chili peppers and tomatoes.

Huevos Rancheros. Fried eggs served on tortillas and topped with ranchero sauce.

Jalapenos. The best known of the Mexican chili peppers. They are the small, fat green ones served in most restaurants either as a condiment or included in a dish.

Jalapenos Rellenos. Jalapenos stuffed with a mixture of cream cheese, cheddar and mozzarella cheeses, and chopped onions, then oven-baked.

Machacado. Scrambled eggs made with shredded dried meat.

Maize. Dried corn.

Mandito. Small corn patty marinated in sauce with beans, chicken, lettuce, tomatoes, and sour cream.

Margarita. Popular tequila-based cocktail made also with Cointreau, lime, or lemon juice, and served in a glass rimmed with table salt.

Mole Poblano. The Mexican national dish traditionally made with turkey in Mexico, but with chicken in most restaurants here. The poultry is cooked in a piquant dark sauce flavored with chocolate, chilies, and spices, and sprinkled with sesame seeds.

Mole Verde. A green sauce made with green chilies.

Nachos. Tortilla chips topped with refried beans, melted cheese, and jalapeno peppers.

Nachos Royal. Tortilla chips with chorizos and onions.

Napolitos dip. Cactus, blended with tomatoes, onions, peppers, fresh coriander, and spices, served in a chalupa shell (parador).

Pachola. Ground meat shaped in a thin half circle.

Paella. Not Mexican, but the national dish of Spain. It's served at some Mexican restaurants, and the ingredients can vary. The original Paella is from Valencia and is made from saffron-flavored rice, shellfish, chicken, some vegetables, and pimientos.

Picadillo. Stuffing made of ground or shredded meat.

Polio en Mole Verde de Pepita. Chicken in a sauce made with green tomatoes and pumpkin sauce.

Polio Fundido. Mixture of boned chicken and vegetables, rolled in a tortilla and sprinkled with grated longhorn cheese.

Polio Pibil. Pit-barbecued chicken made with spices, onions, and tomatoes.

Quelite. A wild green.

Quesadilla. A turnover of tortilla dough filled with any number of mixtures, including cheese, meat, potatoes, or chilies.

Quesados. Triangles of corn flour fried and stuffed with cheese, onions, and guacamole.

Queso Con Verduras. Melted-cheese casserole with cheese and vegetables, served with flour tortillas.

Queso de Polio. Melted-cheese casserole with cheese and chicken and ranchera sauce, served with flour tortillas.

Sangria. A wine punch of Spanish origin often served in Mexican restaurants, garnished with slices of fresh fruit.

Sopa de Flor de Calabacita. Squash flower soup, made of zucchini, pablano chilies, corn kernels, and unblended squash flowers.

Sopes. Small, round antojitos of tortilla dough. Smaller and thicker than tortillas, sopes are pinched into pie crust shapes, pan-fried, and topped with grated cheese, chopped onions, and coriander.

Taco. Tortilla filled with beef, pork, cheese, beans, or shellfish, or a combination of those.

Tacos al Carbon. Tacos filled with charbroiled steak.

Tacos de Polio. Tacos filled with chicken that has been marinated in salsa ranchera.

Tacos de Carne. Tacos filled with meat.

Tacos de Queso. Tacos filled with cheese.

Tamal. Corn-based dough or corn beaten with lard and steamed in a corn husk or banana leaf and filled with meat, seafood, cheese, beans, sweets, or fruits and legumes.

Tequila. This powerful alcohol is distilled from the fermented liquid of a Mexican fruit called the *agave*. Tequila can be drunk mixed in a cocktail or in shots, alternating drinks between licks of salt and sucking a lemon or lime.

Tinga Poblana. Cheese entrée with a pablana chili sauce.

Tortitas de Papa. Potato cakes.

Tostada. Flat tortilla stacked with refried beans, shredded chicken, lettuce, tomato, onions, and sour cream.

Totopas Tostaditas. Small, triangular fried tortilla.

Chinese

Agar. A white seaweed used in salads, aspics, and noodles that looks like transparent noodles.

Almond Gai Ding. Diced chicken and vegetables with almonds.

Barbecued spareribs. Pork ribs marinated in a sauce made of garlic, ginger root, soy sauce, and sherry, as well as other ingredients, either roasted or broiled or barbecued over charcoal.

Bean curd. More commonly known as tofu and used as vegetable in many dishes; this versatile food is made of pureed soybeans.

Bean curd with black bean sauce. Dish made of bean curd and black bean sauce.

Bean curd Szechuan style. A hot and spicy bean curd dish with vegetables.

Beche'derMer. A mollusk, also called *sea cucumber* or *sea slug*.

Beef with shiny noodles. Shredded beef with noodles that shimmer; the noodles are sometimes made of mung bean flour.

Beggar's chicken. A classic dish. The chicken is marinated, stuffed with a pork filling, and cooked slowly in a clay pot.

Bird's nest. Edible nests gathered by sea swallows in southern China, cleaned and used in the well-known bird's nest soup.

Black bean sauce. Black sauce made with fermented black beans and used to enhance a variety of other ingredients including fish, pork, and chicken.

Bok choy. Chinese cabbage.

Brown bean sauce. Sauce made from yellow beans, gives a salty taste to bland food.

Buddhist delight. A popular vegetable entrée including as many as a dozen vegetables such as black mushrooms, bean curd, snow peas, celery, broccoli, and bamboo shoots.

Butterfly shrimp. Fried jumbo shrimp made with garlic, sherry, and beer; also sometimes with bacon and onions.

Cantonese. Cooking of the Canton region characterized by very few seasonings (wine, ginger root, and soy sauce), quick stir-frying, and chicken stock as a base. Also known for its roasted meats, poultry, lobster, steamed pork, and fish dishes. The cooking commonly found in New York's Chinatown is Cantonese.

Cantonese duck. The whole cooked ducks seen hanging in Chinese restaurants and meat shops are prepared in the Cantonese fashion. The bird is first blanched, then filled with a liquid seasoned with spices, cooked, and air-dried. Eaten with duck sauce.

Chicken velvet. This dish for special occasions is made with minced chicken breast added to egg whites and lightly fried in oil or poached in a tasty stock. Sometimes called chicken essence or, when creamed corn is added, either corn essence or chicken velvet and corn.

Chili sauce. Hot sauce made with chili paste and garlic. Also called chili paste sauce, chili paste with garlic, or hot sauce.

Chinese broccoli with oyster sauce. A dish made with Chinese broccoli—a leafier, longer variation of the familiar vegetable—and oyster sauce.

Cold noodles with hot sesame sauce. Vermicelli or egg noodles are used for this chilled tasty appetizer, which is made with a piquant sauce.

Diced chicken with walnuts. Stir-fried dish that also has bamboo shoots, sherry, and ginger root.

Dim sum. Finger foods that include meat dumplings, butterfly shrimp, spring rolls, and shrimp toast.

Duck Sauce. A condiment for Cantonese duck. The sauce is made from a combination of different sweet sauces and fruits.

Egg drop soup. A literal name for this soup with swirls of cooked eggs and garnished with chopped scallion tops. The soup is made by dropping a beaten raw egg mixture into the clear boiling stock and stirring until the eggs are cooked and shredded.

Egg roll. A hefty deep-fried pastry appetizer, made of an egg and flour crust wrapped around a combination of meat, often pork, and shrimp and vegetables.

Fried rice. Cooked rice fried with meat or seafood, eggs, scallions, vegetables, and sherry.

Fortune cookies. These message-bearing, sweet twisted wafer cookies generally arrive with the bill at restaurants, but they likely won't be found in China. Theories of their origin are numerous; one is that they were first made by a transplanted Chinese man living in Los Angeles named George Jung, who was a noodle maker.

Fukien. Cooking of the Fukien province in the southeast includes seafood dishes and clear, light soups, as well as pork dishes and popia—a special pancake used for wrapping cooked fillings at the table. The region is also famous for its soy sauce.

Gai kew. Diced chicken with Chinese vegetables and mushrooms.

Ginger sauce. Tasty sauce made with shallots or scallions, sherry, soy sauce, and ginger.

Green jade. Usually means the dish includes an abundance of green vegetables such as snow peas or broccoli.

Hacked chicken. Chicken cut in small pieces and topped with sesame sauce.

Happy family. Dish made of Beche-de-mer, chicken, pork, ham, bamboo shoots, snow peas, sherry, and soy sauce.

Hoisin sauce. A dark sauce with a sweet and spicy taste, made from garlic, chili peppers, soybeans, and spices.

Hot and sour soup. Popular soup that has a spicy and sour taste and is made with pork, Chinese mushrooms, bean curd, and bamboo shoots.

Hunan. Cooking of the province of Hunan in western China. Hunan-style is the spiciest and hottest of Chinese cooking; the dishes often are seasoned with raw chili peppers. The region is also known for its smoked meats, sweet-and-sour combinations, rich seasonings, black teas, and rice. Also spelled *Honan* and *Hunam*.

Lemon chicken. Batter-fried chicken breast in fresh lemon and sweet sauce.

Lobster sauce. This rich sauce is made to be used over lobster but has no lobster in it. It's made with garlic, scallions, eggs, and chicken stock.

Lo mein. The Chinese version of pasta. Egg noodles cooked and served with a meat and vegetables.

Moo goo gai pan. A bland dish of chicken pieces and vegetables.

Moo shu pork. Dish served with a tasty pork filling and pancakes for wrapping it in. Also made with chicken.

Orange chicken or beef. Chicken breast or sliced beef seasoned with orange rind, dried chilies, garlic, and scallions.

Oyster sauce. A sauce served with meats, made from oysters and soy sauce.

Peking. Cooking of the north, particularly the capital (Peking or Beijing), which includes light, elegant sauces mildly seasoned and the liberal use of garlic, scallions, leeks, and chives. The region is most famous for the classic Peking duck and also is the only area where lamb is eaten regularly.

Peking Duck. The classic duck dish from the north. It has a crisp and savory skin. The duck is prepared by filling it with air and then roasting.

Seafood delight. Lobster, prawns, scallops, and Alaskan king crabmeat, stir-fried with assorted vegetables.

Sesame beef. Flank steak marinated with garlic, wine, brown beans, hot peppers, black mushrooms, and water chestnuts in light, white sauce.

Sesame chicken. Dark chicken meat with brown sauce, surrounded with broccoli flowers and sprinkled with sesame seeds.

Shanghai. Cooking of the eastern part of China. Famous for its seafood and fish entrées and slow-cooked dishes such as steamed chicken and robust casseroles. Also known for dim sum and beggar's chicken.

Shiny noodles. Noodles with a sheen and often made of mung bean flour. Also called *cellophane*, *transluscent*, or *bean thread* noodles.

Shrimp toast. A deep fried hors d'oeuvre prepared by spreading a shrimp based spread on white bread and frying it in hot oil.

Soong. A meat dish that is cut in small pieces and wrapped in lettuce leaves.

Spring roll. Uses lighter ingredients and is smaller than the better-known egg roll. It looks like a small egg roll, but the pastry is made without the egg, as in an egg roll; the filling is generally a combination of vegetables and often shrimp.

Szechuan. Not as hot to taste as Hunan foods but spicy and peppery as well. Dishes include deep-fried chicken wrapped in paper, vegetables prepared in chicken fat, chicken and hot peppers, as well as mushroom dishes. Also spelled *Szechwan*.

Wonton. A meat- or seafood-filled dumpling that can either be part of a dish, such as in wonton soup, or be served separately as a main course or an appetizer. May be steamed, boiled, or deep-fried.

INDEX